Research Methods in Education

Research Methods in Education

Louis Cohen and Lawrence Manion

CROOM HELM LONDON

© 1980 Louis Cohen and Lawrence Manion
Croom Helm Ltd, 2-10 St John's Road, London SW11

British Library Cataloguing in Publication Data

Cohen, Louis
    Research methods in education.
    1. Educational research
    I. Title   II. Manion, Lawrence
    370'.78   LB1028

    ISBN 0−85664−917−1
    ISBN 0−7099−0217−4 Pbk

Reprinted 1981

Printed and bound in Great Britain

CONTENTS

Contents

Contents

Contents

Contents

LIST OF JOURNALS ABBREVIATED IN TEXT

Journal of Experimental Education
Journal of Educational Psychology
Psychological Bulletin
American Educational Research Journal
Journal of Educational Sociology
Journal of Personality and Social Psychology
Educational and Psychological Measurement
Journal of Experimental Social Psychology
American Journal of Psychology
American Journal of Sociology
British Journal of Medical Psychology
British Journal of Social and Clinical Psychology
British Journal of Psychology
British Educational Research Journal
British Journal of Educational Psychology
American Psychologist

Our thanks are due to the following publishers and authors for permission to include materials in the text:

Wadsworth Publishing Co. Inc. Belmont, Cal. Notes in **Box 5.3** p. 105 from Lofland, J., *Analysing Social Settings* (1971)

American Psychological Association, Washington D.C. **Box 6.4** p. 140 from Eron, L.D. *et al.*, *American Psychologist* (April 1972) 253-63

Box 10.4 p. 200 from Forgas, J.P., *Journ. Pers. and Soc. Psychol.*, 34, 2 (1976) 199-209

Box 10.6 p. 203 from Peevers, B.H. and Secord, P.F., *Journ. Pers. and Soc. Psychol.*, 27, 1 (1973) 120-8

Open Books, London **Box 15.4** p. 289 from Bennett, N., *Teaching Styles and Pupil Progress* (1975)

Box 5.4 pp. 106 and 107 from Rutter M. *et al.*, *Fifteen Thousand Hours* (1979)

Prentice-Hall Inc. Englewood Cliffs N.J. quotes and **Box 4.8** p. 93 from Best, J.W., *Research in Education* 2nd edn (1970)

Box 2.1 p. 33 from Good, C.V., *Essentials of Educational Research* (1963)

Academic Press New York N.Y. **Box 10.5** p. 202 from Forgas, J.P., *Journ. Exp. Social Psychol.*, 14, (1978) 434-48

Associated Book Publishers Ltd., London **Box 14.3** p. 269 from Fransella, F., *Need to Change?* (1975)

Box 12.4 p. 230 from Brown, R. and Herrnstein, R.J., *Psychology* (1975)

Addison Wesley Publishing Co. Reading Ma. **Box 2.5** p. 45 from Holsti, O.R. in *Handbook of Social Psychology, Vol. 2 Research Methods* (1968) 604

Routledge and Kegan Paul Ltd., London Words p. 62-5 and **Box 3.6**

p. 63 from J. and E. Newson, in M.D. Shipman, *The Organisation and Impact of Social Research* (1976)

Dr. R. Shields, **Box 5.9** p. 122

Harcourt Brace Jovanovich, Inc., New York N.Y. **Box 6.2** p. 129 and **Box 13.1** p. 242 from Tuckman, B.W., *Conducting Educational Research* (1969)

C.B.S. International Publishing, New York, N.Y.

Box 5.7 p. 119 and **Box 5.8** p. 121 from Adams, R.S. and Biddle, B.J., *Realities of Teaching* (1970)

Box 4.4 p. 83 from Selltiz, C. *et al.*, *Research Methods in Social Relations* (1976)

Pergamon Press Ltd., Oxford **Box 14.4** p. 278 from Ravenette, A.T., *Journ. Child Psychol. and Psychiat.*, 16 (1975) 79-83

Weidenfeld Publishers Ltd., London **Box 5.5** p. 112, **Box 5.6** p. 114 and part of questionnaire p. 113 from Lambert R. *et al.*, *The Chance of Lifetime?* (1975) and Lambert R. *et al.*, *A Manual to the Sociology of the School* (1970)

Harper and Row Publishers, London **Box 15.1** p. 285, **Boxes 15.2** and **15.3** p. 286, **Box 15.14** p. 304, **Box 15.15** p. 305, **Box 15.16** p. 306, **Box 15.17** p. 307 from Cohen, L., *Educational Research in Classrooms and Schools: A Manual of Materials and Methods* (1976)

National Foundation For Educational Research, Slough **Box 3.3** p. 58, **Box 3.4** p. 59 from Jelinek, M.M. and Brittan, E.M., *Educational Research*, 18, 1 (1975) 44-53, and *Educational Research*, 19, 2 (1977) 129-41

Box 10.7 p. 205 from McAleese, R. and Hamilton, D., *Understanding Classroom Life* (1978)

Curtis Brown Ltd., London Words from Shipman, M.D., *Inside a Curriculum Project* (1974)

Scottish Academic Press Ltd., Edinburgh **Box 15.5** p. 292, **Box 15.6** p. 293, **Box 15.7** p. 295, **Box 15.8** p. 296 from Coulson, A.A., *British Journ. Educat. Psychol.*, 46 (1976) 244-52

Manchester University Press, Manchester **Box 7.3** p. 156 from Christie, T. and Oliver, R.A.C., *Research in Education*, 2 (1969) 13-31

The Open University, Milton Keynes Words from Pilliner, A., *Experiment in Educational Research* E 341, Block 5 (1973)

Academic Press Inc. London **Box 14.2** p. 268 from Bannister, D. and Mair, J.M.M., *The Evaluation of Personal Constructs* (1968)

Northwestern University Press, Evanston II p. 95-7 from Backstrom, C.H. and Hursh, G.D., *Survey Research* (1963)

Hodder and Stoughton Educational, Sevenoaks **Box 9.1** p. 177, **Box 9.4** p. 186 from Butcher, H.J. and Pont, H.B., *Educational Research in Britain 3* (1973)

Her Majesty's Stationery Office, London **Box 3.7** p. 66 from *Annexe I: D.E.S. A Study of School Buildings* (1977)

Countryside Commission, Cheltenham **Box 4.1** p. 72 from Davidson, J., *Outdoor Recreation Surveys: The Design and Use of Questionnaires For Site Surveys* (1970)

Heinemann Educational Books Ltd. p. 85-8 and **Box 4.5** p. 89 from Hoinville, G. and Jowell, R., *Survey Research Practice* (1978)

FOREWORD

There are three common types of books on research methods. The first leads the reader through the stages of research as if there was a mechanical sequence that, if followed, arrives invariably at reliable and valid evidence. The second type supports one approach in opposition to others. Here the reader is made aware that there are a variety of approaches and that there is disagreement over their relative virtues. But there is still an attempt to sell one of many possible ways of collecting evidence. The third type of book introduces the reader to the variety of research methods without taking sides. In all three types of book, the intended audience is the minority who undertake research.

There are a few books of a fourth type which can introduce research methods not only to those who will become researchers, but to the majority who will use the evidence produced.

Louis Cohen and Lawrence Manion have added to the small number of books that can serve both researchers and consumers of research evidence. A wide range of methods used in education are presented and these include both traditional and more recent approaches. The book is striking for its breadth, wealth of examples and balanced content. This balance is obtained by describing the method, providing examples and commenting on strengths and weaknesses. It is written in an engagingly straightforward style. Above all, it should provide an excellent introduction to the rich variety on the research menu!

Marten Shipman
Professor of Education
University of Warwick

ACKNOWLEDGEMENTS

We should like to record our sincere thanks to colleagues at Loughborough University of Technology and at Manchester Polytechnic, Didsbury School of Education, for their comments on initial drafts of several chapters and for their suggestions on a variety of materials for inclusion in the text. We are particularly grateful to Derek Blease, Duncan Case, Keith Hodgkinson, Mike Holliday, Jim Hough, Mike Johnson, Morry van Ments, John Mundy, Alan Radley, Cyril Simmons, Don Smedley and Zena Stansbie.

Our special thanks go to Dora Durbidge for the indefatigable way in which she located sources of crucial information that otherwise would have escaped our notice.

Any omissions or mistakes we readily attribute to each other.

1 INTRODUCTION: THE NATURE OF ENQUIRY

The Search for Truth

Man has long been concerned to come to grips with his environment and to understand the nature of the phenomena it presents to his senses. The means by which he sets out to achieve these ends may be classified into three broad categories: *experience, reasoning* and *research* (1). Far from being independent and mutually exclusive, however, these categories must be seen as complementary and overlapping, features most readily in evidence where solutions to complex modern problems are sought.

The first of these categories, *experience*, does itself subsume a number of sources of information that may be called upon in a problem-solving situation. The one most immediately at hand for all people, both children and adults, is personal experience: a person may thus draw upon his own individually accumulated body of knowledge and skills derived from encounters and acquaintance with facts and events in his environment — a child repairs a puncture in a bicycle inner tube speedily and efficiently because he has done it several times previously; and an adult anticipates the problems and difficulties of buying a house because he has gone through the procedures before. Where solutions to problems clearly lie beyond this corpus of personal knowledge, a person may make use of the wider or different experience of other, often older, people in his immediate circle — a child turns to a parent or teacher; an adult consults a friend or colleague; a local manager rings up the regional supervisor. Alternatively, where these sources fail, a person may search out sources beyond his immediate circle, ones we may designate as *authoritative*. Rooted in the past or very much part of the present, these may include recognised experts in particular fields — a Dr Spock on child-rearing, for instance; a figurehead or leader, as in a religious community; or an authority source hallowed by tradition and custom — the Bible, for example.

In our endeavours to come to terms with the problems of day-to-day living, we are heavily dependent upon experience and authority and their value in this context should not be underestimated. Nor should their respective roles be overlooked in the specialist sphere of research where they provide richly fertile sources of hypotheses and questions about the world, though, of course, it must be remembered that as tools for uncovering ultimate truth they have decided limitations. The limitations of personal experience in the form of 'common-sense knowing', for instance, can quickly be exposed when compared with features of the scientific approach to problem-solving. Consider, for example, the striking differences in the way in which theories are used. The layman bases them on haphazard events and uses them in a loose and uncritical manner. When he is required to test them, he does so in a selective fashion, often choosing only that evidence that is consistent with his hunches and ignoring that which is counter to them. The scientist, by contrast, constructs his theories carefully and systematically. Whatever hypotheses he formulates have to be tested empirically so that his explanations have a firm basis in fact. And there is the concept of 'control' distinguishing the layman's and the scientist's attitude to experience. The layman generally makes no attempt to control any extraneous sources of influence when trying to explain an occurrence. The scientist, on the other hand, only too conscious of the multiplicity of causes for a given occurrence, resorts to definite techniques and procedures to isolate and test the effect of one or more of the alleged causes. Finally, there is the difference of attitude to the relationships among phenomena. The layman's concern with such relationships is loose, unsystematic and uncontrolled. The chance occurrence of two events in close proximity is sufficient for him to predicate a causal link between them. The scientist, however, displays a much more serious professional concern with relationships and only as a result of rigorous experimentation will he postulate a relationship between two phenomena.

Similar warnings have been made against the unconditional acceptance of pronouncements of authorities:

Experts are essential, particularly in a complex culture such as ours, where knowledge is expanding so rapidly that no one can be an expert at everything. And obviously certain individuals have such wide experience and deep insight that their advice can be of immense benefit. Yet, it must be remembered that no one is infallible, and even the best and most competent are not exclusive possessors of 'the truth, the whole truth, and nothing but the truth'. It would be highly desirable that an 'authority' be still living; as new evidence accumulates, authorities have been known to change their mind. Thorndike reversed himself concerning the negative components of the law of effect, and Spock has changed his views concerning permissive upbringing. Ancient authorities, confronted with today's greater enlightenment, would very probably want to change their position. In fact, in many instances their views are of greater *historical* than *substantive* interest (1).

The second category by means of which man attempts to comprehend the world around him, namely, *reasoning*, consists of three types: deductive reasoning, inductive reasoning, and the combined inductive-deductive approach. Deductive reasoning is based on the syllogism which was Aristotle's great contribution to formal logic. In its simplest form the syllogism consists of a major premiss based on an *a priori* or self-evident proposition, a minor premiss providing a particular instance, and a conclusion. Thus:

All planets orbit the sun;
The earth is a planet;
Therefore the earth orbits the sun.

The assumption underlying the syllogism is that through a sequence of formal steps of logic, from the general to the particular, a valid conclusion can be deduced from a valid premiss. Its chief limitation is that it can handle only certain kinds of statement. The syllogism formed the basis of systematic reasoning from the time of its inception until the Renaissance. Thereafter its effectiveness was diminished because it was no longer related to observation and experience and became merely a mental exercise. One of the consequences of this was that empirical evidence as the basis of proof was superseded by authority and the more authorities one could quote, the stronger one's position. Naturally, with such abuse of its principal tool, science became sterile.

The history of reasoning was to undergo a dramatic change in the 1600s when Francis Bacon began to lay increasing stress on the observational basis of science. Being critical of the model of deductive reasoning on the grounds that its major premisses were often preconceived notions which inevitably bias the conclusions, he proposed in its place the method of inductive reasoning by means of which the study of a number of individual cases would lead to an hypothesis and eventually to a generalisation. Mouly (1) explains it like this: 'His basic premiss was that if one collected enough data without any preconceived notion about their significance and orientation — thus maintaining complete objectivity — inherent relationships pertaining to the general case would emerge to be seen by the alert observer.' Bacon's major contribution to science was thus that he was able to rescue it from the death-grip of the deductive method whose abuse had brought scientific progress to a standstill. He thus directed the attention of scientists to nature for solutions to man's problems, demanding empirical evidence for verification. Logic and authority in themselves were no longer regarded as conclusive means of proof and instead became sources of hypotheses about the world and its phenomena.

Bacon's inductive method was eventually followed by the inductive-deductive approach which combines Aristotelian deduction with Baconian induction. In Mouly's words, this consisted of:

a back-and-forth movement in which the investigator first operates inductively from observations to hypotheses, and then deductively from these hypotheses to their implications, in order to check their validity from the standpoint of compatibility with accepted knowledge. After revision, where necessary, these hypotheses are submitted to further test through the collection of data specifically designed to test their validity at the empirical level. This dual approach is the essence of the modern scientific method and marks the last stage of man's progress toward empirical science, a path that took him through folklore and mysticism, dogma and tradition, casual observation, and finally to systematic observation.

Although both deduction and induction have their weaknesses, their contributions to the development of science are enormous and fall into three categories: (1) the suggestion of hypotheses; (2) the logical development of these hypotheses; and (3) the clarification and interpretation of scientific findings and their synthesis into a conceptual framework.

The third means by which man sets out to discover truth is *research*. This has been defined by Kerlinger (2) as the systematic, controlled, empirical and critical investigation of hypothetical propositions about the presumed relations among natural phenomena. Research has three characteristics in particular which distinguish it from the first means of problem-solving identified earlier, namely, experience. First, whereas experience deals with events occurring in a haphazard manner, research is systematic and controlled, basing its operations on the inductive-deductive model outlined above. Second, research is empirical. The scientist turns to experience for validation. As Kerlinger puts it, 'subjective belief . . . must be checked against objective reality. The scientist must always subject his notions to the court of empirical inquiry and test.' And third, research is self-correcting. Not only does the scientific method have built-in mechanisms to protect the scientist from error as far as is humanly possible, his procedures and results are open to public scrutiny by fellow professionals. As Mouly says, 'This self-corrective function is the most important single aspect of science, guaranteeing that incorrect results will in time be found to be incorrect and duly revised or discarded'. Research is a combination of both experience and reasoning and must be regarded as the most successful approach to the discovery of truth, particularly as far as the natural sciences are concerned.

The Nature of Science

Since a number of the research methods we describe in this book draw heavily on the scientific method either implicitly or explicitly and can only be fully understood within the total framework of its principles and assumptions, we will here examine some of the characteristics of science a little more closely.

We begin with an examination of the tenets of scientific faith: the kinds of assumptions held by scientists, often implicitly, as they go about their daily work. First, there is the assumption of *determinism*. This means simply that events have causes, that events are determined by other circumstances; and science proceeds on the belief that these causal links can eventually be uncovered and understood, that the events are explicable in terms of their antecedents. Moreover, not only are events in the natural world determined by other circumstances, but there is regularity about the way they are determined: the universe does not behave capriciously. It is the ultimate aim of the scientist to formulate laws to account for the happenings in the world around him, thus giving him a firm basis for prediction and control.

The second assumption is that of *empiricism*. We have already touched upon this viewpoint, which holds that certain kinds of reliable knowledge can only originate in experience. In practice, therefore, this means scientifically that the tenability of a theory or hypothesis depends on the nature of the empirical evidence for its support. 'Empirical' here means that which is verifiable by observation; and 'evidence', data yielding proof or strong confirmation, in probability terms, of a theory or hypothesis in a research setting. The viewpoint has been summed up by Barratt (3) who writes, 'The decision for empiricism as an act of scientific faith signifies that the best way to acquire reliable knowledge is the way of evidence obtained by direct experience'.

Mouly has identified five steps in the process of empirical science (1):

(a) *experience* — the starting point of scientific endeavour at the most elementary level; (b) *classification* — the formal systemisation of other-wise incomprehensible masses of data; (c) *quantification* — a more sophisticated stage where precision of measurement allows more adequate analysis of phenomena by mathematical means; (d) *discovery of relationships* — the identification and classification of functional relationships among phenomena; and (e) *approximation to the truth* — science proceeds by gradual approximations to the truth.

The third assumption underlying the work of the scientist is the *principle of parsimony*. The basic idea is that phenomena should be explained in the most economical way possible. The first historical statement of the principle was by William of Occam when he said that explanatory principles (entities) should not be needlessly multiplied. It may, of course, be interpreted in various ways: that it is preferable to account for a phenomenon by two concepts rather than three; that a simple theory is to be preferred to a complex one; or as Lloyd Morgan did as a guide to the study of animal behaviour — 'In no case may we interpret an action as the outcome of the exercise of a higher psychical faculty, if it can be interpreted as the outcome of the exercise of one which stands lower in the psychological scale.'

The final assumption, that of *generality*, played an important part in both the deductive and inductive methods of reasoning. Indeed, historically speaking, it was the problematic relationship between the concrete particular and the abstract general that was to result in two competing theories of knowledge — the rational and the empirical. Beginning with observations of the particular, the scientist sets out to generalise his findings to the world at large. This is so because he is concerned ultimately with explanation. Of course, the concept of generality presents much less of a problem to the natural scientist working chiefly with inanimate matter than to the human scientist who, of necessity having to deal with samples of larger human popu-lations, has to exercise great caution when generalising his findings to the particular parent populations.

Having identified the basic assumptions of science, we come now to the core question: What is science? Kerlinger (2) points out that in the scientific world itself two broad views of science may be found: the *static* and the *dynamic*. The static view, which incidentally has particular appeal for laymen, is that science is an activity that contri-butes systematised information to the world. The work of the scientist is to uncover new facts and add them to the existing corpus of know-ledge. Science is thus seen as an accumulated body of findings, the emphasis being chiefly on the 'present state of knowledge and adding to it'. The dynamic view, by contrast, conceives science more as an activity, as something that scientists *do*. According to this conception, it is important to have an accumulated body of knowledge of course, but what really matter most are the discoveries that scientists make. The emphasis here, then, is more on the heuristic nature of science.

Two views similarly prevail with regard to the *function* of science. Some see it as, in Kerlinger's words, 'a discipline or activity aimed at improving things, at making progress'. This again is a characteristic lay view. That of the professional scientist and theorist is very different, however. They see science as a way of comprehending the world; as a means of explanation and understanding, of prediction and control. For them the ultimate aim of science is *theory*.

Theory has been defined by Kerlinger as 'a set of interrelated constructs [concepts], definitions, and propositions that presents a systematic view of phenomena by specifying relations among variables, with the purpose of explaining and predicting the phenomena'. In a sense, theory gathers together all the isolated bits of empirical data into a coherent conceptual framework of wider applicability. Mouly expresses it thus: 'If nothing else, a theory is a convenience — a necessity, really — organizing a whole slough of unassorted facts, laws, concepts, constructs, principles, into a meaningful and manageable form. It constitutes an attempt to make sense out of what we know concerning a given phenomenon.' More than this, however, theory is itself a potential source of further information and discoveries. It is in this way a source of new hypotheses and hitherto unasked questions; it identifies critical areas for further investigation; it discloses gaps in our knowledge; and enables a researcher to postulate the existence of previously unknown phenomena.

The status of theory varies quite considerably according to the discipline or area of knowledge in question. Some theories, as in the natural sciences, are characterised by a high degree of elegance and sophistication; others, like educational theory, are only at the early stages of formulation and are thus characterised by great unevenness. Mouly identifies the following characteristics of a good theory which may serve as suitable criteria (1):

1. A theoretical system must permit deductions that can be tested empirically; that is, it must provide the means for its conformation or rejection. One can test the validity of a theory only through the validity of the propositions (hypotheses) that can be derived from it.

If repeated attempts to disconfirm its various hypotheses fail, then greater confidence can be placed in its validity. This can go on indefinitely, until possibly some hypothesis proves untenable. This would constitute indirect evidence of the inadequacy of the theory and could lead to its rejection (or more commonly to its replacement by a more adequate theory that can incorporate the exception).

2. Theory must be compatible with both observation and previously validated theories. It must be grounded in empirical data that have been verified and must rest on sound postulates and hypotheses. The better the theory, the more adequately it can explain the phenomena under consideration, and the more facts it can incorporate into a meaningful structure of ever-greater generalisability.

3. Theories must be stated in simple terms; that theory is best that explains the most in the simplest way. This is the law of parsimony. A theory must explain the data more adequately and yet must not be so comprehensive as to be unwieldy. On the other hand, it must not overlook variables simply because they are difficult to explain.

Sometimes the word *model* is used instead of, or interchangeably with, *theory*. Both may be seen as explanatory devices or schemes having a broadly conceptual framework, though models are often characterised by the use of analogies to give a more graphic or visual representation of a particular phenomenon. Providing they are accurate and do not misrepresent the facts, models can be of great help in achieving clarity and focusing on key issues in the nature of phenomena.

Scientific theories must, by their very nature, be provisional. A theory can never be complete in the sense that it encompasses all that can be known or understood about a given phenomenon. As Mouly says, 'Invariably, scientific theories are replaced by more sophisticated theories embodying more of the advanced state of the question so that science widens its horizons to include more and more of the facts as they accumulate. No doubt, many of the things about which there is agreement today will be found inadequate by future standards. But we must begin where we are.' We have already implied that the quality of a theory is determined by the state of development of the particular discipline. The early stages of a science must be dominated by empirical work, that is, the accumulation and classification of data. This is why, as we shall see, much of educational research is descriptive. Only as a discipline matures can an adequate body of theory be developed. Too premature a formulation of theory before the necessary empirical spadework has been done can lead to a slowing down of progress.

Mouly optimistically suggests that some day a single theoretical system, unknown to us at the present time, will be used to explain the behaviour of molecules, animals and people.

Further Aspects of Science

We here take our examination of the nature of science further by looking at three concepts crucial to an understanding of its workings: *causation*, *explanation* and *the hypothesis*.

Causation

For a long time in the history of science, research addressed itself to the task of identifying relationships among phenomena on a cause-and-effect basis; causal rather than concomitant relationships were sought. It has come to be realised, however, that a phenomenon invariably occurs as a result of multiple causation and that the problem of establishing the actual cause of a particular phenomenon, especially in the behavioural sciences, is virtually insoluble. Even in rigorous experimental situations where variables can be manipulated, it is impossible to control all the factors in such a way as to be able to identify conclusively the causal factor or factors. The result of this difficulty is that the notion of *causation* is no longer as prevalent in the vocabulary of science as it used to be. There has consequently been a shift of emphasis, as Mouly points out, in the direction of discovering functional relationships that can be expressed in terms of probability of occurrence — 'Science is now reconciled to the idea that all that can be expected in the situational realities under which science must operate is prediction — and eventual control — at a high level of probability. We must also realize that the establishment of causation is not essential; we can predict that learning will take place even though we cannot identify its "causes", just as we can predict the movements of the planets even though we cannot control these movements.'

This change of emphasis in no way invalidates the assumption of *determinism* discussed earlier. Events *do* have causes and the desirability of knowing what they are and of being able to tease out the particular cause-and-effect relationships is in no way diminished because of human limitations at our present stage of development. As Mouly says, such relationships would be much more conducive to the development of control and complete explanation than is simple concomitance. As it is, science can only be approximate and continue to function on a probabilistic basis.

Explanation

We have earlier stated that one of the ultimate aims of science and the scientific enterprise is to arrive at explanations of whatever phenomena are being studied. *Explanation* is to be distinguished from *description* in that not only does it tell us what happens, but why. The emphasis is on the evaluation of the relationships between the variables or factors involved. Kaplan (4) enlarges on this point when he says:

> An explanation may be said to be a concatenated description. It does its work, not by invoking something beyond what might be described, but by putting one fact or law into relation with others. Because of the concatenation, each element of what is being described shines, as it were, with light reflected from all the others; it is because they come to a common focus that together they throw light on what is being explained. We see why something happens when we see better − in more detail, or in broader perspective − just what does happen. The difference between explanation and description may nevertheless be worth emphasizing to counter the illusion . . . that describing the same thing all over again, but in other terms, provides an explanation of it.

The most distinctive attribute of explanations − especially in the context of human behaviour − and one which they share with laws and theories is 'openness'. In no sense can an explanation, in this context at least, be said to be final. Indeed, Kaplan points out that the functions explanations perform cannot be appreciated without a full awareness of how far from finality they are in the actual conduct of enquiry. He goes on to distinguish eight ways in which explanations in the behavioural sciences can be open: (1) explanations are *partial*: only some of the factors determining the phenomena being explained are taken into account; (2) explanations are *conditional*: they hold true only of a certain range of phenomena, and are applicable only when certain conditions are satisfied; (3) explanations are *approximate*: the magnitudes they yield are more or less inexact, the qualities they ascribe are a shade different from what is observed; (4) explanations are *indeterminate* in their application to particular instances: they are statistical in content if not in explicit form, and may be true generally speaking but not in every single case; (5) explanations are *inconclusive*: they do not show why what is being explained must be so, but why it was very likely that it would be so; (6) explanations are *uncertain*: the laws and theories invoked, as well as the data applying to the particular cases, are confirmed only to some degree. The history of science is a history of the successive replacement of one explanation by another; (7) explanations are *intermediate*: every explanation is in turn subject to being explained. The circumstance that what we adduce for an explanation is not self-evident does not mean that the explanation is not truly explanatory; and (8) explanations are *limited*: they are appropriate to particular contexts in which they serve as explanations, not to every possible circumstance of enquiry.

The Hypothesis

Possibly the most important working tool of the scientist for discovering truths is the *hypothesis*. It is from this that much of research proceeds, especially when cause-and-effect or concomitant relationships are being investigated. The hypothesis has been defined by Kerlinger as a conjectural statement of the relation between two or more variables. More simply, it has been described as an 'educated guess'. Kerlinger considers that there are two criteria for 'good' hypotheses and hypothesis statements. The first is that hypotheses are statements about the relations between variables; and second, that hypotheses carry clear implications for testing the stated relations. To these, two ancillary criteria may be added: that they disclose compatability with current knowledge; and that they are expressed as economically as possible. Thus if we conjecture that social class background determines academic achievement, we have a relationship between one variable, social class, and another variable, academic achievement. And since both variables can be measured, the criteria specified by Kerlinger are clearly satisfied. Neither do they violate the stated ancillary criteria. A *null hypothesis* is one expressed in negative form and declares, for example, that there is no dependence of one variable on another, or that there is no significant difference between two measures of the same variable.

There are principally four reasons for the importance of hypotheses as tools of research. First, they organise the efforts of the researcher. The relationships expressed in the hypotheses indicate what he should do. They enable him to understand the problem with greater clarity and provide him with a framework for collecting, analysing and interpreting his data. Second, they are, in Kerlinger's words, the working instruments of theory. They can be deduced from theory or from other hypotheses. Third, they can be tested, either empirically or experimentally, thus resulting in confirmation or rejection. There is always the possibility that a hypothesis, once confirmed and established, may become a law. And fourth, hypotheses are powerful tools for the advancement of knowledge because, as Kerlinger explains, they enable man to get outside himself.

Positivism: the Application of the Scientific Method to the Study of Human Behaviour

In the preceding section, we sketched the broad outlines of what we might for convenience refer to as the scientific method. So successful has been the application of its principles to the problems of natural phenomena and so breath-taking have been the outcomes in terms of material and technological progress that it was felt that comparable achievements would eventually distinguish the work of social scientists if this same approach to problem-solving were to be applied to the world of social phenomena. One of the earliest thinkers associated with the founding of this movement was the Frenchman, Auguste Comte, who referred to its underlying philosophy as *positivism*. The term may be said to refer to 'a broadly defined movement in the history of man's intellectual development, the distinguishing feature of which is the attempt to apply to the affairs of man the methods and principles of the natural sciences' (5).

It is the scientific method that has become the basis of the *normative* approaches to the study of man which seek to explain his behaviour in society. The word refers to a view of society as composed of numerous institutions, each consisting of networks of interrelated positions for whose occupants specific role expectations are held (6). Behaviour from this perspective is synonymous with the individual's response to such expectations. In attempting to explain man's behaviour, this approach tends to portray him in mechanistic terms, as operating in the way he does as a result of internal and/or external causes. Explaining man's behaviour from this point of view requires the social scientist to adopt the perspective of a detached, outside observer intent upon classifying what he sees and hears in the light of some theory he holds about the way in which society is structured or some hunch he has about the range and variety of the needs that man must satisfy. This approach is essentially the same as the natural scientist's and we may thus designate it positivistic.

Two particularly important aspects of this approach to the study of man are: (1) the mechanistic image of man it implies; and (2) as a consequence, the concept of behaviour as being man's response to the press of his environment.

Two cogent criticisms are commonly levelled at the positivistic approach to the study of human behaviour. First, it fails to take account of man's unique ability to interpret his experiences and represent them to himself. Man can, and does, construct theories about himself and his world; moreover, he acts upon these theories. In failing to recognise this, positivistic social science is said to ignore the profound differences between the natural and the social sciences. Social science, unlike natural science, 'stands in a subject-subject relation to its "field of study", not a subject-object relation; it deals with a pre-interpreted world in which the meanings developed by active subjects actually enter into the actual constitution or production of that world' (7).

Second, the findings of positivistic social science are often said to be so banal and trivial that they are of little consequence to those for whom they are intended — teachers, social workers, counsellors, personnel managers and the like (6). The more effort, it seems, that the researcher puts into his scientific experimentation in, for example, the social psychology laboratory, by restricting, simplifying and controlling variables, the more likely he is to end up with a 'pruned, synthetic version of the whole, a constructed play of puppets in a restricted environment' (8). We go on to consider an alternative approach to positivistic social science suggested by its critics. To give the arguments sharper focus we concentrate on recent developments in social psychology, though parallel schools of thought may be discerned in psychology and sociology.

Proposals that social psychology should devote itself to becoming a 'science of persons' have been strengthened by recent developments in analytical philosophy concerned to elucidate the concept of *person* as used in everyday language and in philosophy. Because of man's self-awareness and powers of language, it is argued (9), man must be seen as a system of such a different order of complexity from any other existing system whether natural (an animal, for example) or artificial (a computer), that no other system is capable of providing a sufficiently powerful model to advance our understanding of him as a person.

What must we do then? We must use *ourselves*, it is suggested, to further our understanding of others and conversely our understanding of others as a way of finding out about ourselves. What is called for is an 'anthropomorphic model of man'. Since anthropomorphism means, literally, the attribution of human form and personality, the implied criticism is that social psychology has singularly failed, so far, *to model man as he really is*. As one wry commentator has pleaded, 'for scientific purposes, treat people as if they were human beings'.

What exactly would this involve? It would entail working from a model of man that takes account of the following uniquely human attributes:

> Man is an entity who is capable of monitoring his own performance. Further, because he is aware of this self-monitoring and has the power of speech, man is able to provide commentaries on those performances and to plan ahead of them as well. Such an entity, it is held, is much inclined to using rules, to devising plans, to developing strategies in getting things done the way he wants them doing (9).

The researcher's task is to understand man in the light of this anthropomorphic model. But what specifically would this involve? Proponents of a 'science of persons' approach place great store on the systematic and painstaking analysis of *social episodes*. The approach to analysing these is known as the *ethogenic method*. Unlike positivistic approaches, which ignore or presume its subjects' interpretations of situations, ethogenic approaches concentrate upon the ways in which a person construes his social world. By probing at his accounts of his actions, it endeavours to come up with an understanding of what that person was doing in the particular episode.

Critics of the interpretive approach, as this perspective has come to be known, have wasted no time in pointing out what they regard as its weaknesses. They argue that whilst it is undeniable that our understanding of the actions of our fellow men necessarily requires knowledge of their intentions, this, surely, cannot be said to comprise *the* purpose of a social science. As Rex (10) observes:

> Whilst patterns of social relations and institutions may be the product of the actors' definition of the situation there is also the possibility that those actors might be falsely conscious and that sociologists have an obligation to seek an objective perspective which is not necessarily that of any of the participating actors at all . . . we need not be confined purely and simply to that . . . social reality which is made available to us by participant actors themselves.

Giddens (7) argues similarly, 'No specific person can possess detailed knowledge of anything more than the particular sector of society in which he participates, so that there still remains the task of making into an explicit and comprehensive body of knowledge that which is only known in a partial way by lay actors themselves.'

Bernstein's (11) criticism focuses upon the overriding concern of interpretive researchers with the *meaning of situations* and the ways in which these meanings are negotiated by the actors involved. What is overlooked about such negotiated meanings, observes Bernstein, is that they 'presuppose a structure of meanings (and their history) wider than the area of negotiation. Situated activities presuppose a situation; they presuppose relationships between situations; they presuppose sets of situations'. His point is that the very process whereby one interprets and defines a situation is itself a product of the circumstances in which one is placed. One important factor in such circumstances that must be considered is the *power* of others to impose *their* definitions of situations upon participants.

In presenting what appear to be competing paradigms in social research we have avoided discussion of normative versus interpretive approaches. Both perspectives are necessary and inseparable aspects of a fuller understanding of man's behaviour and experience. Rather than viewing each approach as separate and self-enclosed, it is more profitable, as Giddens has suggested, to see 'all paradigms as mediated by the others'.

In Box 1.1 we identify a selection of contrasting features of the two approaches, the normative and the interpretive.

Box 1.1

Differing approaches to social psychology

Normative	*Interpretive*
Society and the social system	The individual
Impersonal, anonymous forces regulating behaviour	Human actions continuously recreating social life
'Objectivity'	'Subjectivity'
Generalising from the specific	Interpreting the specific
Explaining behaviour	Understanding actions
Assuming the taken-for-granted	Investigating the taken-for-granted
Macro-concepts: society, institutions, norms, positions, roles, expectations	Micro-concepts: individual perspective, personal constructs, negotiated meanings, definitions of situations
Structuralists	Symbolic interactionists, phenomenologists, ethnomethodologists

---

Source: Cohen and Manion (6)

Methods and Methodology

This book is concerned with methods and methodology. By *methods*, we mean that range of approaches used in educational research to gather data which are to be used as a basis for inference and interpretation, for explanation and prediction. Traditionally, the word refers to those techniques associated with the positivistic model – eliciting responses to predetermined questions, recording measurements, describing phenomena and performing experiments. For our purposes, we will extend the meaning to include not only the methods of normative research but also those associated with the interpretive paradigm – participant observation, role-playing, non-directive interviewing, episodes and accounts. Although methods may also be taken to include the more specific features of the scientific enterprise such as forming concepts and hypotheses, building models and theories, and sampling procedures, we will limit ourselves principally to the more general techniques which researchers use.

If methods refer to techniques and procedures used in the process of data-gathering, the aim of *methodology* then is, in Kaplan's (4) words

> to describe and analyse these methods, throwing light on their limitations and resources, clarifying their presuppositions and consequences, relating their potentialities to the twilight zone at the frontiers of knowledge. It is to venture generalizations from the success of particular techniques, suggesting new applications, and to unfold the specific bearings of logical and metaphysical principles on concrete problems, suggesting new formulations.

In summary, he suggests, the aim of methodology is to help us to understand, in the broadest possible terms, not the products of scientific enquiry but the process itself.

Our review will begin by examining those techniques associated with normative studies (with the exception of historical research) and will proceed to those used by interpretive researchers. We, for our part, will attempt to present the two perspectives in complementary light and will try to lessen the tension that is sometimes generated between them. Merton and Kendall (12) express the same sentiment when they say, 'Social scientists have come to abandon the spurious choice between qualitative and quantitative data; they are concerned rather with that combination of both which makes use of the most valuable features of each. The problem becomes one of determining *at which points* they should adopt the one, and at which the other, approach.'

A paradigm* consists of a set of assumptions; and two contrasting paradigms will embrace contrasting assumptions. Depending on the particular paradigm he espouses, whether normative or interpretive, the researcher will identify certain issues as of interest to him and ignore others; he will ask certain questions and not others; he will adopt certain research methods rather than others; and he will show a preference for certain kinds of analysis, explanation and theory (13). By way of example, let us examine in a more extended way the kinds of contrasting assumptions that normative and interpretive researchers hold about the *notion of data*. The term *data* is used in social research to represent the information gathered by investigators with the aid of their instruments, techniques and other means. They have two important characteristics which have been identified by Travers (14): they are clearly identifiable information collected under conditions that are precisely specified; and they have meaning only in relation to the particular problems being investigated. Data constitute the basis for decisions as to whether certain theoretical hypotheses should be confirmed, for the interpretation and explanation of human behaviour and for making inferences and reconstructions. In *normative studies*, data are always data for some hypothesis or other (4); if they are what is *given*, then the researcher must have hypotheses to be eligible to receive them. Data in *interpretive studies*, on the other hand, are the source of hypotheses, of interpretation; they precede any theorising or explanation which takes place. Before taking our consideration of data further, let us see how the normative and the interpretive researcher respectively would each go about his task of data collection. The former would undertake his research with attitudes, values, skills and objectives derived from the positivistic model. He is concerned with the outer social world and, as far as he is able, adopts a detached and neutral role. He is thus free to stand apart and apply whatever conceptual

---

* Gelwick's (15) extended definition of a paradigm is worth quoting in full: 'A paradigm expresses the configuration of beliefs, values, and techniques by which normal science is pursued. It represents the outlook and methods by which a discipline of study conducts its routine life, interprets data, and does research. A paradigm provides metaphors, analogies, explanations, and standards for solutions to puzzles. Paradigms are adopted because they both win adherence of followers and are sufficiently open-ended to allow focus upon further research. The breakdown of old paradigms and the emergence of new ones is a case of major revolution, usually involving preceding periods of crisis and the search for new directions. The establishment of new paradigms is a moment of synthesis and of originality.'

schema he chooses to the phenomena he has selected for investigation (6). A researcher assuming an interpretive perspective, by contrast, favours an inner view of social reality and is therefore much more involved, an involvement which frequently demands participation in the ongoing action as a member of the group he is studying. There is no question of his being neutral; most likely he himself will be changed by the events he becomes part of. Indeed, this kind of change will provide him with the fresh insights he seeks; with first-hand knowledge of the way the group conceives the world and the meanings its members impute to such conceptions. The traditionalist approaches social reality with preconceptions and hypotheses, manifest in his choice of questionnaires, attitude-scales and structured interview schedules. The interpretive researcher, however, will start with the social world *as it is* and, almost in the spirit of an eavesdropper, will tune in to it on its terms with unstructured interviews, natural conversation and the like.

The data thus gathered by the normative researcher may be described variously as *objective, external, quantifiable, explanatory, publicly verifiable* and *replicable*. Interpretive data, by contrast, may be referred to as *subjective, internal, qualitative* (that is, expressed in symbolic form − language or gesture, for instance), *interpretative, unique* and *negotiable*. To the extent that both types of researchers are trying to understand and explain social phenomena, they have a common purpose. It is in their respective attitudes to the data they have gathered that they diverge. How, then, do these differing attitudes manifest themselves in practice? What do the respective researchers *do* with their data? The normative researcher, committed to the view that there are general and universal laws determining social behaviour, uses his data to check out his hunches about objective reality or absolute truth. In a sense he tries to strait-jacket social reality with his models of man. Not so the interpretive researcher. He searches out modes of explanation *from the data themselves,* be they descriptive, analytical or conceptual. He would share the views of one observer (16) who said, 'Knowledge needed to understand human behaviour is embedded in the complex network of social interaction. To assume what it is without attempting to tap it; to refuse to tap it on the grounds of scientific objectivity; or to define this knowledge with constricting operational definitions, is to do grave injustice to the character and nature of the empirical social world that sociologists seek to know and understand.'

Kaplan has drawn our attention to a particular problem concerning the handling of data in social research. Stemming from the common humanity of the researcher and his subject, it is that behaviour has meaning to the person engaging in it as well as to the observer — the scientist — and that the two meanings do not necessarily coincide. He distinguishes the two kinds as *act meaning* and *action meaning*. The former refers to the meaning an act has for the actor; and the latter, its meaning for the researcher, the observer. The normative researcher, in interpreting an act through the mediation of his chosen theory or hypothesis, does so on the presumption that shared meanings exist between his subject and himself. The validity of his data rests on this presumption. The validity of the interpretive researcher's data and the inferences he draws from them, however, rest on no such presumption, since he is in a position to negotiate and reconstruct meanings from the data with the actor himself.

Conclusion: the Role of Research in Education

Our earlier remarks on the *nature of research* may best be summarised by quoting Mouly's definitive statement on the subject. He writes, 'Research is best conceived as the process of arriving at dependable solutions to problems through the planned and systematic collection, analysis, and interpretation of data. It is a most important tool for advancing knowledge, for promoting progress, and for enabling man to relate more effectively to his environment, to accomplish his purposes, and to resolve his conflicts.'

The term *research* itself may take on a range of meanings and thereby be legitimately applied to a variety of contexts from, say, an investigation into the techniques of Dutch painters of the seventeenth century to the problem of finding more efficient means of improving traffic flow in major city centres. For our purposes, however, we will restrict its usages to those activities and undertakings aimed at developing *a science of behaviour*, the word 'science' itself implying both normative and interpretive perspectives. Accordingly, when we speak of social research, we have in mind the systematic and scholarly application of the principles of a science of behaviour to the problems of man within his social context; and when we use the term educational research, we likewise have in mind the application of these selfsame principles to the problems of teaching and learning within the formal educational framework and to the clarification of issues having direct or indirect bearing on these concepts.

A characteristic of education in the Western world has been its uneven progress. This has been attributed to a general reluctance to apply the principles of the scientific method to educational problems and to too great a reliance on authority and experience as a means of making progress. Borg (17) has succinctly highlighted the difficulty:

> Perhaps a major reason for the slow and unsure progress in education has been the inefficient and unscientific methods used by educators in acquiring knowledge and solving their problems. An uncritical acceptance of authority opinion that is not supported by objective evidence and an overdependence upon personal experience have been characteristic of the educator's problem-solving techniques.

The particular value of scientific research in education is that it will enable educators to develop the kind of sound knowledge base that characterises other professions and disciplines; and one that will ensure education a maturity and sense of progression it at present lacks.

References

1.   Mouly, G.J., *Educational Research: the Art and Science of Investigation* (Allyn and Bacon, Boston, 1978).
2.   Kerlinger, F.N., *Foundations of Behavioural Research* (Holt, Rinehart and Winston, New York, 1970).
3.   Barratt, P.E.H., *Bases of Psychological Methods* (John Wiley and Sons, Australasia Pty Ltd 1971).
4.   Kaplan, A., *The Conduct of Inquiry* (Intertext Books, Aylesbury, 1973).
5.   Heather, N., *Radical Perspectives in Psychology* (Methuen, London, 1976).
6.   Cohen, L. and Manion, L., *Perspectives on Classrooms and Schools* (Holt-Saunders, Eastbourne, in preparation).
7.   Giddens, A., *New Rules of Sociological Method: a Positive Critique of Interpretative Sociologies* (Hutchinson, London, 1976).
8.   Shipman, M.D., *The Limitations of Social Research* (Longmans, London, 1972).
9.   Harré, R. and Secord, P.F., *The Explanation of Social Behaviour* (Basil Blackwell, Oxford, 1972).
10. Rex, J. (ed.), *Approaches to Sociology: an Introduction to Major Trends in British Sociology* (Routledge and Kegan Paul, London, 1974).
11. Bernstein, B., 'Sociology and the sociology of education: a brief account' in J. Rex (ed.), *Approaches to Sociology*.
12. Merton, R.K. and Kendall, P.L., 'The focused interview', *American Journal of Sociology*, 51 (1946) 541-57.
13. Hargreaves, D.H., Hester, S.K. and Mellor, F.J., *Deviance in Classrooms* (Routledge and Kegan Paul, London, 1975).
14. Travers, R.M.W., *An Introduction to Educational Research* (Collier-Macmillan, London, 1969).
15. Gelwick, R., *The Way of Discovery: an Introduction to the Thought of Michael Polanyi* (Oxford University Press, New York, 1977).
16. Filstead, W.J. (ed.), *Qualitative Methodology: Firsthand Involvement with the Social World* (Markham Pub. Co., Chicago, 1970.
17. Borg, W.R., *Educational Research: an Introduction* (Longmans, London, 1963).

2 HISTORICAL RESEARCH

Introduction

It must seem strange, on the face of it, that among an assemblage of research methods based on the normative and interpretive paradigms we should include, and even begin with, *historical research*. A chapter devoted to a method apparently so fundamentally different from methods having a scientific or 'science of persons' basis must at first glance seem out of place. This notwithstanding, we feel it is essential to include it and base our justifications partly on reasons advanced by Travers (1) and partly on our own views. First, a considerable number of education students do pursue historical research into their subject and so the method does have topical relevance. Second, the review of the literature which an empirical researcher is required to undertake is in itself a kind of historical study because he is reconstructing what was done in the past in a particular respect; so the principles of historical research have some bearing on part of his work at least. Third, recent years have witnessed a *rapprochement* between historical research and research into other areas such as sociology and psychology, although until now historians have tended to borrow data and methods from these disciplines and to use them to enhance historical knowledge rather than radically to change its nature. And fourth, historical research does have some features in common with both normative and interpretive approaches to research. In the case of the former, it shares the quest for objectivity and the desire to minimise bias and distortion; and with the latter, it likewise sets out to describe *all* aspects of the particular situation under study, or as many as are accessible, in its search for the *whole* truth. In summary, then, we may agree with Mouly (2) who says that while historical research cannot meet some of the tests of the scientific method interpreted in the specific sense of its use in the physical sciences (it cannot depend, for instance, on direct observation or experimentation, but must make use of reports that cannot be repeated), it qualifies as a scientific endeavour from the standpoint of its subscription to the same principles and the same general scholarship that characterise all scientific research.

Historical research has been defined as the systematic and objective location, evaluation and synthesis of evidence in order to establish facts and draw conclusions about past events (3). It is an act of reconstruction

31

undertaken in a spirit of critical enquiry designed to achieve a faithful representation of a previous age. In seeking data from the personal experiences and observations of others, from documents and records, the researcher has often to contend with inadequate information so that his reconstruction tends to be a sketch rather than a portrait. Indeed, the difficulty of obtaining adequate data makes historical research one of the most taxing kinds of enquiry to conduct satisfactorily.* Reconstruction implies a holistic perspective in that the method of enquiry characterising historical research attempts to 'encompass and then explain the whole realm of man's past in a perspective that greatly accents his social, cultural, economic, and intellectual development' (4). Ultimately, historical research is concerned with a broad view of the conditions and not necessarily the specifics which bring them about, although such a synthesis is rarely achieved without intense debate or controversy, especially on matters of detail. The act of historical research involves the identification and limitation of a problem or an area of study; sometimes the formulation of an hypothesis (or set of questions); the collection, organisation, verification, validation, analysis and selection of data; testing the hypothesis (or answering the questions) where appropriate; and writing a research report. This sequence leads to a new understanding of the past and its relevance to the present and future.

The values of historical research have been categorised by Hill and Kerber (4) as follows: (a) it enables solutions to contemporary problems to be sought in the past; (b) it throws light on present and future trends; (c) it stresses the relative importance and the effects of the various interactions that are to be found within all cultures; and (d) it allows for the revaluation of data in relation to selected hypotheses, theories and generalisations that are presently held about the past. As the writers point out, the ability of history to employ the past to predict the future, and to use the present to explain the past, gives it a dual and unique quality which makes it especially useful for all sorts of scholarly study and research.†

---

* By contrast, the historian of the modern period, i.e. the nineteenth and twentieth centuries, is more often faced in the initial stages with the problem of selecting from too much material, both at the stage of analysis and writing. Here the two most common criteria for such selection are (1) the degree of significance to be attached to data, and (2) the extent to which a specific detail may be considered typical of the whole.

† However, historians themselves usually reject such a direct application of their work and rarely indulge in it on the grounds that no two events or contexual circumstances, separated geographically and temporally, can possibly be equated. As the popular sayings go, 'History never repeats itself' and so 'the only thing we can learn from History is that we can learn nothing from History'.

The particular value of historical research in the field of education is unquestioned. Although one of the most difficult areas in which to undertake research, the outcomes of enquiry into this domain can bring great benefit to educationalists and the community at large. It can, for example, yield insights into some educational problems that could not be achieved by any other means. Further, the historical study of an educational idea or institution can do much to help us understand how our present educational system has come about; and this kind of understanding can in turn help to establish a sound basis for further progress. Historical research in education can also show how and why educational theories and practices developed. It enables educationalists to use former practices to evaluate newer, emerging ones. Recurrent trends can be more easily identified and assessed from an historical standpoint — witness, for example, the various guises in which progressivism in education appears. And it can contribute to a fuller understanding of the relationship between politics and education, between school and society, between local and central government, and between teacher and pupil.* Specific individual competencies that can be developed through instruction in the history of education have been listed in Box 2.1.

Box 2.1

Specific competencies to be developed through instruction in the history of education

1. Understanding the dynamics of educational change.
2. Increased understanding of the relationship between education and the culture in which it operates.
3. Increased understanding of contemporary educational problems.
4. Understanding the functions and limitations of historical evidence in analysing educational problems.
5. Development of elementary ability in locating, analysing and appraising historical evidence.
6. Development of a sense of the dignity and responsibility of the teaching profession.

Source: Good (5)

Historical research in education may concern itself with an individual, a group, a movement, an idea or an institution. As Best (6)

---

* The present status of the history of education as an academic discipline is well summarised and illustrated in Sutherland (7).

Box 2.2

Some historical interrelations between men, movements and institutions			
Men	Movements	Institutions	
		Type	Specific
Ignatius Loyola	Counter-Reformation	Religious teaching order	Society of Jesus, 1534
Benjamin Franklin	Scientific movement; Education for Life	Academy	Philadelphia Academy, 1751
John Dewey	Experimentalism Progressive education	Experimental School	University of Chicago Elementary School, 1896

Source: Adapted from Best (6)

points out, however, no one of these objects of historical interest and observation can be considered in isolation. No one person can be subjected to historical investigation without some consideration of his contribution to the ideas, movements or institutions of a particular time or place. These elements are always interrelated. The focus merely determines the point of emphasis towards which the historical researcher directs his attention. Box 2.2 illustrates some of these relationships from the history of education. For example, no matter whether the historian chooses for study the Jesuit order, religious teaching orders, the Counter-Reformation or Ignatius Loyola, each of the other elements appears as a prominent influence or result, and an indispensable part of the narrative.

Choice of Subject

As with other methods we shall be considering in this book, historical research may be structured by a flexible sequence of stages, beginning with the selection and evaluation of a problem or area of study. Then follows the definition of the problem (or area of study) in more precise terms, the selection of suitable sources of data, the collection of data, the classification and processing of the data, and finally, the evaluation and synthesis of the data into a balanced and objective account of the subject under investigation. There are, however, some important differences between the method of historical research and other research methods used in education. The principal difference has been highlighted by Borg (3):

> In historical research, it is especially important that the student carefully defines his problem and appraises its appropriateness before committing himself too fully. Many problems are not adaptable to historical research methods and cannot be adequately treated using this approach. Other problems have little or no chance of producing significant results either because of the lack of pertinent data or because the problem is a trivial one.

One can see from Borg's observations that the choice of a problem can sometimes be a daunting business for the potential researcher. Once a topic has been selected, however, and its potential and significance for historical research evaluated, the next stage is to define it more precisely or, perhaps more pertinently, delimit it so that a more potent analysis will result. Too broad or too vague a statement can result in the final report lacking direction or impact. Best expresses it like this: 'The experienced historian realizes that research must be a penetrating analysis of a limited problem, rather than the superficial examination of a broad area. The weapon of research is the rifle not the shotgun.' Various prescriptions exist for helping to define historical topics. Such a one has been suggested by Gottschalk (8) who recommends that four questions should be asked in identifying a topic:

1. Where do the events take place?
2. Who are the persons involved?
3. When do the events occur?
4. What kinds of human activity are involved?

As Travers (1) suggests, the scope of a topic can be modified by adjusting the focus of any one of the four categories: the geographical area involved can be increased or decreased; more or fewer persons can be included in the topic; the time span involved can be increased or decreased; and the human activity category can be broadened or narrowed. It sometimes happens that a piece of historical research can only begin with a rough idea of what the topic involves; and that delimitation of it can only take place after the pertinent material has been assembled.

In hand with the careful specification of the problem goes the need, where this is appropriate, for an equally specific and testable hypothesis (sometimes a sequence of questions may be substituted). As in empirical research, the hypothesis gives direction and focus to data collection and analysis. It imposes a selection, a structure on what would otherwise be an overwhelming mass of information. As Borg (3) observes:

> Without hypotheses, historical research often becomes little more than an aimless gathering of facts. In searching the materials that make up the sources of historical research data, unless the student's attention is aimed at information relating to specific questions or concerned with specific hypotheses, he has little chance of extracting a body of data from the available documents that can be synthesized to provide new knowledge or new understanding of the topic studied. Even after specific hypotheses have been established, the student must exercise strict self-control in his study of historical documents, or he will find himself collecting much information that is interesting but is not related to his area of inquiry. If the student's hypotheses are not sufficiently delimited or specific, it is an easy matter for him to become distracted and led astray by information that is not really related to his field of investigation.

Hill and Kerber (4) have pointed out that the evaluation and formulation of a problem associated with historical research often involve the personality of the researcher to a greater extent than do other basic types of research. They suggest that personal factors of the investigator such as interest, motivation, historical curiosity, and educational background for the interpretation of historical facts tend to influence the selection of the problem to a great extent.

Although it has been overshadowed to some extent in the past decade by a growing interest in empirical research, historical research has still a significant role to play in education, a role that will enable us to use the past to understand and explain the present more satisfactorily and also enable us to make predictions about educational trends, practices and outcomes with greater confidence. One of the commonest forms of historical research in education is the biography: a study of the life, teachings and subsequent influence of one or other of the great educators. Yet if there are priorities in this area, as determined by current needs, more fruitful problem areas exist. One of these concerns the study of present-day practices in education and how these developed. Studies of this kind often show that current practices were developed in the first place to meet needs that no longer exist. A cognate area is the realm of educational thought and ideas and the way in

Box 2.3   An example of an historical study in education

Loughborough: From College to University. A History of Higher Education at Loughborough 1909-66

This study provides a fine example of research into an educational institution or, rather, a complex of institutions. Yet it is more than this, for in providing a case study of the pre-war development of the relationship between a local college, a local education authority, and central government and the subsequent emergence of the college as a higher technological institute, the research captures the full flavour of the struggles and achievements of individuals caught in the sweep of history during one of the most expansionist periods in the history of British Higher Education.

Here is a brief extract summarising what had been achieved by the year 1939:

'By the outbreak of war in 1939, Loughborough College had become a remarkable educational establishment. In the preceding twenty years, Schofield had enlarged it very considerably and put together a uniquely idiosyncratic institution which, thanks partly to its own very considerable merits and partly to his superb flair for gathering favourable publicity, had acquired an international reputation. An odd amalgam of red-brick buildings and huts in the centre of Loughborough, imposing collegiate-looking residences and splendid sporting facilities on the playing field site, country houses and dignified mansions in Loughborough and the surrounding district, and an aerodrome on the edge of the town, it had, like Topsy, 'just growed'. Thanks to Schofield's entrepreneurial genius and willingness to try his hand at anything, he had grafted onto its engineering staple, such apparently odd bed-fellows as teacher-training and physical education. The previous twenty years had been a period of unparalleled growth so that by 1939 Schofield could boast that his College consisted of Departments of Mechanical and Civil, Electrical, Automobile, and Aeronautical Engineering; the East Midlands Teachers' Training College; a School of Athletics, Games, and Physical Training; Departments of Industrial and Fine Art, Extra-Mural Education, and Continuative Education; and, last but not least, Loughborough College School.'

Source: Cantor and Matthews (9)

which they have influenced educational practices. Travers (1) observes,
'So often education has moved through cycles of ideas only to return,
ultimately, to the starting point. A better understanding of the history
of ideas in education would prevent much activity that has been called
"rediscovering the wheel". So often a great new educational program is
little more than one that had been in vogue thirty years previously.'
An investigation, for example, of the factors contributing to the demise
of progressive education in the United States some years ago would
have striking relevance to the future of current informal and open
movements in Great Britain and the United States.

Data Collection

One of the principal differences between historical research and other
forms of research is that historical research must deal with data that
already exist. Hockett (10) expresses it thus:

> History is not a science of *direct* observation, like chemistry and
> physics. The historian like the geologist interprets past events by the
> traces they have left; he deals with the evidence of man's past acts
> and thoughts. But the historian, no less than the scientist, must
> utilize evidence resting on reliable observation. The difference in
> procedure is due to the fact that the historian usually does not make
> his own observations, and that those upon whose observations he
> must depend are, or were, often if not usually untrained observers.
> Historical method is, strictly speaking, a process *supplementary* to
> observations, a process by which the historian attempts to test the
> truthfulness of the reports of observations made by others. Like the
> scientist, he examines his data and formulates hypotheses, i.e.,
> tentative conclusions. These conjectures he must test by seeking
> fresh evidence or re-examining the old, and this process he must
> continue until, in the light of all available evidence, the hypotheses
> are abandoned as untenable or modified until they are brought into
> conformity with the available evidence.

Sources of data in historical research may be classified into two main
groups: *primary sources*, which are the life-blood of historical research;
and *secondary sources*, which may be used in the absence of, or to
supplement, primary data.

Primary sources of data have been described as those items that are
original to the problem under study and may be thought of as being in
two categories, thus:

1. The remains or relics of a given period. Although such remains and artefacts as skeletons, fossils, weapons, tools, utensils, buildings, pictures, furniture, coins and *objets d'art* were not meant to transmit information to subsequent eras, nevertheless they may be useful sources providing sound evidence about the past.
2. Those items that have had a direct physical relationship with the events being reconstructed. This category would include not only the written and oral testimony provided by actual participants in, or witnesses of, an event, but also the participants themselves. Documents considered as primary sources include manuscripts, charters, laws; archives cover official minutes or records, files, letters, memoranda, memoirs, biography, official publications, wills, newspapers and magazines, maps, diagrams, catalogues, films, paintings, inscriptions, recordings, transcriptions, log books and research reports. All these are, intentionally or unintentionally, capable of transmitting a first-hand account of an event and are therefore considered as sources of primary data. Historical research in education draws chiefly on the kind of sources identified in this second category.

Secondary sources are those that do not bear a direct physical relationship to the event being studied. They are made up of data that cannot be described as original. A secondary source would thus be one in which the person describing the event was not actually present but who obtained his descriptions from another person or source. These may or may not have been primary sources. Other instances of secondary sources used in historical research include: quoted material, textbooks, encyclopedias, other reproductions of material or information, prints of paintings or replicas of art objects. Best (6) points out that secondary sources of data are usually of limited worth because of the errors that result when information is passed on from one person to another.

Various commentators stress the importance of using primary sources of data where possible. Hill and Kerber (4) say in this connection for instance:

> In the process of conducting historical research the investigator should never be satisfied with copies of documents that can be obtained in original form . . . Relatively insignificant errors in reproduction processes may, through additive or multiplicative effects, produce a resultant error of comparatively great magnitude in the final form of the data. This condition is particularly well illustrated in reporting census data in various forms and indexes, where these

final forms are derived through the operations of addition, subtraction, multiplication, and/or division.

The value, too, of secondary sources should not be minimised. There are numerous occasions where a secondary source can contribute significantly to more valid and reliable historical research than would otherwise be the case.

One further point: the review of the literature in other forms of educational research is regarded as a preparatory stage to gathering data and serves to acquaint the researcher with previous research on the topic he himself is studying. It thus enables him to continue in a tradition, to place his work in context, and to learn from earlier endeavours. The function of the review of the literature in historical research, however, is different in that it provides the data for research; the researcher's acceptance or otherwise of his hypothesis will depend on his selection of information from the review and the interpretation he puts on it. Borg (3) has identified other differences: one is that the historical researcher will have to peruse longer documents than the empirical researcher who normally studies articles very much more succinct and precise. Further, documents required in historical research often date back much further than those in empirical research. And one final point: documents in education often consist of unpublished material and are therefore less accessible than reports of empirical studies in professional journals.

Evaluation

Because a worker in the field of historical research gathers much of his data and information from records and documents, they must be carefully evaluated so as to attest their worth for the purposes of the particular study. Evaluation of historical data and information is often referred to as historical criticism and the reliable data yielded by the process is known as historical evidence. Historical evidence has thus been described as that body of validated facts and information which can be accepted as trustworthy, as a valid basis for the testing and interpretation of hypotheses. Historical criticism is usually undertaken in two stages: first, the *authenticity* of the source is appraised; and second, the *accuracy* or *worth* of the data is evaluated. The two processes are known as *external* and *internal* criticism respectively, and since they each present problems of evaluation they merit further inspection.

External Criticism

External criticism is concerned with establishing the authenticity or genuineness of data. It is therefore aimed at the document (or other source) itself rather than the statements it contains; with analytic forms of the data rather than with the interpretation or meaning of them in relation to the study. It therefore sets out to uncover frauds, forgeries, hoaxes, inventions or distortions. To this end, the tasks of establishing the age or authorship of a document may involve tests of factors such as signatures, handwriting, script, type, style, spelling and place-names. Further, was the knowledge it purports to transmit available at the time and is it consistent with what is known about the author or period from another source? Increasingly sophisticated analyses of physical factors can also yield clues establishing authenticity or otherwise: physical and chemical tests of ink, paper, parchment, cloth and other materials, for example. Investigations in the field of educational history are less likely to encounter deliberate forgeries than in, say, political or social history, though it is possible to find that official documents, correspondence and autobiographies have been 'ghosted', that is, pre-pared by a person other than the alleged author or signer.

Internal Criticism

Having established the authenticity of the document, the researcher's next task is to evaluate the accuracy and worth of the data contained therein. While they may be genuine, they may not necessarily disclose the most faithful picture. In his concern to establish the meaning and reliability of data, the investigator is confronted with a more difficult problem than external criticism because he has to establish the credi-bility of the author of the document. Travers (1) has listed those characteristics commonly considered in making evaluations of writers, thus: was he a trained or untrained observer of the event? In other words, how competent was he? What was his relationship to the event? To what extent was he under pressure, from fear or vanity, say, to distort or omit facts? What was the intent of the writer of the docu-ment? To what extent was he an expert at recording the particular event? Were the habits of the author such that they might interfere with the accuracy of recording? Was he too antagonistic or too sympa-thetic to give a true picture? How long after the event did he record his testimony? And was he able to remember accurately? Finally, is he in agreement with other independent witnesses?

Many documents in the history of education tend to be neutral in character, though it is possible that some may be in error because of these kinds of observer-characteristics.

Writing the Research Report

Once the data have been gathered and subjected to external criticism for authenticity and to internal criticism for accuracy, the researcher is next confronted with the task of piecing together an account of the events embraced by the research problem. This stage is known as the *process of synthesis*. It is probably the most difficult phase in the project and calls for considerable imagination and resourcefulness. The resulting pattern is then applied to the testing of the hypothesis.

The writing of the final report is equally demanding and calls for creativity and high standards of objective and systematic analysis.

Best (6) has listed the kinds of problems occurring in the various types of historical research projects submitted by students. These include:

1. Problem too broadly stated.
2. Tendency to use easy-to-find secondary sources of data rather than sufficient primary sources which are harder to locate but usually more trustworthy.
3. Inadequate historical criticism of data, due to failure to establish authenticity of sources and trustworthiness of data. For example, there is often a tendency to accept a statement as necessarily true when several observers agree. It is possible that one may have influenced the others, or that all were influenced by the same inaccurate source of information.
4. Poor logical analysis resulting from:
   (a) Oversimplification — failure to recognise the fact that causes of events are more often multiple and complex than single and simple.
   (b) Overgeneralisation on the basis of insufficient evidence, and false reasoning by analogy, basing conclusions upon superficial similarities of situations.
   (c) Failure to interpret words and expression in the light of their accepted meaning in an earlier period.
   (d) Failure to distinguish between significant facts in a situation and those that are irrelevant or unimportant.
5. Expression of personal bias, as revealed by statements lifted out of context for purposes of persuasion, assuming too generous or uncritical an attitude towards a person or idea (or being too unfriendly or critical), excessive admiration for the past (sometimes known as

the 'old oaken bucket' delusion), or an equally unrealistic admiration for the new or contemporary, assuming that all change represents progress.

6. Poor reporting in a style that is dull and colourless, too flowery or flippant, too persuasive or of the 'soap-box' type, or lacking in proper usage.

In addition to these, Sutherland (7) has brilliantly illustrated two further common errors among historians of education. These are: (a) projecting current battles backwards onto an historical background which leads to distortion; and (b) 'description in a vacuum' which fails to illustrate the relationship of the educational system to the structure of society.

To conclude on a more positive note, we refer you to Box 2.4 which itemises five basic criteria for evaluating historical research.

Box 2.4

Criteria for evaluating historical research

1. *Problem:* Has the problem been clearly defined? It is difficult enough to conduct historical research adequately without adding to the confusion by starting out with a nebulous problem. Is the problem capable of solution? Is it within the competence of the investigator?

2. *Data:* Are data of a primary nature available in sufficient completeness to provide a solution, or has there been an overdependence on secondary or unverifiable sources?

3. *Analysis:* Has the dependability of the data been adequately established? Has the relevance of the data been adequately explored?

4. *Interpretation:* Does the author display adequate mastery of his data and insight into their relative significance? Does he display adequate historical perspective? Does he maintain his objectivity or does he allow personal bias to distort the evidence? Are his hypotheses plausible? Have they been adequately tested? Does he take a sufficiently broad view of the total situation? Does he see the relationship between his data and other 'historical facts'?

5. *Presentation:* Does the style of writing attract as well as inform? Does the report make a contribution on the basis of newly discovered data or new interpretation, or is it simply 'uninspired hack-work'? Does it reflect scholarliness?

Source: From Mouly (2)

The Use of Quantitative Methods

By far the greater part of research in historical studies is qualitative in nature. This is so because the proper subject-matter of historical research consists to a great extent of verbal and other symbolic material emanating from a society's or a culture's past. The basic skills required of the researcher to analyse this kind of qualitative or symbolic material involve collecting, classifying, ordering, synthesising, evaluating and interpreting. At the basis of all these acts lies sound personal judgement. In the comparatively recent past, however, attempts have been made to apply the quantitative methods of the scientist to the solution of historical problems (11). Of these methods, the one having greatest relevance to historical research is that of *content analysis*, the basic goal of which is to take a verbal, non-quantitative document and transform it into quantitative data (12).

Content analysis itself has been defined as 'a multipurpose research method developed specifically for investigating a broad spectrum of problems in which the content of communication serves as a basis of inference' (13). The use of content analysis as a technique in social research dates from the early years of this century and since then the method has gone through a number of phases. The earliest attempts at using content analysis involve word counts. As Travers (1) explains, 'Writers typically use particular words at their own frequency rates. A word that has a high usage rate by one writer may have a low usage rate by another. The usage rates of different words can be studied to throw light on the authenticity of the source of a document. Word-usage rates can also be used as a basis for inferring inner emotional states, such as anxiety.' More sophisticated approaches to content analysis are careful to identify appropriate *categories* and *units of analysis*, both of which will reflect the nature of the document being analysed and the purpose of the research. *Categories* are normally determined after initial inspection of the document and will cover the main areas of content (categories identifying trends in newspaper content, for example, may include (1) domestic news; (2) foreign affairs; (3) business and financial news; (4) sport; (5) art criticism; (6) television and radio; (7) children's items; and (8) cartoons). *Units of analysis* may include (1) the single word; (2) a theme; (3) a character (of a play or novel); (4) a sentence; and (5) a paragraph.

We can readily see how the technique of content analysis may be applied to selected aspects of historical research in education. It could be used, for instance, in the analysis of educational documents. In addition to elucidating the content of the document, the method may throw additional light on the source of the communication, its author, and on its intended recipients, those to whom the message is directed. Further, an analysis of this kind would tell us more about the social context and the kinds of factors stressed or ignored, and of the influence of political factors, for instance. It follows from this that content analysis may form the basis of comparative or cross-cultural studies. Another usage that comes readily to mind would be an examination of the content of textbooks at different points in recent history as a means of indicating, say, cultural differences, cultural censorship or cultural change. Box 2.5 itemises the seven purposes of content analysis identified by Holsti (13).

Box 2.5

The purposes of content analysis

1. To describe trends in communication content.
2. To relate known characteristics of sources to messages they produce.
3. To audit communication content against standards.
4. To analyse techniques of persuasion.
5. To analyse style.
6. To relate known attributes of the audience to messages produced for them.
7. To describe patterns of communication.

Source: From Holsti (13)

An Example of Historical Research in Education

We conclude this chapter with a short review of an example of a piece of historical research (14) in education which investigated the role of the local church school at Sowerby, Yorkshire, from the middle of the nineteenth century to the 1970s. The study set out to examine four specific aspects of the life of the school during this period. Briefly, these were:

1. the factors which influenced the building of the school, its original character, and the changes in status and organisation which took place from 1859 to 1978;
2. the changes in curriculum and teaching methods which took place in the school;
3. the facilities available for the children within the school and the

effect that legislation has had on the provisions and running of the school; and

4. the role of the church in running the school.

Of particular interest to us are the numerous *primary sources* on which the researcher drew as principal sources of information. These included: the trust deeds of the church; school admission books; school log books; inspectors' annual reports; important Education Acts during the period, in particular those passed from 1902 to 1944; the Hadow Report; HMI's reports; and extracts from a local newspaper, the *Halifax Courier*.

By using these original sources, the researcher was able to build up a detailed picture of the factors resulting in the building of the school in the early nineteenth century; subsequent developments and changes in its organisation; the content of the curriculum and the changes it underwent; the teaching methods used; the facilities available to the children and the influence of prevailing environmental and social conditions on them; the impact of successive Education Acts on various aspects of school life, including the welfare of the children; the part played by the church and its agents in the running and maintenance of the school; and the relationship between church and state as focused on the particular school in question.

This study is a good example of what can be modestly achieved using primary sources which are not too difficult to locate and which meet the criteria referred to earlier.

References

1. Travers, R.M.W., *An Introduction to Educational Research* (Collier-Macmillan, London, 1969).
2. Mouly, G.J., *Educational Research: The Art and Science of Investigation* (Allyn and Bacon, Boston, 1978).
3. Borg, W.R., *Educational Research: An Introduction* (Longmans, London, 1963).
4. Hill, J.E. and Kerber, A., *Models, Methods, and Analytical Procedures in Educational Research* (Wayne State University Press, Detroit, 1967).
5. Good, C.V., *Essentials of Educational Research* (Appleton Century Crofts, New York, 1963).
6. Best, J.W., *Research in Education* (Prentice Hall, Englewood Cliffs, New Jersey, 1970).
7. Sutherland, G., 'The study of the history of education', *History*, vol. 54, no. 180 (February 1969).
8. Gottschalk, L., *Understanding History* (Alfred A. Knopf, New York, 1951).
9. Cantor, L.M. and Matthews, G.F., *Loughborough: From College to*

University. A History of Higher Education at Loughborough 1909-1966 (Loughborough University of Technology, 1977).

10. Hockett, H.C., *The Critical Method in Historical Research and Writing* (Macmillan, London, 1955).
11. Travers, R.M.W., *An Introduction to Educational Research.* See also the Social Science Research Council's *Research in Economic and Social History* (Heinemann, London, 1971), Chapters 2 and 3.
12. Bailey, K.D., *Methods of Social Research* (Collier-Macmillan, London, 1978).
13. Holsti, O.R., 'Content analysis' in G. Linzey and E. Aronson (eds), *The Handbook of Social Psychology*, vol. 2, *Research Methods* (Addison-Wesley, New York, 1968).
14. Law, B. 'The role of the church school at Sowerby in local education', unpublished study submitted for the Certificate in Education (University of Leeds, 1978).

3 DEVELOPMENTAL RESEARCH

Introduction

Most educational research methods are descriptive; that is, they set out to describe and to interpret *what is* (1). Descriptive research, according to Best, is concerned with

> conditions or relationships that exist; practices that prevail; beliefs, points of view, or attitudes that are held; processes that are going on; effects that are being felt; or trends that are developing. At times, descriptive research is concerned with how *what is* or *what exists* is related to some preceding event that has influenced or affected a present condition or event.

The previous and the present chapter and, indeed, most of the chapters that follow deal with descriptive research. Chapter 8, 'Experiments and Quasi-experiments', is a clear exception, descriptive research being fundamentally different from experimental research in that in the former, the researcher accounts for what has already occurred; in the latter, he arranges for events to happen (1). This overall balance in the text reflects the fact that the majority of education studies that are reported in the literature are descriptive rather than experimental. They look at individuals, groups, institutions, methods and materials in order to describe, compare, contrast, classify, analyse and interpret the entities and the events that constitute their various fields of enquiry.

This chapter deals with three types of descriptive research which for the present we shall refer to loosely as longitudinal, cross-sectional and trend or prediction studies. Collectively they are termed *developmental research* because they are concerned both to describe what the present relationships are among variables in a given situation and to account for changes occurring in those relationships as a function of time. The term 'developmental' is primarily biological, having to do with the organisation and the life processes of living things. The concept has been appropriated and applied to diverse educational, historical, sociological and psychological phenomena (2). In education, developmental studies often retain the original biological orientation of the term, having to do with the acquisition of motor and perceptual skills in young children. However, the designation 'developmental' has wider application in education, for example, in connection with Piaget's studies of qualitative changes occurring in children's thinking, and Kohlberg's work on moral development.

Because education is primarily concerned with the individual's physical, social, intellectual and emotional growth, developmental studies continue to occupy a central place in the methodologies used by the educational researcher.

The Terminology of Developmental Research

The term *longitudinal* is used to describe a variety of studies that are conducted over a period of time. Often, as we have seen, the word *developmental* is employed in connection with longitudinal studies that deal specifically with aspects of human growth.

A clear distinction is drawn between *longitudinal* and *cross-sectional* studies. The longitudinal study gathers data over an extended period of time; a short-term investigation may take several weeks or months; a long-term study can extend over many years. Where successive measures are taken at different points in time from the *same* respondents, the term *follow-up study* or *cohort study* is used in the British literature, the equivalent term in the United States being the *panel study*. Where *different* respondents are studied at different points in time, the study is called *cross-sectional*. Where a few selected factors are studied continously over time, the term *trend study* is employed.

Cohort studies and trend studies are *prospective* longitudinal methods in that they are ongoing in their collection of information about individuals or their monitoring of specific events. *Retrospective* longitudinal studies, on the other hand, focus upon individuals who have reached some defined end-point or state (3). For example, a group of young people may be the researcher's particular interest (intending social workers, convicted drug offenders or university dropouts, for example), and the questions to which he will address himself are likely to include ones such as: is there anything about the previous experience of these individuals that can account for their present situation (3)?

A cross-sectional study is one that produces a 'snapshot' of a population at a particular point in time. The epitome of the cross-sectional study is a national census in which a representative sample of the population consisting of individuals of different ages, different occupations, different educational and income levels, and residing in different parts of the country, is interviewed on the same day (4). More typically in education, cross-sectional studies involve indirect measures of the nature and rate of changes in the physical and intellectual development of samples of children drawn from representative age levels. The single 'snapshot' of the cross-sectional study provides the researcher with data for either a retrospective or a prospective enquiry.

Trend or *prediction studies* have an obvious importance to the educational administrator or planner. Like cohort studies, they may be of relatively short or long duration. Essentially, the trend study examines recorded data to establish patterns of change that have already occurred in order to predict what will be likely to occur in the future. A major difficulty the researcher faces in conducting trend analyses is the intrusion of unpredictable factors that invalidate forecasts formulated on past data. For this reason, short-term trend studies tend to be more accurate than long-term analyses. The distinctions we have drawn between the various terms used in developmental research are illustrated in Box 3.1.

Strengths and Weaknesses of Cohort and Cross-sectional Studies

Longitudinal studies of the cohort analysis type have an important place in the research armoury of the educational investigator. Cohort studies of human growth and development conducted on representative samples of populations are uniquely able to identify typical patterns of development and to reveal factors operating on those samples which elude other research designs. They permit the researcher to examine individual variations in characteristics or traits, and to produce individual growth curves. Cohort studies, too, are particularly appropriate when the investigator attempts to establish causal relationships, for this task involves identifying changes in certain characteristics that result in changes in others. Cross-sectional designs are inappropriate in causal research. Cohort analysis is especially useful in sociological research because it can show how changing properties of individuals fit together into changing properties of social systems as a whole (5). For example, the study of staff morale and its association with the emerging organisational climate of a newly-opened school would lend itself to this type of developmental research. A further strength of cohort studies in schools is that they provide longitudinal records whose value derives in part from the known fallibility of any single test or assessment (3). Finally, *time*, always a limiting factor in experimental and interview settings, is generally more readily available in cohort studies, allowing the researcher greater opportunity to observe trends and to distinguish 'real' changes from chance occurrences (4).

Longitudinal studies suffer several disadvantages, though the gravity of these weaknesses is challenged by supporters of cohort analysis (see

Box 3.1
Types of developmental research

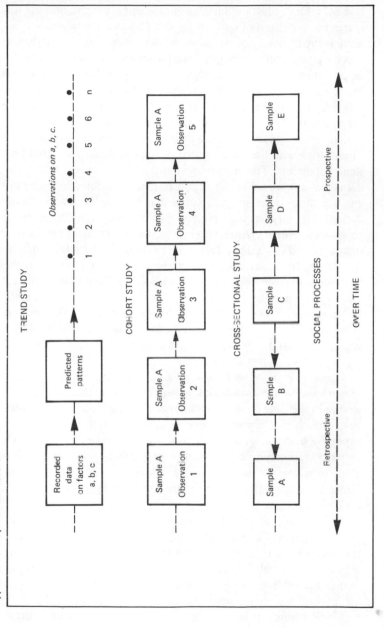

Box 3.2). First, they are time-consuming and expensive because the researcher is obliged to wait for growth data to accumulate. Second, there is the difficulty of *sample mortality*. Inevitably during the course of a long-term cohort study, subjects drop out, are lost or refuse further co-operation. Such attrition makes it unlikely that those who remain in the study are as representative of the population as the sample that was originally drawn. Sometimes attempts are made to lessen the effects of sample mortality by introducing aspects of cross-sectional study design, that is, 'topping up' the original cohort sample size at each time of re-testing with the same number of respondents drawn from the same population. The problem here is that differences arising in the data from one survey to the next may then be accounted for by differences in the persons surveyed rather than by genuine changes or trends. A third difficulty has been termed *control effect* (sometimes referred to as *measurement effect*). Often, repeated interviewing results in an undesired and confusing effect on the actions or attitudes under study, influencing the behavior of subjects, sensitising them to matters that have hitherto passed unnoticed, or stimulating them to communication with others on unwanted topics (5). Finally, cohort studies in education pose considerable problems of organisation due to the continuous changes that occur in pupils, staff, teaching methods and the like. Such changes make it highly unlikely that a study will be completed in the way that it was originally planned.

Cohort studies, as we have seen, are particularly appropriate in research on human growth and development. Why then are so many studies in this area cross-sectional in design? The reason is that they have a number of advantages over cohort studies: they are less expensive than cohort analyses; they produce findings more quickly; they are less likely to suffer from control effects; and they are more likely to secure the co-operation of respondents on a 'one-off' basis. Generally, cross-sectional designs are able to include more subjects than are cohort designs.

The strengths of cohort analysis are the weaknesses of the cross-sectional design. The cross-sectional study is a less effective method for the researcher who is concerned to identify individual variations in growth or to establish causal relationships between variables. Sampling in the cross-sectional study is complicated because different subjects are involved at each age level and may not be comparable. Further problems arising out of selection effects and the obscuring of irregularities in growth weaken the cross-sectional study so much that one observer (6) dismisses the method as a highly unsatisfactory way of obtaining developmental data except for the crudest purposes.

Douglas (7), who pioneered the first national cohort study to be undertaken in any country, makes a spirited defence of the method against the common criticisms that are levelled against it — that it is expensive and time-consuming. We summarise his account of the advantages of cohort analysis over cross-sectional designs in Box 3.2.

Box 3.2

Advantages of cohort over cross-sectional designs

1. Some types of information, for example, on attitudes or assessment of potential ability, are only meaningful if collected contemporaneously. Other types are more complete or more accurate if collected during the course of a longitudinal survey, though they are likely to have some value even if collected retrospectively, for example, length of schooling, job history, geographical movement.

2. In cohort studies, no duplication of information occurs, whereas in cross-sectional studies the same type of backgroup information has to be collected on each occasion. This increases the interviewing costs.

3. The omission of even a single variable, later found to be important, from a cross-sectional study is a disaster, whereas it is usually possible in a cohort study to fill the gap, even if only partially, in a subsequent interview.

4. A cohort study allows the accumulation of a much larger number of variables, extending over a much wider area of knowledge than would be possible in a cross-sectional study. This is of course because the collection can be spread over many interviews. Moreover, information may be obtained at the most appropriate time, for example, information on job entry may be obtained when it occurs even if this varies from one member of the sample to another.

5. Starting with a birth cohort removes later problems of sampling and allows the extensive use of subsamples. It also eases problems of estimating bias and reliability.

6. Longitudinal studies are free of one of the major obstacles to causal analysis, namely, the re-interpretation of remembered information so that it conforms with conventional views on causation. It also provides the means to assess the direction of effect.

Source: Adapted from Douglas (7)

Strategies in Developmental Research

Having identified some strengths and weaknesses in cohort and cross-sectional analyses, we now look at actual decisions made by researchers in planning their studies in light of the phenomena with which they have to deal and the support upon which they can draw. In this section, we examine a number of developmental studies in education to see the constraints under which they have been conducted, the techniques that have been employed, and the retrospective views of the researchers themselves about their design decisions.

Example 1   A Cohort Study: Douglas (7) The 1946 National Cohort Study

For more than a quarter of a century, Douglas was concerned with a longitudinal study for the Medical Research Council involving over 5,000 children born in the year 1946. Among the numerous books and research reports (9) that have arisen out of the study of this cohort, *The Home and the School* (1964) is perhaps the most widely known by educationalists.

At its inception in 1946, Douglas's study had the support of the Royal Commission on Population and the financial backing of the Nuffield Foundation and the National Birthday Trust Fund. The research followed a national cohort of children from birth, through adolescence and into adulthood. At each stage, the study involved a lengthy questionnaire enquiry beginning in 1946 with detailed descriptions of maternity care and child-rearing practices, and extended as the children grew older with information on physical, intellectual and social characteristics gathered from school records and teachers' assessments. In 1961 when the sample reached statutory school-leaving age, 62 per cent who left for employment were followed up by youth employment officers, contact with those remaining at school being maintained through headteachers and their staffs. In 1972, approximately 100 professional interviewers were recruited to make contact with the total sample in one-and-a-quarter-hour interviews, and to obtain data on family and household affairs, employment histories, religious beliefs and membership of clubs and other organisations.

Over the 26 years of the study, contact was maintained with between 80 per cent and 90 per cent of the original sample and a mass of data were accumulated from earliest infant experiences to adult employment and family affairs. Complete longitudinal data exist for 70 per cent of the sample with an additional 10 per cent of information on respondents marred only by occasional loss of contact. Detailed accounts of the main survey findings and of subsidiary investigations are reported in Douglas (9). For present purposes, Douglas (7) discusses a number of problems in the design and execution of the 1946 National Cohort Study which we now relate to our previous account of the strengths and weaknesses of cohort analysis.

Sampling decisions. Douglas's decision to select a single week's births in Great Britain (some 15,000 in number) in the week beginning 3 March 1946 was governed primarily by questions of finance and the availability of coding help. Spreading the sample throughout the year by selecting six separate days would have made it more representative but would have proved more costly than funds permitted. Because the only source of coders of questionnaire data were students available only in the summer vacation, Douglas 'worked backwards' from the early summer, and allowing time for the administration of interviews and the initial processing of questionnaire data, arrived at the most propitious week, 3-9 March.

In 1947, financial constraints led to the decision to cut the original 15,000 sample to approximately 5,000. The interests of the research team in *equality of opportunity* led to the retention of the total number of children in the non-manual working-class group and the group designated agricultural workers. All in all, some 5,362 children constituted the cohort in 1947 of whom approximately half had parents who were non-manual workers. Retrospectively, Douglas (7) says of his original sampling decisions:

> If I were to repeat the 1946 study I would take a six-day sample spread throughout the year. For the whole sample I would get minimal birth information and for the follow-up would divide each day's births into two random groups. One would be used largely as a control, the other would be followed up in detail. This would give a main sample of about 7,000 and an equal number of controls. The controls would show up any biases introduced by the exposure of the main longitudinal sample to repeated interviews, examinations, and tests. They could also provide additional information, at widely spaced intervals, on major and checkable events such as accidents, hospital admissions and school achievement. By spreading the sample over the year the dangers of seasonal bias would be avoided. Moreover, the load of examinations and interviewing would be spread evenly and this would make it reasonable to ask for yearly contacts.

In addition to financial constraints then, the specific interests of the research team and the seasonal availability of assistance governed the sampling decisions taken by Douglas and his associates.

Sampling mortality. The very low sample mortality reported by Douglas stemmed in part from the fact that in a national cohort study internal migration is more a problem of contact than of outright losses and renewed contact was made easier because the intervals between interviews was never more than two years (7). Comparisons of the characteristics of those who were lost with those of the remaining sample revealed that the resulting bias was not large enough to cause concern.

Control effects. Douglas's check for bias introduced as a result of control effects involved taking one quarter of the manual working-class children in the 1946 sample (that is, some 5,000 of those in the original 15,000 sample) and using them as a control group. Eleven years later, using data collected from interviews and from school medical records, Douglas found no evidence of bias apart from a greater incidence of treatment for minor speech and eye defects in the longitudinal sample.

Interviewers – professional or amateur? The dangers arising out of the use of health visitors, nurses, employment officers and school teachers rather than trained professional interviewers as data collectors are discussed at length by Douglas. On balance, he concluded that the lack of medical, industrial and educational knowledge in the trained group outweighed any advantages that might have accrued as a result of their professional interviewing skills.

In conclusion, the National Cohort Study of Douglas and his associates serves as an excellent example of what can be achieved by the long-term cohort analysis, based upon a large representative sample and backed by adequate funding agencies. Those aspects of the study that are of particular interest to educationalists are to do with the wastage of ability among working-class children during their primary and secondary schooling. The cohort design enabled Douglas to establish causal relationships between variables. Thus, he was able to show the extent to which adverse effects of local educational provision were cumulative as his sample of children grew older. Other analyses were able to relate early illnesses and adverse home conditions to indices of health and behaviour in early adulthood. By using a large sampling frame, Douglas was able to introduce controls when examining relationships between independent and dependent variables (see Chapter 8 for the meaning of dependent and independent variables). Thus, geographical variation in the provision of selective school places, he found, accounted for approximately half of the social inequalities in secondary education after controlling for ability. Douglas makes a strong case for the retention of cohort studies:

> My contention is that cohort studies provide the most efficient and also the cheapest opportunities to assess the effectiveness of new services and new policies . . . If we need to know what benefits accrue, for example, from spending £X million on pre-school education and which sections of the population are receiving the greatest benefits from this provision, comparisons between cohorts will provide the best answers.

Example 2   A Cross-Sectional Study: Jelinek and Brittan (10)
Multiracial Education

One of the first large-scale attempts to explore pupils' attitudes towards multiracial education is chosen as an example of cross-sectional research. A national sample of boys and girls in multiracial schools in England answered questions about their actual and their desired friendship choices and completed a 20-item questionnaire about their attitudes towards (a) the atmosphere of the multiracial school; (b) their school work; and (c) the school in general.

Inter-ethnic friendship patterns. Three questions to do with friendships in a sample consisting of 677 eight year olds, 611 ten year olds, 1,507 twelve years olds, and 1,505 fourteen year olds, who were further differentiated by sex and by ethnic group (British, Indian, Pakistani, West Indian, Kenyan, Asian, Cypriot, Italian, Others).

The Criswell Index of Self-preference was used to obtain indices of in-group and out-group friendship choices. Basically, the Criswell Index is a ratio of two ratios, one giving the relative strengths of observed in-group and out-group choices, the other giving the relative strengths which could be expected on the basis of chance alone. In the present study, out-group was defined as all other ethnic groups in the particular school other than that of the chooser. The Criswell Index allows for variability in the size of the groups and variability in the number of friendship choices that are made.

Where the Criswell Index is equal to 1.0 it indicates that a completely balanced pattern of choice between in-group and out-group choices has been made. Values *less than 1.0* indicate a tendency

Box 3.3

In-group, out-group actual friendship choices by age and ethnic group

Junior School No.	Age 8+ (N = 677)								Age 10+ (N = 611)							
	B	I	P	K	AS	WI	C	IT	B	I	P	K	AS	WI	C	IT
1	1		7		10	6			3		2		4	2		
2	2	.7	3		3	3			2	2	4		2	4		
4	3	.2	0		2	2			.7	1		4	2	7		
5	2	2			2	5			2	3			4	1		
6	2	4	0		3	2			3	1	5	10	3	6		
7	2					1			2					1		
8	2				8		1		2					.3	2	
10	1				2		3		2					1	2	
11	3	13			13				11							
13	3	3			3	.6		6	3	3			4	3	2	3

Secondary School No.	Age 12+ (N = 1507)								Age 14+ (N = 1505)							
	B	I	P	K	AS	WI	C	IT	B	I	P	K	AS	WI	C	IT
14 (1)	2	6	12	42	10	7			4	3	7		7	6		
15 (2)	5	4		13	6	6			5	6	4	1	12	6		
16 (4)	4	5	4	3	2	31			9	4	0	4	8	13		
17 (4)	8	2	10	4	4	9			13	.6	4	3	2	15		
18 (6)	3	4	3		6	6			2	23	39	4	31	4		
19 (7)	2				5	3			2				3	7		
20 (8)	4				3	7	8		4				7	9	4	
21 (10)	2				.9	4	4		3				3	6	4	
22 (11)	5	14			5	15			4	12			7	13		
23 (11)	2	5			3	4			7	6			3	5		
24 (13)	4	17				16		8	3	17			9	7		4
25 (13)	4	9			3	16	20	10	2	17		33	27	3		20

Note:
1. The numbers of brackets refer to the junior school situated in the same locality as each secondary school: 3 infant schools are excluded from the list as having no pupils in the age-group involved in this aspect of the study.
2. The indices for 'Asians' are derived from the combined data of Indian, Pakistani and Kenyan Asian pupils.
3. Key to Ethnic Groups:
   B — British   I — Indian   P — Pakistani   K — Kenyan Asian
   AS — Asian   WI — West Indian   C — Cypriot   IT — Italian

Source: From Jelinek and Brittan (10)

Box 3.4

In-group, out-group desired friendship choices by age and ethnic origin

Junior School No.	Age 8+ (N = 677)								Age 10+ (N = 611)							
	B	I	P	K	AS	WI	C	IT	B	I	P	K	AS	WI	C	IT
1	.5		1		1	2			3	.2			.1	2		
2	1	2			1	4			2	2	4		2	2		
4	1	.9	3		9	2			.7	.9		3	2	3		
5	2	0			.2	2			2	1			1	1		
6	3	2			2	1			3	1	1	0	2	3		
7	2					1			.9					2		
8	2					2	.6		1					3	1	
10	1					.6	2		2					2	1	
11	5	2			2				8							
13	2	.7			.7	1		2	3	.9		2	.8	.9		2

Secondary School No.	Age 12+ (N = 1507)								Age 14+ (N = 1505)							
	B	I	P	K	AS	WI	C	IT	B	I	P	K	AS	WI	C	IT
14 (1)	2	0	5	19	4	5			7	0	9		7	1		
15 (2)	4	6			3	4			3	4	2	3	7	5		
16 (4)	3	1	4	2	3	8			10	6		3	4	8		
17 (4)	4	1	3	4	3	9			8	5		2	3	35		
18 (6)	2	5	2	4	3	3			1	45	36		35	6		
19 (7)	2				4	2			1				0	2		
20 (8)	2				4	4	2		2				3	14	5	
21 (10)	1				0	2	2		1				0	4	4	
22 (11)	7	2			.8	1			5	5			4	8		
23 (11)	4	4			2				12	3			3	5		
24 (13)	3	4			4		6		4	14			12	4	2	
25 (13)	2	0		13	4	7		2	2	3			4	4	8	7

Note:

1. The numbers of brackets refer to the junior school situated in the same locality as each secondary school: 3 infant schools are excluded from the list as having no pupils in the age-group involved in this aspect of the study.
2. The indices for 'Asians' are derived from the combined data of Indian, Pakistani and Kenyan Asian pupils.
3. Key to Ethnic Groups:

B — British	I — Indian	P — Pakistani	K — Kenyan Asian
AS — Asian	WI — West Indian	C — Cypriot	IT — Italian

Source: From Jelinek and Brittan (10)

towards *out-group* friendship choices; and values *greater than 1.0*
indicate a tendency towards *in-group* friendship choices. Boxes 3.3 and
3.4 show the Criswell Indices for each of the age-based samples in
respect of *actual* and *desired* friendship choices.

The most striking feature of the data in Boxes 3.3 and 3.4 is the high
incidence of own-group preferences and the noticeable increase in own-
group preferences that occurs in the older age groups. One important
finding of the study is the relatively early age (8+) at which ethnicity
features in friendship choices in the context of British schools. Another
is the greater incidence of balanced indices in respect of desired friendship choices (Box 3.4) as compared with actual friendship choices (Box
3.3), implying that barriers exist to inter-ethnic friendships.

These data raise tantalising questions, the answers to which are
beyond the scope of a cross-sectional enquiry. Why, for example, are
there such striking differences in the sizes of the indices between
schools with roughly the same ethnic mixes? And to what extent does
the Criswell Index's lumping together of all other ethnic groups from
that of the chooser disguise complex differences which might reveal a
very different state of affairs to that shown in Boxes 3.3 and 3.4?

Pupils' attitudes. A glance at the analysis of pupils' attitudes shown in
Box 3.5 reveals the strengths and the weaknesses of the cross-sectional
design. In this part of the study, the researchers were able to contact a
large sample of children (n = 3,551), gather attitudinal data which were
then subdivided by age and ethnic origin, and compute mean scores for
each subsample. Analysis of variance and t-tests were then used to test
for significance. With such large numbers in the various subsamples,
very small mean score differences reach statistical significance. Thus
(10):

> Relative to the others, Asian pupils held favourable attitudes to the
> multiracial school but were also much more concerned about their
> work . . . The European pupils, like the indigenous pupils, were
> generally less anxious than those from other ethnic backgrounds.
> West Indian pupils held distinctly different views (from other
> groups) about the multiracial school. Their attitude was less favour-
> able than others at 10+, most favourable at 12+, and average at 14+.

Par excellence, the cross-sectional design is able to show the pattern of
differences that exist between the various age/ethnic subsamples. The
problem arises when an interpretation of the differences is attempted.

Box 3.5

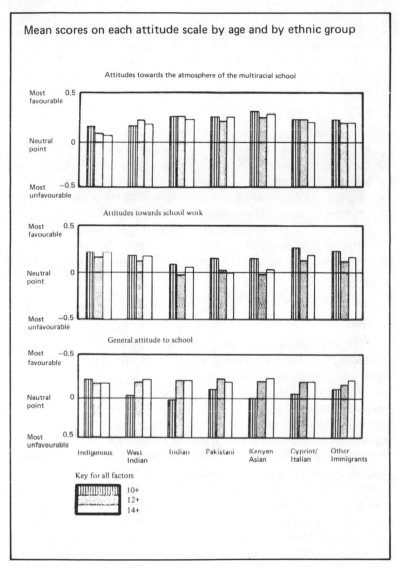

Mean scores on each attitude scale by age and by ethnic group

Attitudes towards the atmosphere of the multiracial school

Attitudes towards school work

General attitude to school

Key for all factors

10+
12+
14+

Indigenous | West Indian | Indian | Pakistani | Kenyan Asian | Cypriot/ Italian | Other Immigrants

Source: From Jelinek and Brittan (10)

The researchers are justly cautious (10):

> The attitude of pupils from minority ethnic groups toward school
> was less favourable in the lowest age group but was found to have
> improved among older children. On the other hand, this might
> reflect how they became gradually used to the existing norms as
> they came to know the whole system better, or they acquired a
> better knowledge of English and perhaps some English friends.
>
> In an ideal solution, the cohorts of pupils would be followed
> throughout their school career to allow for thorough observation of
> the development of their attitudes within the school situation. This
> was however a cross-sectional study . . . so any conclusions about
> trends in the development of the pupils' attitudes to school can only
> be assumptions . . . The observed differences could have originated
> in three different ways: from differences between cohorts, from
> different perceptions of the core items, or from the influence of
> items added for the two older groups. A more precise explanation
> can only be supplied by further studies.

*Example 3:   A Cohort/Cross-sectional Design: The Newsons' Child
Development Research Unit Study (11)*

The long-term research into child upbringing undertaken by the
Newsons at the Child Development Research Unit at Nottingham University is of major importance as a developmental study and, for our
purposes, a useful illustration of a combination of cohort and cross-
sectional designs.

Each of the publication (11) that has arisen out of this ongoing
investigation has an immediate appeal in the way that the researchers
have captured the richness and variety of life in contemporary urban
society. At one, four and seven years of age (and more studies are
promised) the reader is presented with descriptive accounts of the social
and material contexts of the lives of some 700 Nottingham children.
The Newsons' objective is to obtain detailed pictures of these children
at successive stages of their development from babyhood, through
adolescence and into adulthood − pictures, they say, built up from the
children's behaviour in the natural habitats of the homes, backyards
and neighbourhoods that constitute the 'Kaleidoscope of their everyday
environment'. Our particular interest is in the design decisions governing the research itself and with the constraints under which those
decisions were taken.

At the beginning of the study the sample target aimed at by the Newsons was 700 completed interviews with mothers about a variety of infant-rearing practices. To obtain 700 completed schedules, 773 interviews were attempted altogether.

At the initial and subsequent stages in the ongoing study the researchers worked with a class-stratified random sample. To begin with, a fully random sample was drawn from the birth records of the City of Nottingham Health Department. Because the study is primarily concerned with normal children in ordinary family situations, illegitimate children and those known to have gross disabilities were excluded from the outset. So too were children not in the care of their mothers and children whose parents were recent immigrants to Britain. This allowed the Newsons to establish the social class composition of the sample. In this way, 500 completed interviews were obtained. At the second stage of the initial survey, the researchers began by drawing random samples which were then interviewed by health visitors who forwarded details of the social class composition of these groups to the investigators. With this information, the researchers were able to adjust their sample numbers to increase the overall representation of groups that were not numerically well-represented by simple random sampling procedures. Stage two, then, involved stratified random sampling on the basis of social class data. This sampling practice has been carried out at each successive stage, the strategy being to include at least 100 cases in each of the numerically smaller social class groups. In Box 3.6, which

Box 3.6

Class composition of interviewed sample compared with (bracketed) expected composition of unstratified sample

	social class					summary		
	I&II	*IIIwc*	*III man*	*IV*	*V*	*I&II, IIIwc*	*IIIman, IV, V*	*Total*
	N	N	N	N	N	N	N	N
boys	69	58	105	81	57	127	243	370
	(49)	(45)	(175)	(52)	(27)	(94)	(254)	(348)
girls	65	49	99	75	39	114	213	327
	(49)	(45)	(175)	(52)	(27)	(94)	(254)	(348)
both	134	107	204	156	96	241	456	697
	(98)	(90)	(350)	(104)	(54)	(188)	(508)	(696)
	14%	13%	50%	15%	8%	27%	73%	100%

Source: From J. and E. Newson (11)

shows the sample interviewed at the seven-year-old stage of the study, the numbers in brackets identify the expected composition of the groups had simple random sampling rather than stratified random sampling been adopted. It will be seen that the total group for Social Class V just fails to meet the 100-cases criterion that the Newsons aimed for.

Losses from the study. Out of 708 children whose mothers were interviewed when their children were one year old, 274 matched follow-up cases were made at the four-year-old stage, making possible cohort-type analyses of the sort undertaken by Douglas and his associates in the previously reported study. There were 426 new cases whose mothers were seen for the first time when their children were four years old. Figure 3.1 (from a personal communication, Dr. J. Newson, 9 March 1979) shows losses and additions at each stage of the study to date (1979).

Figure 3.1: Losses and additions at each stage of the study from 1 year through to 16 years of age

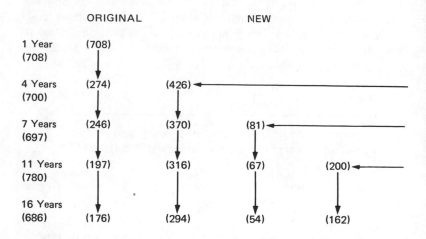

Cohort analyses are being undertaken in respect of a variety of longitudinal data. With successive losses from the original cohort at each stage of the enquiry and the 'topping up' of the sample to around 700, it seems that the cross-sectional nature of the data must take on increasing importance, restricting the ability of the researchers to speculate about causal relationships.

The retrospective account of the early years of this research study
stands in stark contrast to that of Douglas (9). 'How do you get a good
idea off the ground if you have no money, no resources, no academic
patron, and no one has ever heard of you?' The Newsons go on to say
how — and leave the reader full of admiration for their tenacity,
single-mindedness and diligence. Without the resources of the national
cohort-type study, they opted for a sophisticated use of the interview
as a research tool, a decision which they freely admit was influenced by
factors of practical expediency rather than an original commitment to
the interview as a research instrument. None the less, their detailed
account of the use of the interview technique bears close reading. In
contrast to Douglas's faith in the interview data collected by his health
visitor teams, it was the disparity which the Newsons found between
their own focused interviews and those conducted by health visitors
which led them to develop the tape-recorded interview as a research
instrument (8).

*Example 4   A Trend or Prediction Study: Department of Education
and Science, A Study of School Buildings (12)*

As an example of a trend or prediction study, we present an outline of
the work involved in estimating the overall number of school children
in 1986 who will need to be catered for in school buildings, and the
consequent scale of work involved in 'basic need' and 'improvement'
building programmes. The phase of the Department of Education and
Science study that we describe only partly follows the lines of the trend
study set out in Box 3.1 in so far as its primary concern is with predicting future demands.

First, past and projected numbers of births are used to arrive at a
projection of the overall school population in 1986. (In practice, a
series of projections is made based upon different assumptions about
birth trends. The graphs in Box 3.7 show three such projections.) This
overall population is then differentiated by regions of England and
Wales. Estimates are then made of the number of pupils who will be in
school places provided between now (1976) and 1986 under basic
need building programmes. Finally, the number of pupils who will
need to be catered for in 1986 in the then existing buildings is arrived
at: 3,069,000 primary and 2,871,000 secondary school pupils.

Box 3.7 shows the run of previous figures and projected figures of
the number of pupils of primary and secondary age in maintained
schools in England and Wales up to the year 1996. The graphs for
primary and secondary projections are similar in shape, though

Box 3.7

Previous and projected figures of pupil numbers in England and Wales

Pupils of Primary age (5 and over) in maintained primary and secondary schools in England and Wales: 1965 to 1976 and projections to 1996

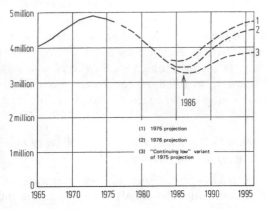

Pupils of Secondary age in maintained primary and secondary schools in England and Wales 1965 to 1976 and projections to 1996

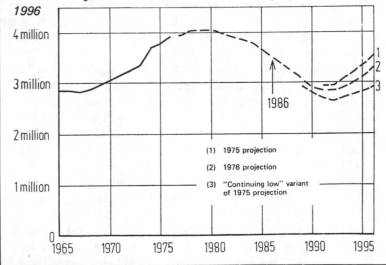

Source: HMSO (12)

differently sequenced chronologically, each showing an upturn towards the 1990s. The upturns are based on a number of assumptions:

one of the reasons for the low numbers of births in the last few years is that many women have postponed, rather than abandoned, starting or adding to their families. The annual number of births is therefore projected to recover quite soon as these women 'catch up'.
    The projection also incorporates the assumption that the average completed family size in the medium-term future will be about 2.1 children.

What these projections mean in the actual scale of the decline in school numbers between the years 1976 and 1986 is shown in Table 3.1.

Table 3.1: The decline in the numbers of pupils aged 5 and over in maintained primary and secondary schools, 1976 to 1986: England and Wales

| | School population ('000) | | Projected decline 1976 to 1986 | |
	1976	1986 (projected)	Thousands	As a percentage of the 1976 population
Pupils of primary age	4,763	3,429	1,334	28.0%
Pupils of secondary age	3,900	3,545	335	9.1%

Source: HMSO (12)

Table 3.1 shows a 28 per cent decline in the primary school population by the year 1986, the corresponding decline in the secondary school age being some 9 per cent. The researchers then go on to estimate the percentage declines in the various regions of England and Wales. These data are shown in Table 3.2. Estimates are then made of the number of places that will be made available through the basic need building programme between 1976 and 1986. Finally, projected needs and estimated availability are brought together to arrive at 'hard' data on which policy decisions can be made for regional planning and expenditure forecasting.

Problems in trend or prediction studies. We referred earlier to the intrusion of unpredictable factors in trend analyses that make long-term

Table 3.2: Projected percentage declines in the number of pupils in maintained primary and secondary schools, 1976 to 1986: England and Wales

Area	Pupils of primary age	Pupils of secondary age
Non-Metropolitan Counties		
North	30%	15%
Yorkshire & Humberside	26%	9%
North West	24%	6%
East Midlands	23%	6%
West Midlands	21%	4%
East Anglia	18%	4%
South East	28%	5%
South West	25%	9%
Metropolitan Counties		
North	37%	22%
Yorkshire & Humberside	28%	12%
North West	33%	15%
West Midlands	27%	5%
Greater London	34%	14%
Wales	27%	9%
England and Wales	28%	9%

Source: HMSO (12)

forecasting hazardous. In the present study the researchers identify a number of uncertainties in connection with their predictions.

First, projections of the number of pupils aged under five in 1986 are subject to uncertainty, the number depending upon the number of three and four year olds in the population, the amount of available space, the various admission policies for this age group and the amount of money available. Projections about this age group are therefore excluded from the calculations. As a matter of interest, there were 380,000 under-fives in schools in 1976 and 32,000 in nursery classes. Clearly, these groups must figure in long-term estimates of school building needs. Second, the definition of basic need school building is somewhat ambiguous. Conventionally, say the researchers, school building in a given year comprises basic need building plus improvement building. The basic need part covers places that are built to cater for local increases in the school population. In the past, the demand for basic need building has been thought of as comprising two elements — an overall growth in the school population, and an allowance for pupils shifting from one area of the country to another. In times of growth in pupil numbers the shift allowance hardly figures in estimates when compared with the overall growth aspect. With the decline in school population, the basic need school building becomes simply an estimate of the shift element, a factor that is open to a variety of unknown influences over the projected period of the study.

Third, the estimate of basic need building between 1976 and 1986 is based upon projects actually started, on local authority bids for work from 1976 onwards, and on expectations that the shift-based demand during the 1980s will fall faster than the school population, it being assumed that migration will be proportional to the school population but that more empty places will be available to accommodate the migrants (12).

It can be seen how difficult the task of the school building planner is in having to work not only with uncertainties but with imprecise criteria in respect of the very trends that he is trying to predict.

References

1. Best, J.W., *Research in Education* (Prentice Hall, New York, 1970).
2. Good, C.V., *Introduction to Educational Research* (Appleton Century Crofts, New York, 1963).
3. Davie, R., 'The longitudinal approach', *Trends in Education*, 28 (1972) 8-13.
4. Bailey, K.D., *Methods of Social Research* (Collier-Macmillan, London, 1978).
5. Riley, M.W., *Sociological Research I· A Case Approach* (Harcourt, Brace and World, New York, 1963).
6. Travers, R.M.W., *An Introduction to Educational Research* (Collier-Macmillan, London, 1964).
7. Douglas, J.W.B., 'The use and abuse of national cohorts' in M.D. Shipman, *The Organization and Impact of Social Research* (Routledge and Kegan Paul, London, 1976).
8. The discussion draws upon several papers in M.D. Shipman: *The Organization and Impact of Social Research* (Routledge and Kegan Paul, London, 1976).
9. See also: Douglas, J.W.B. and Blomfield, J.M., *Maternity in Great Britain* (Oxford University Press, London, 1948); Douglas, J.W.B. and Blomfield, J.M., *Children Under Five* (Allen and Unwin, London 1958); Douglas, J.W.B., Ross, J.M. and Simpson, H.R., *All Our Future* (P. Davies, London, 1968).
10. Jelinek, M.M. and Brittan, E.M., 'Multiracial education 1. Inter-ethnic friendship patterns', *Educational Research*, 18, 1 (1975) 44-53; Jelinek, M.M., 'Multiracial education 3. Pupils' attitudes to the multiracial school', *Educational Research*, 19, 2 (1977) 129-41.
11. J. and E. Newson, *Infant Care in an Urban Community* (Allen and Unwin, London, 1963); *Four Years Old in an Urban Community* (Allen and Unwin,

London, 1968); *Seven Years Old in an Urban Community* (Allen and Unwin, London, 1976); *Perspectives on School at Seven Years Old* (Allen and Unwin, London, 1977).

12.   HMSO, Annex 1: Department of Education and Science, *A Study of School Buildings* (London, 1977).

4 SURVEYS

Introduction

In this chapter we discuss what is perhaps the most commonly used descriptive method in educational research — *the survey*. Typically, surveys gather data at a particular point in time with the intention of (a) describing the nature of existing conditions, or (b) identifying standards against which existing conditions can be compared, or (c) determining the relationships that exist between specific events. Thus, surveys may vary in their levels of complexity from those which provide simple frequency counts to those which present relational analyses.

Surveys may be further differentiated in terms of their scope. A study of contemporary developments in post-secondary education, for example, might encompass the whole of Western Europe; a study of subject choice, on the other hand, might be confined to one secondary school. The complexity and scope of surveys in education can be illustrated by reference to familiar examples. The surveys undertaken for the Plowden Committee on primary school children (1) collected a wealth of information on children, teachers and parents and used sophisticated analytical techniques to predict pupil attainment. By contrast, the small-scale survey of Jackson and Marsden (2) involved a detailed study of the backgrounds and values of 88 working-class adults who had achieved success through selective secondary education.

Whether the survey is large-scale and undertaken by some governmental bureau or small-scale and carried out by the lone researcher, the collection of information typically involves one or more of the following data-gathering techniques: structured or semi-structured interviews, self-completion or postal questionnaires, standardised tests of attainment or performance, and attitude scales. Typically, too, surveys proceed through well-defined stages, though not every stage that we outline in Box 4.1 is required for the successful completion of a survey.

We begin with a consideration of some necessary preliminaries to survey planning before going on to outline a variety of sampling strategies that are used in survey research. We then discuss the construction and sequencing of questions in both interviews and questionnaires prior to a detailed examination of the postal questionnaire as a survey technique. Finally, we identify some of the procedures involved in

1.

2.

3.

Box 4.1.

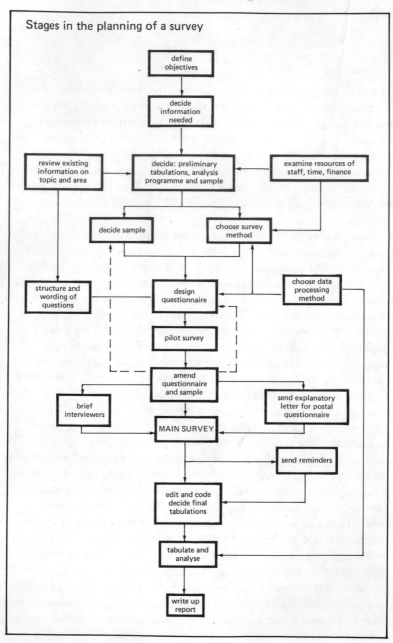

Stages in the planning of a survey

Source: Adapted from Davidson (4)

processing and analysing the results of survey research. Our discussion follows the sequential stages in survey design set out in Box 4.1.

Some Preliminary Considerations

Three prerequisites to the design of any survey are the specification of (1) the exact purpose of the enquiry; (2) the population on which it is to focus; and (3) the resources that are available. Hoinville and Jowell's (3) consideration of each of these key factors in survey planning can be illustrated in relation to the design of an educational enquiry.

The Purpose of the Enquiry

First, a survey's general purpose must be translated into a specific central aim. Thus, 'to explore teachers' views about in-service work' is somewhat nebulous, whereas 'to obtain a detailed description of primary and secondary teachers' priorities in the provision of in-service education courses' is reasonably specific. Having decided upon and specified the primary objective of the survey, the second phase of the planning involves the identification and itemising of subsidiary topics that relate to its central purpose. In our example, subsidiary issues might well include: (1) the types of courses required; (2) the content of courses; (3) the location of courses; (4) the timing of courses; (5) the design of courses; and (6) the financing of courses.

The third phase follows the identification and itemisation of subsidiary topics and involves formulating specific information requirements relating to each of these issues. For example, with respect to *the type of courses required*, detailed information would be needed about the *duration* of courses (one meeting, several meetings, a week, a month, a term or a year), the *status* of courses (non-award bearing, award bearing, with certificate, diploma, degree granted by college, polytechnic or university), the *orientation* of courses (theoretically oriented involving lectures, readings, etc., or practically oriented involving workshops and the production of curriculum materials).

As these details unfold, note Hoinville and Jowell, consideration would have to be given to the most appropriate ways of collecting items of information (interviews with selected teachers, postal questionnaires to selected schools, etc.).

The Population upon which the Survey is Focused

The second prerequisite to survey design, the specification of the population to which the enquiry is addressed, affects decisions that the researcher must make both about sampling and resources. In our hypothetical survey of in-service requirements, for example, we might specify the population as 'those primary and secondary teachers employed in schools within a thirty-mile radius of Loughborough University of Technology'. In this case, the population is readily identifiable and, given sufficient resources to contact every member of the designated group, sampling decisions do not arise. Things are rarely so straightforward, however. Often the criteria by which populations are specified ('severely handicapped', 'underachievers', 'intending teachers' or 'highly anxious') are difficult to operationalise. Populations, moreover, vary considerably in their accessibility; pupils and student teachers are relatively easy to survey, gypsy children and headteachers are more elusive. More importantly, in a large survey the researcher usually draws a sample from the population to be studied; rarely does he attempt to contact every member. We deal with the question of sampling shortly.

The Resources Available

The third important factor in designing and planning a survey is the financial cost. Sample surveys are labour-intensive (4), the largest single expenditure being the fieldwork where costs arise out of the interviewing time, travel time and transport claims of the interviewers themselves. There are additional demands on the survey budget. Training and supervising the panel of interviewers can often be as expensive as the costs incurred during the time that they actually spend in the field. Questionnaire construction, piloting, printing, posting, coding, together with card punching, card correction, computer programming – all eat into financial resources.

Proposals from intending education researchers seeking governmental or private funding are often weakest in the amount of time and thought devoted to a detailed planning of the financial implications of the projected enquiries. (In this chapter we confine ourselves from this point to a discussion of surveys based on *self-completion questionnaires*. A full account of the interview as a research technique is given in Chapter 13.)

Survey Sampling

Because questions to do with sampling arise directly from the second of our preliminary considerations, that is, defining the population upon which the survey is to focus, the researcher must take sampling decisions early in the overall planning of a survey (see Box 4.1). We have already seen that due to factors of expense, time and accessibility,

it is not always possible or practical to obtain measures from a population. The researcher endeavours therefore to collect information from
a smaller group or subset of the population in such a way that the
knowledge gained is representative of the total population under study.
This smaller group or subset is a *sample*. Notice how the competent
researcher starts with the total population and works down to the
sample. By contrast, the novice works from the bottom up, that is, he
determines the minimum number of respondents needed to conduct a
successful survey (5). However, unless he identifies the total population
in advance, it is virtually impossible for him to assess how representative the sample is that he has drawn. There are two methods of
sampling. One yields *probability samples* in which, as the term implies,
the probability of selection of each respondent is known. The other
yields *non-probability samples* in which the probability of selection
is unknown. We deal first with various methods of probability
sampling (6).

Simple Random Sampling

In simple random sampling, each member of the population under
study has an equal chance of being selected. The method involves
selecting at random from a list of the population (a sampling frame) the
required number of subjects for the sample. Because of probability and
chance, the sample should contain subjects with characteristics similar
to the population as a whole, i.e. some old, some young, some tall,
some short, some fit, some unfit, some rich, some poor, etc. One
problem associated with this particular sampling method is that a
complete list of the population is needed and this is not always readily
available.

Systematic Sampling

This method is a modified form of simple random sampling. It involves
selecting subjects from a population list in a systematic rather than a
random fashion. For example, if from a population of, say, 2,000, a
sample of 100 is required, then every twentieth person can be selected.
The starting point for the selection is chosen at random.

Stratified Sampling

Stratified sampling involves dividing the population into homogeneous
groups, each group containing subjects with similar characteristics. For
example, group A might contain males and group B, females. In order
to obtain a sample representative of the whole population in terms of

sex, a random selection of subjects from group A and group B must be taken. If needed, the exact proportion of males to females in the whole population can be reflected in the sample.

Cluster Sampling

When the population is large and widely dispersed, gathering a simple random sample poses administrative problems. Suppose we want to survey children's fitness levels in a particularly large community. It would be quite impractical randomly to select children and spend an inordinate amount of time travelling about in order to test them. By cluster sampling, we can randomly select a specific number of schools and test all the children in those selected schools.

Stage Sampling

Stage sampling is an extension of cluster sampling. It involves selecting the sample in stages, that is, taking samples from samples. Using the large community example referred to earlier, one type of stage sampling might be to select a number of schools at random, and from within each of these schools select a number of classes at random, and from within these classes select a number of pupils.

Small-scale surveys often resort to the use of non-probability samples because, despite the disadvantages that arise from their non-representativeness, they are far less complicated to set up, they are considerably less expensive, and can prove perfectly adequate where the researcher does not intend to generalise his findings beyond the sample in question or where he is simply piloting a survey questionnaire as a prelude to his main study. The chief kinds of non-probability sampling are as follows:

Convenience Sampling

Convenience sampling – or as it is sometimes called, accidental sampling – involves choosing the nearest individuals to serve as respondents and continuing that process until the required sample size has been obtained. Captive audiences such as pupils or student teachers often serve as respondents in surveys based upon convenience sampling.

Quota Sampling

Quota sampling has been described (5) as the non-probability equivalent of stratified sampling. It attempts to obtain representatives of the various elements of the total population in the proportions in which they occur there. Thus, a researcher interested in race relations in a particular community might set a quota for each ethnic group that is proportionate to its representation in the total population in the area under survey.

Purposive Sampling

In purposive sampling, the researcher handpicks the cases to be included in his sample on the basis of his judgement of their typicality. In this way, he builds up a sample that is satisfactory to his specific needs.

Dimensional Sampling

Dimensional sampling is simply a further refinement of quota sampling. It involves identifying various factors of interest in a population and obtaining at least one respondent for every combination of those factors. Thus, in the study of race relations to which we referred earlier, within each ethnic group the researcher may wish to distinguish between the attitudes of recent immigrants, those who have been in the country for some period of time, and those members of the ethnic group who were born in Great Britain. His sampling plan might take the form of a multidimensional table with *ethnic group* across the top and *length of stay* down the side.

Snowball Sampling

In snowball sampling, the researcher identifies a small number of individuals who have the characteristics that he requires. These people are then used as informants to identify others who qualify for inclusion and these, in turn, identify yet others — hence the term snowball sampling.

Sample Size: An Overview

A question that often plagues the novice researcher is just how large his sample should be in order to conduct an adequate survey. There is, of course, no clear-cut answer, for the correct sample size depends upon the purpose of the study and the nature of the population under scrutiny. However, it is possible to give some advice on this matter. Thus, a sample size of 30 is held by many to be the minimum number of cases if the researcher plans to use some form of statistical analysis on his data, though techniques are available for the analysis of samples below 30. Of more import to the researcher is the need to think out *in advance* of any data collection the sorts of relationships that he wishes to explore within subgroups of his eventual sample. The point is well illustrated in the data contained in Box 15.14 (p. 304). There, the researcher has necessarily obtained a large sample of children in order to examine how *staying on at school after 16* is associated with the *sex* of the pupils, the *types of school* they attend, the *types of ability streams* they are placed in, and their level of *alienation from school*. The number of variables the researcher sets out to control in his analysis and the types of statistical tests he wishes to make must inform his decision about sample size prior to the actual research undertaking.

Sample Size: Some Statistical Considerations

As well as the requirement of a minimum number of cases in order to examine relationships within subgroups, the researcher must obtain the minimum sample size that will accurately represent the population under survey. Where simple random sampling is used, the sample size needed to reflect the population value of a particular variable depends both upon the size of the population and the amount of heterogeneity of the variable in the population (5). Generally, for populations of equal heterogeneity, the larger the population, the larger the sample that must be drawn. For populations of equal size, the greater the heterogeneity on a particular variable, the larger the sample that is needed. To the extent that a sample fails to represent accurately the population under survey, there is *sampling error*.

Sampling Error (6)

If many samples are taken from the same population, it is unlikely that they will all have characteristics identical either with each other or with the population. In brief, there will be sampling error. Sampling error is not necessarily the result of mistakes made in sampling procedures. Rather, variations may occur due to the chance selection of different individuals. For example, if we take a large number of samples from the population and measure the mean value of each sample, then the sample means will not be identical. Some will be relatively high, some relatively low, and many will cluster around an average or mean value of the samples. Why should this occur? We can explain the phenomenon by reference to the *Central Limit Theorem* which is derived from the laws of probability. This states that if random, large samples of equal size are repeatedly drawn from any population, then the means of those samples will be approximately normally distributed. Moreover, the average or mean of the sample means will be approximately the same as the population mean. We show this diagrammatically in Box 4.2.

Box 4.2

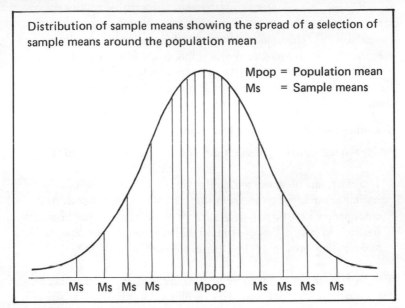

Distribution of sample means showing the spread of a selection of sample means around the population mean

Mpop = Population mean
Ms   = Sample means

Ms   Ms   Ms   Ms   Mpop   Ms   Ms   Ms   Ms

Source: Cohen and Holliday (6)

By drawing a large number of samples of equal size from a population, we create a sampling distribution. We can calculate the error involved in such sampling. The standard deviation of the theoretical distribution of sample means is a measure of sampling error and is called the *standard error of the mean* (SE_M). Thus,

$$SE_M = \frac{SD_s}{N}$$

where SD_s = the standard deviation of the sample and,
      N = the number in the sample

Strictly speaking, the formula for the standard error of the mean is:

$$SE_M = \frac{SD_{pop}}{N}$$

where SD_{pop} = the standard deviation of the population

However, as we are usually unable to ascertain the SD of the total population, the standard deviation of the sample is used instead. The standard error of the mean provides the best estimate of the sampling error. Clearly, the sampling error depends upon the variability (i.e. the heterogeneity) in the population as measured by SD_{pop} as well as the sample size (N). The smaller the SD_{pop}, the smaller the sampling error; the larger the N, the smaller the sampling error. Where the SD_{pop} is very large, then N needs to be very large to counteract it. Where SD_{pop} is very small, then N, too, can be small and still give a reasonably small sampling error.

Designing the Self-completion Questionnaire   *See Ch 13*

An ideal questionnaire possesses the same properties as a good law: *N.B.*

> It is clear, unambiguous and uniformly workable. Its design must minimize potential errors from respondents . . . and coders. And since people's participation in surveys is voluntary, a questionnaire has to help in engaging their interest, encouraging their co-operation, and eliciting answers as close as possible to the truth. (4)

With these qualities in mind, we turn to the problem of designing a self-completion questionnaire. Having identified subsidiary topics of interest in his survey and itemised specific information requirements relating to them, the researcher's task now involves the structure of the questionnaire itself.

At this preliminary stage of design, it can sometimes be helpful to use a flow chart technique to plan the sequencing of questions. In this way, the researcher is able to anticipate the type and range of responses that his questions are likely to elicit. In Box 4.3, we illustrate a flow chart employed in a commercial survey based upon an interview schedule, though the application of the method to a self-completion questionnaire is self-evident.

Using a flow chart in questionnaire design brings home to the researcher the paramount importance of the *question* in any form of survey work. Whole books have been written on the art of questionning. The brief space we are able to allot to this vital topic in no way reflects the priority that should be given to the framing and testing of questions before any survey is undertaken. We discuss various forms of questions (structured, unstructured and the funnel varieties) in Chapter 13 and illustrate some ways in which respondents may record their answers. For the present, we identify some pitfalls in question construction.

Ch 13

Box 4.3

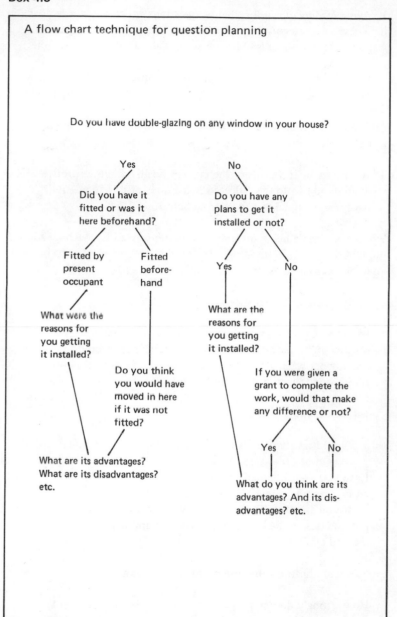

A flow chart technique for question planning

Do you have double-glazing on any window in your house?

Source: Social and Community Planning Research (7)

'Avoid' Questions

1. Avoid *leading* questions, that is, questions which are worded (or their response categories presented) in such a way as to suggest to respondents that there is only one acceptable answer. For example:

> Do you prefer abstract, academic-type courses, or down-to-earth, practical courses that have some pay-off in your day-to-day teaching?

2. Avoid *highbrow* questions even with sophisticated respondents. For example:

> What particular aspects of the current positivistic/interpretive debate would you like to see reflected in a course of developmental psychology aimed at a teacher audience?

Where the sample being surveyed is representative of the whole adult population, misunderstandings of what the researcher takes to be clear, unambiguous language are commonplace.

3. Avoid *complex* questions. For example:

> Would you prefer a short, non-award bearing course (3, 4 or 5 sessions) with part-day release (e.g. Wednesday afternoons) and one evening per week attendance with financial reimbursement for travel, or a longer, non-award bearing course (6, 7 or 8 sessions) with full-day release, or the whole course designed on part-day release without evening attendance?

4. Avoid *irritating* questions or instructions. For example:

> Have you ever attended an in-service course of any kind during your entire teaching career?
> If you are over 40, and have never attended an in-service course, put one tick in the box marked *NEVER* and another in the box marked *OLD*.

5. Avoid questions that use negatives. For example:

> How strongly do you feel that no teacher should enrol on the in-service, award-bearing course who has not completed at least two years full-time teaching?

Box 4.4.

A guide for questionnaire construction

A. *Decisions about question content*
  1. Is the question necessary? Just how will it be useful?
  2. Are several questions needed on the subject matter of this question?
  3. Do respondents have the information necessary to answer the question?
  4. Does the question need to be more concrete, specific and closely related to the respondent's personal experience?
  5. Is the question content sufficiently general and free from spurious concreteness and specificity?
  6. Do the replies express general attitudes and only seem to be as specific as they sound?
  7. Is the question content biased or loaded in one direction, without accompanying questions to balance the emphasis?
  8. Will the respondents give the information that is asked for?

B. *Decisions about question wording*
  1. Can the question be misunderstood? Does it contain difficult or unclear phraseology?
  2. Does the question adequately express the alternative with respect to the point?
  3. Is the question misleading because of unstated assumptions or unseen implications?
  4. Is the wording biased? Is it emotionally loaded or slanted towards a particular kind of answer?
  5. Is the question wording likely to be objectionable to the respondent in any way?
  6. Would a more personalised wording of the question produce better results?
  7. Can the question be better asked in a more direct or a more indirect form?

C. *Decisions about form of response to the question*
  1. Can the question best be asked in a form calling for check answer (or short answer of a word or two, or a number), free answer or check answer with follow-up answer?
  2. If a check answer is used, which is the best type for this question — dichotomous, multiple choice ('cafeteria' question), or scale?
  3. If a checklist is used, does it cover adequately all the significant alternatives without overlapping and in a defensible order? Is it of reasonable length? Is the wording of items impartial and balanced?
  4. Is the form of response easy, definite, uniform and adequate for the purpose?

D. *Decisions about the place of the question in the sequence*
  1. Is the answer to the question likely to be influenced by the content of preceding questions?
  2. Is the question led up to in a natural way? Is it in correct psychological order?
  3. Does the question come too early or too late from the point of view of arousing interest and receiving sufficient attention, avoiding resistance, and so on?

Source: From Selltiz, Wrightsman and Cook (8)

6. Avoid *open-ended* questions on self-completion questionnaires. Because self-completion questionnaires cannot probe the respondent to find out just what he means by a particular response, the open-ended question is a less satisfactory way of eliciting information. (This caution does not hold in the interview situation, however.) Open-ended questions, moreover, are too demanding of most respondents' time. Nothing can be more off-putting than the following format:

> Use pages 5, 6 and 7 respectively to respond to each of the questions about your attitudes to in-service courses in general and your beliefs about their value in the professional life of the serving teacher.

On a more positive note, Selltiz and her associates (8) have provided a fairly exhaustive guide to the researcher in constructing his questionnaire which we summarise in Box 4.4.

Postal Questionnaires

Frequently, the postal questionnaire is the best form of survey in carrying out an educational enquiry. Take, for example, the researcher intent on investigating the adoption and use made of a new curriculum series in secondary schools in England and Wales. An interview survey based upon some sampling of the population of schools would be both expensive and time-consuming. A postal questionnaire, on the other hand, would have several distinct advantages. Moreover, given the usual constraints over finance and resources, it might well prove the only viable way of carrying through such an enquiry.

What evidence we have about the advantages and disadvantages of postal survey derives from settings other than educational. Many of the findings, however, have relevance to the educational researcher. In Box 13.1 (p. 242), we summarize the relative merits of self-completion questionnaires as compared with interview procedures. Here, we focus upon some of the ways in which the educational researcher can maximise the response level that he obtains when using a postal survey.

Research shows (3) that a number of myths about postal questionnaires are not borne out by the evidence. Response levels to postal surveys are not invariably less than those obtained by interview procedures; frequently they equal, and in some cases surpass, those achieved in interviews. Nor does the questionnaire necessarily have to be short in order to obtain a satisfactory response level. With sophisticated respondents, for example, a short questionnaire might appear to trivialise complex issues with which they are familiar. Hoinville and

Jowell (3) identify a number of factors in securing a good response rate to a postal questionnaire:

1. The appearance of the questionnaire is vitally important. It must look easy and attractive. A compressed layout is uninviting; a larger questionnaire with plenty of space for questions and answers is more encouraging to respondents.

2. Clarity of wording and simplicity of design are essential. Clear instructions should guide the respondent – 'Put a tick', for example, invites participation, whereas complicated instructions and complex procedures intimidate respondents.

3. Arrange the contents of the questionnaire in such a way as to maximise co-operation. For example, include questions that are likely to be of general interest. Make sure that questions which appear early in the format do not suggest to respondents that the enquiry is not intended for them. Intersperse attitude questions throughout the schedule to allow respondents to air their views rather than merely describe their behaviour. Such questions relieve boredom and frustration as well as providing valuable information in the process.

At a more detailed level, several aspects of design and layout have been shown to produce high levels of response to postal questionnaires. Thus:

4. Coloured pages can help to clarify the overall structure of the questionnaire and the use of different colours for instructions can assist the respondent.

5. Putting ticks in boxes by way of answering a questionnaire is familiar to most respondents whereas requests to circle precoded numbers at the right-hand side of the questionnaire can be a source of confusion and error.

6. The practice of sublettering questions (e.g. Q9 (a) (b) (c) . . .) is a useful technique for grouping together questions to do with a specific issue. It is also a way of making the questionnaire look smaller than it actually is!

7. Repeating instructions as often as necessary is good practice in a postal questionnaire. Since everything hinges on the respondent knowing exactly what is required of him, clear, unambiguous instructions, boldly and attractively displayed, are essential.

8. Completing a questionnaire can be seen as a learning process in which the respondent becomes more at home with the task as he proceeds. Initial questions should therefore be simple, have high interest value, and encourage participation. The middle section of the questionnaire should contain the difficult questions; the last few questions should be of high interest in order to encourage the respondents to return the completed schedule.

9. It bears repeating that the wording of the self-completion questionnaire is of paramount importance and that pretesting is crucial to its success.

10. Finally, a brief note at the very end of the questionnaire can: (a) ask the respondent to check that no answer has been inadvertently missed out; (b) solicit an early return of the completed schedule; (c) thank the respondent for his participation; and (d) offer to send a short abstract of the major findings when the analysis is completed.

Apart from the design of the questionnaire, Hoinville and Jowell (3) consider the effects of four other factors in maximising the response rate of postal questionnaires. These are: the initial mailing, the covering letter, follow-up letters and incentives.

The following practices are to be recommended in *initial mailing*:

(a) use good quality envelopes, typed and addressed to a named person wherever possible;
(b) use first class postage, stamped rather than franked wherever possible;
(c) enclose a first class stamped envelope for the respondent's reply;
(d) in surveys of the general population, Thursday is the best day for mailing out; in surveys of organisations, Monday or Tuesday are recommended; and
(e) avoid at all costs a December survey.

The purpose of the *covering letter* is to indicate the aim of the survey, to convey to the respondent its importance, to assure him of confidentiality, and to encourage his reply. With these intentions in mind, the following practices are to be recommended:

(a) the appeal in the covering letter must be tailored to suit the particular audience. Thus, a survey of teachers might stress the importance of the study to the profession as a whole;

(b) neither the use of prestigious signatories, nor appeals to altruism, nor the addition of handwritten postscripts affect response levels to postal questionnaires;

(c) the name of the sponsor or the organisation conducting the survey should appear on the letterhead as well as in the body of the covering letter;

(d) a direct reference should be made to the confidentiality of the respondent's answers and the purposes of any serial numbers and codings should be explained;

(e) a presurvey letter advising respondents of the forthcoming questionnaire has been shown to have substantial effect on response rates; and

(f) a short covering letter is most effective; aim at no more than one page.

Of the four factors that Hoinville and Jowell (3) discuss in connection with maximising response levels, the *follow-up letter* has been shown to be the most productive. The following points should be borne in mind in preparing reminder letters:

(a) all of the rules that apply to the covering letter apply even more strongly to the follow-up letter;

(b) the follow-up should re-emphasise the importance of the study and the value of the respondent's participation;

(c) the use of the second person singular, the conveying of an air of disappointment at non-response and some surprise at non-co-operation have been shown to be effective ploys;

(d) nowhere should the follow-up give the impression that non-response is normal or that numerous non-responses have occurred in the particular study; and

(e) the follow-up letter must be accompanied by a further copy of the questionnaire together with a stamped addressed envelope for its return.

Second and third reminder letters suffer from the law of diminishing returns, so how many follow-ups are recommended and what success rates do they achieve? It is difficult to generalise, but the following points are worth bearing in mind. A well-planned postal survey should obtain at least a 40 per cent response rate and with the judicious use of reminders, a 70 per cent to 80 per cent response level should be possible. A preliminary pilot survey is invaluable in that it can indicate the general level of response to be expected. The main survey should generally achieve at least as high as and normally a higher level of return than the pilot enquiry. The Government Social Survey (now the Office of Population Censuses and Surveys) recommends the use of three reminders which, they say, can increase the original return by as much as 30 per cent in surveys of the general public. A typical pattern of responses to the three follow-ups is as follows:

Original despatch	40%
1st follow-up	+20%
2nd follow-up	+10%
3rd follow-up	+ 5%
Total	70%

The fourth and final factor in maximising response rates is the *use of incentives*. Although the use of incentives is comparatively rare in British surveys, it can substantially reduce non-response rates particularly when the chosen incentives accompany the initial mailing rather than being mailed subsequently as rewards for the return of completed schedules. The explanation of the effectiveness of this particular ploy appears to lie in the sense of obligation that is created in the recipient. Care is needed in selecting the most appropriate type of incentive. It should clearly be seen as a token rather than a payment for the respondent's efforts and, according to Hoinville and Jowell, should be as neutral as possible. In this respect, they suggest that books of postage stamps or ballpoint pens are cheap, easily packaged in the

Box 4.5

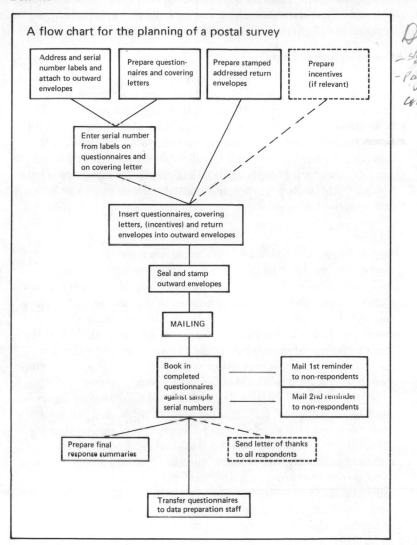

A flow chart for the planning of a postal survey

- Address and serial number labels and attach to outward envelopes
- Prepare questionnaires and covering letters
- Prepare stamped addressed return envelopes
- Prepare incentives (if relevant)

Enter serial number from labels on questionnaires and on covering letter

Insert questionnaires, covering letters, (incentives) and return envelopes into outward envelopes

Seal and stamp outward envelopes

MAILING

Book in completed questionnaires against sample serial numbers

Mail 1st reminder to non-respondents

Mail 2nd reminder to non-respondents

Prepare final response summaries

Send letter of thanks to all respondents

Transfer questionnaires to data preparation staff

Do
- staff charson
- Pay day
collection

Source: Hoinville and Jowell (3)

questionnaire envelopes, and appropriate to the task required of the respondent.

In conclusion, the preparation of a flow chart can help the researcher to plan the timing and the sequencing of the various parts of a postal

N.B. . do.

survey. One such flow chart suggested by Hoinville and Jowell is shown in Box 4.5. The researcher might wish to add a chronological chart alongside it to help plan the exact timing of the events shown here.

Processing Survey Data

Let us assume that the researcher has followed the advice we have given about the planning of postal questionnaires and has secured a high response rate to his survey. His task is now to reduce the mass of data he has obtained to a form suitable for analysis. *Data reduction,* as the process is called, generally consists of coding data in preparation for analysis — by hand in the case of small surveys; by computers when numbers are larger. Both methods of analysis will be illustrated. First, however, prior to coding, the questionnaires have to be checked. This task is referred to as *editing.*

Editing

Editing interview schedules or self-completion questionnaires is intended to identify and eliminate errors made by interviewers or respondents. (In addition to the clerical editing that we discuss in this section, editing checks are also performed by the computer. For an account of computer run *structure* checks and *valid coding range* checks, see Hoinville and Jowell (3) pp. 150-5.) Moser and Kalton (9) point to three central tasks in editing: (1) *completeness*: a check is made that there is an answer to every question. In most surveys, interviewers are required to record an answer to every question (a 'not applicable' category always being available). Missing answers can sometimes be cross-checked from other sections of the survey. At worst, the respondent can be contacted again to supply the missing information. (2) *accuracy*: as far as is possible a check is made that all questions are answered accurately. Inaccuracies arise out of carelessness on the part of either the interviewer or the respondent. Sometimes a deliberate attempt is made to mislead. A tick in the wrong box, a ring round the wrong code, an error in simple arithmetic — all can reduce the validity of the data unless they are picked up in the editing process. (3) *uniformity*: a check is made that interviewers have interpreted instructions and questions uniformly. Sometimes the failure to give explicit instructions over the interpretation of respondents' replies leads to interviewers recording the same answer in a variety of answer codes instead of one. A check on uniformity can help eradicate this source of error.

Coding

The primary task of data reduction is coding, that is, assigning a code number to each answer to a survey question so that responses can be punched onto a computer card (or edge-punched for hand-sort cards) for ease of storage and retrieval. Of course, not all answers to survey questions can be reduced to code numbers. Many open-ended questions, for example, are not reducible in this way for computer analysis.

Coding can be built into the construction of the questionnaire itself. In this case, we talk of *precoded* answers. Where coding is developed after the questionnaire has been administered and answered by respondents, we refer to *postcoded* answers. Precoding is appropriate for closed-ended questions – male 1, female 0, for example; or single 0, married 1, separated 2, divorced 3. For questions such as these whose *answer categories* are known in advance, a *coding frame* is generally developed before the interviewing commences so that it can be printed onto the questionnaire itself. For open-ended questions (Why did you choose this particular in-service course rather than XYZ?), a coding frame has to be devised after the completion of the questionnaire. This is best done by taking a random sample of the questionnaires (10 per cent or more, time permitting) and generating a frequency tally of the range of responses as a preliminary to coding classification. Having devised the coding frame, the researcher can make a further check on its validity by using it to code up a further sample of the questionnaires. It is vital to get coding frames right from the outset – extending them or making alterations at a later point in the study is both expensive and wearisome.

Small Survey Data and Edge-punched Cards

Where surveys involve only a small number of respondents, the researcher may choose to use edge-punched cards in data tabulation. As illustrated in Box 4.6, data are transferred to cards by cutting notches in the numbered holes around the edges of the cards according to a code that is predetermined by the researcher.

In Box 4.7 we illustrate hypothetical data that have been coded onto edge-punched cards.

Sorting out the punched cards (Box 4.8) involves inserting a needle through specific holes to allow the notched cards to fall out of the deck, leaving the others remaining on the needle. It can be seen how much effort in cross tabulation can be saved by this winnowing out process. The various commercial companies producing edge-punch cards provide guides to coding techniques that maximize the flexibility of their particular system.

Box 4.6

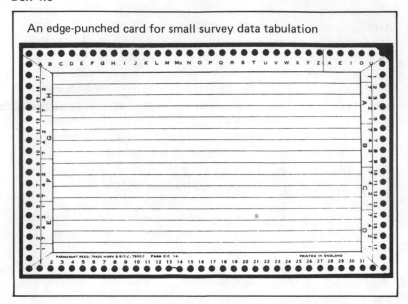

An edge-punched card for small survey data tabulation

Box 4.7

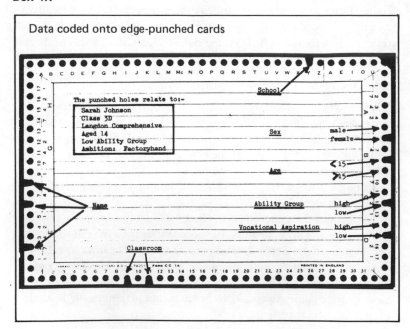

Data coded onto edge-punched cards

The punched holes relate to:-

Sarah Johnson
Class 3D
Langdon Comprehensive
Aged 14
Low Ability Group
Ambition: Factoryhand

School

Sex   male
       female

Age   <15
       >15

Name

Ability Group   high
                 low

Vocational Aspiration   high
                         low

Classroom

Box 4.8

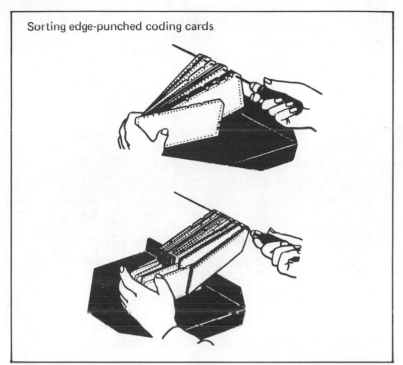

Sorting edge-punched coding cards

Source: Best (10)

Large Survey Data and the Computer Punch Card

Box 4.9 shows the standard 80-column computer punch card commonly used in coding survey data. The card contains 12 rows and 80 columns. The top row, that is, the '12 row' is sometimes called plus (+) or Y; '11 row' being minus (−) or X. Punches 0 to 9 are numbered vertically down each column. One corner of the card is usually cut to make for ease of handling. Data are punched into the cards by a key-punch machine operating rather like a typewriter except that the machine does not punch only in a single horizontal line but punches up and down the column according to the number chosen. Letters are punched into the card as well as numbers, the letters being formed by a multiple number punch, different combinations of numbers forming different letters.

It is up to the researcher to design a coding scheme for transferring his data onto the 80-column punch card. For the novice, the following

Box 4.9

A standard 80-column computer punch card

GENERAL PURPOSE - 16 FIELD WITH ALPHA

CDSL 5020

coding hints repay careful reading (11):

1. Use columns on the machine data card economically. Analysis is far easier if you can get your data on one card per respondent. Naturally, you do not want to sacrifice any information you get, but proper planning may permit compressing the data to the 80 columns on the data card used in this model (see Box 4.9).

2. If you must use more than one card, be sure to differentiate Card 1 from Card 2 in a special column (C 80) so there will be no confusion. Also, most identification items have to be reproduced on both cards — case number, cluster number, study number, respondent classification number — preferably in the same columns on each card.

3. With two cards per respondent, plan to leave a separate block of vacant columns in the second card, in order to reproduce as much of the relevant demographic data from the first card as possible. This greatly simplifies cross-analysis. Other information can also be condensed on the second card through the use of indexes.

4. If you need two or more full cards for each respondent, transpose certain information from each onto a separate analysis deck (set of cards), sometimes called a work deck. The point of this is to make cross-analysis possible for data on both cards. The transposition of data is, of course, done by machine.

5. Remember, each column of the data card used in the model contains 12 punch positions. The uppermost portion is designated by the letter 'R' or 'Y' and the position just below it is designated 'X'. The remaining ten positions are numbered 0 through 9. Use these codes.

6. Use only one column for each question where possible without losing significant variety of response. Answers to open-ended questions can usually be grouped into as many as 12 significant response categories.

7. Two columns can be used together if you desire finer categorical breakdowns. If you have as many as 24 response categories, always use the first column for the first 12 classifications, and the second for the next 12 response types. This is wiser than using the two

columns like a two-digit number. If the first column were used as the ten's digit and the second the unit's digit, no multiple punching is possible, machine printing is useless, and cross-tabulation takes much longer.

8. Some items must be punched in two or three columns, for example, case numbers. Use Column 1, Column 2 and Column 3 for this (if less than 1,000 in the sample). Use all columns for each case number even if the number is less than 100, prefixing zeros to fill the space: 001,099.

9. Usually only one column is necessary to code the date of the interview. If the interviewing period is longer than 12 days, but does not duplicate the same data in different months, two columns could be used. The actual date can be coded rather than an artificial code. 26 July would appear as '26' and 3 August as '03'. Explanations, of course, are provided in the coding manual.

10. Some code should appear for each column. In any column where all 12 positions are not used, and the column is skipped due to interviewing errors or because the respondent was disqualified by a filter question, a uniform punch should be used to show that the column was not missed by the keypuncher. Punch position 'X' can be used for legitimate skips. For example, if the respondent says 'No', he doesn't belong to a union, the next column, 'Which union?' should be coded 'X'. 'R' can stand for interviewer error — that is, the interviewer failed to ask this question, or failed to write down an answer. By having something in each column, you will know the coder considered it, and it will help to keep the keypunch operator in the right place.

11. Some items can be multiple-coded. If the respondent gives two answers that you want to record for a question, simply code both numbers for those answers in that column. So, if the answers to a why-voted question are that 'He was the best man, and besides he is a Democrat', and these answers are to be coded 5 and 2 respectively, write down '2-5' before the column number. For convenience of the keypunch operator write the multiple codes in ascending order, as has just been shown. In the coding manual, instruct coders at each point where multiple coding is permitted. Otherwise their general instructions are: one, and only one, code per column.

12. Two different items sometimes can be coded into the same column to save space. For many questions, not all positions in the column are used. For example, often the possible answers are 'Yes', 'No' and 'Don't know'. These could be coded 1, 2 and 3, respectively. Then you could code the response to the next question in the same column as 4, 5, 6, etc. If you do this, indicate it in the coding manual. Avoid this kind of doubling up if possible as it tends to add confusion for coders and analysts.

13. A further compression can be made if two mutually exclusive answers are followed by explanatory statements. For example, you may have had respondents judge a proposal as 'good' or 'poor'. Each response would likely be followed by 'Why do you think it is (good) (poor)?' All reasons for both 'good' and 'poor' responses can be coded in the *same* column by an additional 'cue' punch, 'X' for 'good' and 'R' for 'poor'. Then the rest of the positions, 0 through 9, can be used twice — once for 'good' reasons and once for 'poor' reasons. If 'X' is punched, you know that the 0 through 9 codes represent the list of positive reasons under 'good'. If 'R' is punched, the 0-9 codes are reasons given for 'poor' reactions.

14. Always provide a code for 'Don't know' and 'Refused'.

15. Code with a blue ballpoint pen to make the code stand out against the black mimeographed column numbers in the left margin of the questionnaire, and the red pen scribblings of the interviewer.

16. Use common sense while coding, rather than mechanically going through the questionnaire. You must empathise with the respondent to understand how his response correctly fits the categories devised for each question. Recognise, of course, that your own predispositions may enter in at this stage. Strive always to maintain an impartial stance.

17. Code only as a member of a group and under supervision. Keep track of all questionnaires. The information on them has not been transcribed, and a loss would negate all the work that has gone into the survey so far.

18. Remind coders of the confidential nature of the data.

In conclusion, we suggest that this chapter be studied alongside Chapter 13 which deals with interviews and interviewing.

References

1. Central Advisory Council for Education, *Children and their Primary Schools* (HMSO, London, 1967).
2. Jackson, B. and Marsden, D., *Education and the Working Class* (Routledge and Kegan Paul, London, 1962).
3. Hoinville, G. and Jowell, R., *Survey Research Practice* (Heinemann Educational Books, London, 1978).
4. Davidson, J., *Outdoor Recreation Surveys: The Design and Use of Questionnaires for Site Surveys* (Countryside Commission, London, 1970).
5. Bailey, K.D., *Methods of Social Research* (Collier-Macmillan, London, 1978).
6. Cohen, L. and Holliday, M., *Statistics for Education and Physical Education* (London, Harper and Row, 1979).
7. Social and Community Planning Research, *Questionnaire Design Manual, No. 5* (London: 16 Duncan Terrace, N1 8BZ, 1972).
8. Selltiz, C., Wrightsman, L.S. and Cook, S.W., *Research Methods in Social Relations* (Holt, Rinehart and Winston, New York, 1976).
9. Moser, C.A. and Kalton, G., *Survey Methods in Social Investigation* (Heinemann Educational Books, London, 1977).
10. Best, J.W., *Research in Education* (Prentice Hall, Englewood Cliffs, NJ, 1970).
11. Backstrom, C.H. and Hursh, G.D., *Survey Research* (Northwestern University Press, Evanston, 1963).

5 CASE STUDIES

Introduction

How can knowledge of the ways in which children learn and the means by which schools achieve their goals be verified, built upon and extended? This is a central question for educational research. The problem of verification and cumulation of educational knowledge is implicit in our discussion of the nature of educational enquiry in the opening chapter of the book. There, we outline two broad approaches to educational research. The first, based on the *scientific* paradigm, rests upon the creation of theoretical frameworks that can be tested by experimentation, replication and refinement. We illustrate this approach in Chapter 8. Against this scientific, experimental paradigm, we posit an alternative perspective which we describe as *interpretive* and *subjective*, a focus we hasten to add that should be seen as complementing rather than competing with the experimental stance.

In the present chapter, although our presentation emphasises the interpretive, subjective dimensions of educational phenomena that are best explored by case study methods, we balance this with examples of quantitative case study research. Our broad treatment of case study techniques follows directly from a *typology of observation studies* that we develop shortly. We begin with a brief description of the case study itself.

The Case Study

Unlike the experimenter who manipulates variables to determine their causal significance or the surveyor who asks standardised questions of large, representative samples of individuals, the case study researcher typically *observes* the characteristics of an individual unit — a child, a clique, a class, a school or a community. The purpose of such observation is to probe deeply and to analyse intensively the multifarious phenomena that constitute the life cycle of the unit with a view to establishing generalisations about the wider population to which that unit belongs.

Present antipathy towards the statistical-experimental paradigm has created something of a boom industry in case study research. Delinquents (1), dropouts (2) and drug-users (3), to say nothing of studies of all types of schools (4), attest to the wide use of the case

Box 5.1

A typology of observation studies

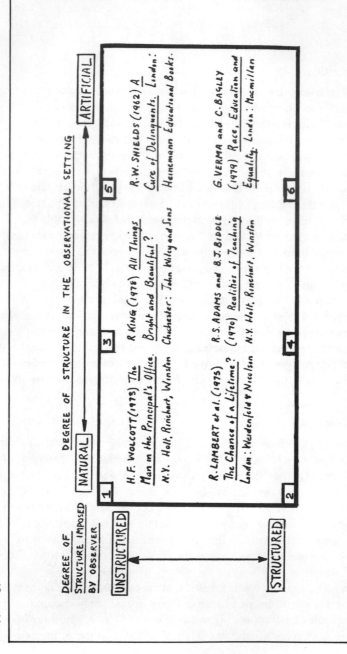

study in contemporary social science and educational research. Such
wide use is marked by an equally diverse range of techniques employed
in the collection and analysis of both qualitative and quantitative data.
Whatever the problem or the approach, at the heart of every case study
lies a *method of observation*.

In this chapter, we discuss six educational case studies. They are
chosen to illustrate the use of a particular *style* of observation within
a particular observational *setting*. In Box 5.1, we set out a typology of
observation studies on the basis of which our six examples are selected.

There are two principal types of observation – *participant observation* and *non-participant observation*. In the former, the observer
engages in the very activities he sets out to observe. Often, his 'cover'
is so complete that as far as the other participants are concerned, he is
simply one of the group. In the case of Patrick (1), for example, born
and bred in Glasgow, his researcher role remained hidden from the
members of the Glasgow gang in whose activities he participated for a
period of four months. Such complete anonymity is not always
possible, however. Thus in Parker's (2) study of downtown Liverpool
adolescents, it was generally known that the researcher was waiting to
take up a post at the university. In the meantime, 'knocking around'
during the day with the lads and frequenting their pub at night rapidly
established that he was 'OK'.

> I was a drinker, a hanger-arounder, and had been tested in illegal
> 'business' matters and could be relied on to say nothing since I
> 'knew the score'.

Cover is not necessarily a prerequisite of participant observation. In
an intensive study of a small group of working-class boys during their
last two years at school and their first months in employment, Willis
(5) attended all the different subject classes in school – 'not as a
teacher, but as a member of the class' – and worked alongside each boy
in industry for a short period.

A non-participant observer, on the other hand, stands aloof from the
group activities he is investigating and eschews group membership – no
great difficulty for King (4), an adult observer in infant classrooms.
Listen to him recounting how he firmly established his *non-participant*
status* with young children:

_____

*King's study as a whole is based upon *unstructured* observations in infant
classrooms. It is different in its approach from other studies by him.

I rapidly learnt that children in infants' classrooms define any adult as another teacher or teacher surrogate. To avoid being engaged in conversation, being asked to spell words or admire pictures, I evolved the following technique.

To begin with, I kept standing so that physical height created social distance . . . Next, I did not show immediate interest in what the children were doing, or talk to them. When I was talked to I smiled politely and if necessary I referred the child asking a question to the teacher. Most importantly, I avoided eye contact; if you do not look you will not be seen.

The best illustration of the non-participant observer role is perhaps the case of the researcher sitting at the back of a classroom coding up every three seconds the verbal exchanges between teacher and pupils by means of a structured set of observational categories.

It is frequently the case that the *type of observation* undertaken by the researcher is associated with the *type of setting* in which the research takes place. In Box 5.1 we identify a continuum of settings ranging from the artificial environments of the therapist's clinic (Cell 5) and the social psychological laboratory (Cell 6) to the natural environments of the community in which the professional life of a headteacher is embedded (Cell 1) and the academic, social and religious life associated with boarding school education (Cell 2). Because our continuum is crude and arbitrary, we are at liberty to locate a study of infant schools (Cell 3) somewhere between the artificial and natural poles.

Although in theory each of the six examples of case studies in Box 5.1 could have been undertaken either as a participant or as a non-participant observation study, a number of factors intrude to make one or other of the observational strategies the dominant mode of enquiry in a particular type of setting. Bailey (6) explains as follows:

In a natural setting it is difficult for the researcher who wishes to be covert not to act as a participant. If the researcher does not participate, there is little to explain his presence, as he is very obvious to the actual participants . . . Most studies in a natural setting are unstructured participant observation studies . . . Much the opposite is true in an artificial environment. Since there is no natural setting, in a sense none of the persons being studied are really participants of long standing, and thus may accept a non-participant observer more readily . . . Laboratory settings also enable a non-participant observer to use sophisticated equipment such as videotape and tape recordings . . . Thus most studies in an artificial laboratory setting will be structured and will be non-participant studies.

What we are saying is simply this: that the unstructured, ethnographic account of the headteacher (Cell 1) is the most typical method of observation in the natural surroundings of school, home, church and community in which that study was conducted. Similarly, the structured questions and the quantitative techniques employed in the study of the black adolescent (Cell 6) reflect a common approach in the artificial setting of a social psychological laboratory.

Why Participant Observation?

The current vogue enjoyed by the case study conducted on participant observation lines is not difficult to account for. This form of research is eminently suitable to many of the problems that the educational investigator faces.

The natural scientist, Schutz (7) points out, explores a field that means nothing to the molecules, atoms and electrons therein. By contrast, the subject matter of the world in which the educational researcher is interested is composed of people and is essentially meaningful. That world is subjectively structured, possessing particular meanings for its inhabitants. The task of the educational investigator is very often to explain the means by which an orderly social world is established and maintained in terms of its shared meanings. How do participant observation techniques assist the researcher in this task? Bailey (6) identifies some inherent advantages in the participant observation approach:

1. Observation studies are superior to experiments and surveys when data are being collected on non-verbal behaviour.

2. In the observation study, the investigator is able to discern ongoing behaviour as it occurs and is able to make appropriate notes about its salient features.

3. Because case study observations take place over an extended period of time, the researcher can develop a more intimate and informal relationship with those he is observing, generally in more natural environments than those in which experiments and surveys are conducted.

4. Case study observations are less reactive than other types of data-gathering methods. For example, in laboratory-based experiments and in surveys that depend upon verbal responses to structured questions, bias can be introduced in the very data that the researcher is attempting to study.

On the other hand, participant observation studies are not without their critics. The accounts that typically emerge from participant observations are often decried as subjective, biased, impressionistic, idiosyncratic and lacking in the precise quantifiable measures that are the hallmark of survey research and experimentation. Whilst it is probably true that nothing can give better insight into the life of a gang of juvenile delinquents than going to live with them for an extended period of time, the critic of participant observation studies will point to the dangers of 'going native' as a result of playing a role within such a group. How do we know that the observer does not lose his perspective and become blind to the peculiarities that he is supposed to be investigating?

These criticisms raise questions about two types of validity in

Box 5.2

Steps in participant observation
1. A rough definition of the phenomenon is formulated.
2. A hypothetical explanation of that phenomenon is formulated.
3. One case is studied in the light of the hypothesis, with the object of determining whether or not the hypothesis fits the facts in that case.
4. If the hypothesis does not fit the facts, either the hypothesis is reformulated or the phenomenon to be explained is redefined so that the case is excluded.
5. Practical certainty may be attained after a small number of cases has been examined, but the discovery of negative cases disproves the explanation and requires a reformulation.
6. This procedure of examining cases, redefining the phenomenon, and reformulating the hypothesis is continued until a universal relationship is established, each negative case calling for a redefinition of a reformulation.

Source: Denzin (8)

observation-based research. In effect, comments about the subjective and idiosyncratic nature of the participant observation study are to do with its *external validity*. How do we know that the results of this one piece of research are applicable to other situations? Fears that the observer's judgement will be affected by his close involvement in the group relate to the *internal validity* of the method. How do we know that the results of this one piece of research represent the real thing, the genuine product? In our outline of one of the educational case study examples we refer to a number of techniques (quota sampling, snowball sampling, the search for exceptions) that researchers employ as a way of checking on the representativeness of the events that they observe and of cross checking their interpretations of the meanings of those events (see also our discussion in Chapter 10, 'Accounts'). We can best illustrate the concern of the participant observer for the validity of his data by the following brief outline of a typical strategy in participant observation research. Denzin (8) uses the term 'analytical induction' to describe a broad strategy of participant observation which we set out in Box 5.2.

Box 5.3

Field notes in observation studies

1. Record the notes as quickly as possible after observation, since the quantity of information forgotten is very slight over a short period of time but accelerates quickly as more time passes.
2. Discipline yourself to write notes quickly and reconcile yourself to the fact that although it may seem ironic, recording of field notes can be expected to take as long as is spent in actual observation.
3. Dictating rather than writing is acceptable if one can afford it, but writing has the advantage of stimulating thought.
4. Typing field notes is vastly preferable to handwriting because it is faster and easier to read, especially when making multiple copies.
5. It is advisable to make at least two copies of field notes and preferable to type on a master for reproduction. One original copy is retained for reference and other copies can be used as rough draft to be cut up, reorganised and rewritten.
6. The notes ought to be full enough adequately to summon up for one again, months later, a reasonably vivid picture of any described event. This probably means that one ought to be writing up, at the very minimum, at least a couple of single space typed pages for every hour of observation.

Source: Lofland (9)

Box 5.4.

A structured observation schedule for the classroom

1. Number		Late
2. Pencils		
3. Uniform		
4. Overcoats		
5. Chairs		
6. Windows		
7. Condition	Clean	
	Tidy	
	Plants	
	Posters	
	Pictures	
Total		
8. Work on walls	0 1 2 3 4	
9. Graffiti	0 1 2 3 4	

Classroom observation schedule – definitions

This observation schedule was used during the series of classroom observations of the third year and during the administration of the pupil questionnaire.

1. The number of pupils in the class and the number who arrived after the start of the lesson.
2. The number of pencils borrowed from the researchers during the administration of the questionnaire.
3. The number of children not in correct school uniform (as defined by the school).
4. The number of children in outdoor coats or anoraks.
5. The number of broken chairs in the classroom.
6. The number of broken or cracked windows.
7. The decorative condition of the room. One point was given for each of the five items and a total score assigned to each room.
8. The amount of children's work on the walls, coded from 0 to 4. $0 =$ none, $1 =$ one quarter of available wall space, $2 =$ one half of available wall space, $3 =$ three quarters of available wall space, $4 =$ all available wall space.
9. The amount of graffiti, coded as item 8.

Source: Rutter *et al*. (11)

Checklist for beginning and ending of lessons

TO LESSON

33	Start/after break/N.K.		0
	Same room/Double		1
	V. slow		2

34	Lost	0	1
35	Fight	0	1
36	750 yards	0	1

START

37	Outside:	Mill	0
		Enter room	1
		Line up	2
	Inside:	Muddle	0
		Sit	1
		Stand	2

39	Off-task chat to T	0	1
40	Silence	0	1
41	Greeting	0	1
42	Register	0	1
43	Ritual	0	1

44	Seating:	Chosen by children	0
		T directs some	1
		T directs all	2
		N/K	9
45	Resources:	Brought by children	0
		On desk	1
		Distrib. by T	2
		Distrib. by monitors	3
		Collected by children	4

46–7 Time to start of work:

48 No. Late:

END

49	Timing:	Long	0
		Good	1
		Short	2
		Dismiss before bell	3

50	Stand behind chairs	0	1
51	Silence	0	1
52	Farewell	0	1
53	Line-up	0	1
54	Off-task chat to T	0	1
55	Tidy room	0	1
56	Dismiss by row/group/sex	0	1
57	Reports:	Individual	0	1
58		Class	0	1

59	*Resources:*	
	Collected by T	0
	Collected by monitor	1
	Replaced by children	2
	Kept by children	3

CHECKLIST

60	Homework set	0	1
61	Homework returned	0	1

Outings/trips

Formal punishments:

Formal rewards:

Jobs of e.g. monitors

Recording Observations

> I filled thirty-two notebooks with about half a million words of
> notes made during nearly six hundred hours [of observation]
> (King (4)).

The recording of observations is a frequent source of concern to the
inexperienced case study researcher. How much ought to be recorded?
In what form should the recordings be made? What does one do with
the mass of recorded data? Lofland (9) gives a number of useful suggestions about collecting field notes which we summarise in Box 5.3.

The sort of note-taking recommended by Lofland (9) and actually
undertaken by King (4) and Wolcott (10) in their ethnographic
accounts grows out of the nature of the unstructured observation
study. Note-taking, confessed Wolcott, helped him fight the acute boredom that he sometimes felt when observing the interminable meetings
that are the daily lot of the school principal. Occasionally, however, a
series of events would occur so quickly that Wolcott had time only to
make cursory notes which he supplemented later with fuller accounts.
One useful tip from this experienced ethnographer is worth noting:
never resume your observations until the notes from the preceding
observation are complete. There is nothing to be gained merely by your
presence as an observer. Until your observations and impressions from
one visit are a matter of record, there is little point in returning to the
classroom or school and reducing the impact of one set of events by
superimposing another and more recent set.

Recording observations in structured settings calls for quite different
techniques as the observation schedule in Box 5.4 clearly shows.
Because Rutter and his colleagues (11) were aiming to collect fairly
simple descriptive data about lessons and classrooms, the observation
schedules that we show in Box 5.4 were entirely adequate for their
purposes.

Educational Case Study Examples

We turn now to a brief exposition of each of the case study examples
identified in our observation typology in Box 5.1.

Cell 1: Wolcott (10) The Man in the Principal's Office

Participant observation has been described as a 'process of waiting to
be impressed by recurrent themes that reappear in various contexts'.
Wolcott's account (10) of the career of an elementary school principal
well illustrates the 'waiting role' of the participant observer. Wolcott

shadowed Ed Bell, the school principal, for a period of two years,
spending several days every week with him in school, at home, at
church meetings, accompanying him on school business away from the
school building and even going to the local store with him to purchase
household requirements. During all of these events, Wolcott maintained
a constant written record of the behaviour he saw and the conversations
he heard between the school principal and staff, children, family and
friends. With the principal's permission, the researcher sifted through
his notes, files and personal records. Extensive tape recordings were
made of interviews with members of the school staff. The principal
himself was persuaded to keep an account of recurring school problems
for a period of several weeks. A further observational device used by
Wolcott involved noting the activity and the social interaction patterns
of the school principal every minute for periods of two hours at a time.
This procedure included recording the person with whom the principal
interacted, who initiated the interaction, where and when, who was
talking, and how many people were involved. Over a period of several
weeks Wolcott generated a set of categories for tabulating these interactions. By a careful sampling of the data from these two-hour recordings over ten consecutive school days, the researcher built up a detailed
picture of the multifarious demands made upon the school principal in
his day-to-day life.

To what end? The objective of this particularly intensive form of
participant observation has been cogently put by Diesing (12) as
follows:

> The . . . method involves taking data as they come, and they usually
> come in scattered, disconnected fragments. Unlike the experi-
> mentalist, who can demand evidence on a specific question from his
> subject matter, the participant observer must adapt his thinking to
> what his subject happens to be doing. He has to observe each casual
> interchange as it happens, participate in the ceremony of the day
> since it may not occur again for two years, talk to the informants
> who are available, and get involved in whatever problems and contro-
> versies are prominent at the moment. At the end of the day he
> comes home with a wealth of information on a variety of points, but
> nothing conclusive on any one point. Over the weeks and months his
> evidence on a given point gradually accumulates and the various
> points start to fit together into a tentative pattern.

Wolcott's painstaking and detailed observing and recording led to the gradual identification and piecing together of several important strands in the professional life of the school principal. The researcher reveals the complex demands that are made of a school leader and the degree to which Ed Bell succeeds both in his own estimation and in the judgements of those who have to work with him. We illustrate the point with an example.

One particulary difficult task that American school principals face each year is staff evaluation. Because permanence of tenure and financial advancement hang upon a satisfactory evaluation from the principal, the exercise is charged with tension and anxiety on the part of the teachers and principal alike. (The common practice in North America is that the teacher reads what the school principal has to say about her teaching ability and signs the document in his presence.) Wolcott's observation and recording of the evaluation exercise gathered information from the principal and from various teachers. His account shows how the task of teacher evaluation set the principal most clearly apart from his staff and challenged him with difficult decisions which he tackled with an indecisiveness that only added to the stress that everyone involved experienced:

> After I read the evaluation, I said to Ed, 'So you're going to try to stop me from teaching by saying such things as: I expect that ten years from now you'll be teaching the same way as you're teaching now! On what grounds can anyone say this? Why, I wasn't teaching the same way as I was a year ago, and certainly not ten years ago . . .

Ed Bell is not at all happy with one of his teachers, Mrs Alma Skirmish, and is all set to write a report that will exclude her from his school for the following session. In the end, however, he has a change of heart following evaluation meetings with her such as the one we report above.

> She really seemed to listen to the things I had to say . . . She runs her classroom like a classroom now, not a Sunday school class . . . She's doing a better job . . . Maybe next year I'll regret it. But right now I feel I'm right.

Outside of the actual interchanges between principal and teachers, Wolcott is able to look at the staff evaluation exercise and bring to it his own assessment of the principal's leadership:

> I could never escape a personal feeling that Ed made his assessments

about new staff quickly (probably on first impression), independent of performance observed in the classroom, and then subsequently accumulated whatever evidence he felt he needed to support those impressions. Although he tended to be cautious when screening candidates for his school or the district, once he decided to accept a candidate for the Taft faculty, the extent of his enthusiasm and optimism took a predictable upward swing.

Wolcott's ethnographic study is a very readable and 'real' account of the life of a school principal. The researcher himself is a strong advocate of this particular method of participant observation.* At the same time, he is concerned that would-be researchers are aware of the pitfalls of the approach. It is, he says, an excellent method for obtaining certain kinds of data, but it cannot by itself provide the whole picture. One always faces the problem of generalisability in pursuing an in-depth study of a single case. The participant observer approach, Wolcott adds, is a high-risk, low-yield adventure. It is high risk because unless the fieldwork is eventually translated into a significant, readable (and read) monograph, the only possible gain is that made by the researcher in terms of his own research experience. The participant observer approach is low yield because of the considerable investment of time and personal effort that has to be made in order to obtain basic and often commonplace data. Finally, Wolcott adds, the researcher contemplating ethnographic studies in educational settings faces unique problems in that he assumes the role of formal observer in an institutional framework with which he has probably been in continuous contact since the age of five. It should make any intending researcher consider the crucial nature of *himself as an instrument* in collecting data through participant observation and interviewing techniques.

Cell 2: Lambert et al. (13) *The Chance of a Lifetime?*

Like Wolcott, Lambert and his associates (13) used a variety of techniques including focused, depth interviews in gathering data in their massive study of 66 boarding schools throughout England and Wales. In the *intensive* sample of seven schools with which we deal here, the bulk of the information was obtained from a lengthy questionnaire which was completed by 1,238 senior pupils under examination conditions. More importantly, the questionnaire was designed to provide statistical

---

* See also: H.F. Wolcott, 'Criteria for an ethnographic approach to research in schools', *Human Organization*, 34, 2 (1975) 111-27.

evidence by means of which the researchers could test a number of
hypotheses arising out of their view of the school as an organisation.
Lambert describes the theoretical orientation of his study as largely
deriving from a *conflict* view of society although he concedes that
the approach 'combines *functional* and *conflict* models and adds a third
sociological approach. This is a *developmental* approach which
emphasizes the ways in which the [school as an] organization has
changed or developed over a period of time'. The model of the school
that guided the research is set out in Box 5.5.

Box 5.5.

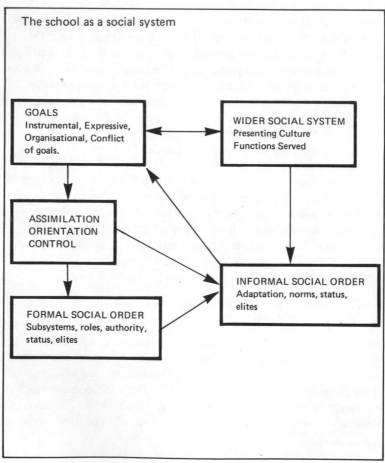

Source: Lambert *et al.* (13)

To convey to the reader the flavour of the highly structured approach used in the intensive sample study we include part of the questionnaire in which the researchers sought information on the effects of boarding school life on the emotional and sexual life of the pupils. By way of introducing the section we give details from the *Manual* (13) in which Lambert outlines the theoretical ideas which guided the choice of questions.

Questions 51, 52, 53, 54, 55, 56, 57:

Besides giving further data on peer associations both within and outside or based on the school, these questions are some of several which explore reactions to the opposite sex. They relate thus to the sections on *adaptation, patterns of association, sexual adaptations,* and *school and society*. The data on the opposite sex correlates with that gained from the Thematic Apperception Test which we used and that based on Merton's paradigm (conformity, ritualism, innovation, retreatism, rebellion). It also refers to the following hypotheses:

H. 57: The age of boarding influences the boarder's affective relationships in depth.

H. 59: Boarders from single sex boarding schools find difficulty in responding to the other sex in a natural way on leaving.

H. 60: The more total the one sex institution the greater is the incidence of deviant sexual adaptations to it.

H. 61: Where the expressive stress and provision of the school is limited deviant sexual adaptations will be more dominant.

H. 62: While there is no evidence that boarding schools produce more homosexuals than day schools it is likely that those that have homosexual and heterosexual tendencies are sensitized more on the homosexual side than in a day school.

H. 74: Boarding reduces superficial strains in family relationships but inhibits communications at deeper levels.

The section of the questionnaire to which these hypotheses are directed is set out in Box 5.6.

Lambert and his colleagues tested their hypotheses in percentage comparisons between boarding school boys' responses and those of control groups drawn from single-sex day schools. Thus, in respect of Hypothesis 59 they reported:

A majority of boarders (56 to 67%) were uneasy or lacking in

Box 5.6

Effects of boarding on emotional and sexual life

Q.51 Have you any close friends of your own age and sex near here
(apart from boys actually at this school now)?
Tick:
              Yes, connected with the school ....
              Yes, not connected with the school ....
              No ....

Q.52 Have you a girl friend near here at present (apart from one you may
have at home)?
Tick:
              Yes ....
              No ....

Q.53 Do you think that the senior boys at this school (tick which one)

              see too much of the other sex ....
              see about enough of them ....
              see too little of them ....
              anything else ....

Q.54 What about *you* personally:
Would you like to have more to do with girls here if it were possible?
(Tick)
              Yes ....
              No ....
              Don't know ....

Q.55 Which of the following most nearly describes your own reaction
when in the company of a girl? (Tick)

              I'm usually quite at ease ....
              I look self-confident but don't feel it ....
              I tend to put on a bit of a show ....
              I feel a bit embarrassed ....
              I feel uneasy ....
              Any alternatives or additions ....

Q.56 Has being away from girls and women had any effect on your
attitudes or reactions to them?

              ....

              ....

Q.57 In your experience are there any good or bad effects produced by
living in a community all of your own sex?

       (a)   the good effects ....

       (b)   the bad effects ....

Source: Lambert *et al.* (13)

assurance with girls compared with a majority of day boys in the same or similar single sex schools (58 to 63%) who claimed to be perfectly at ease in the company of the other sex.

Our reasons for classifying this study at the natural end of the observational setting continuum become clear from the details that Lambert and his associates give about the overall framework of the research programme.

In the extensive sample of 59 schools, the researchers visited each school for usually two weeks or more, living and sleeping on the premises, joining in the everyday pattern of life in an endeavour to experience all aspects of the school — 'classroom, chapel, games, social services, corps, the pupil world, the staff common room, meetings and social life'. Subsequent visits were made to about a quarter of the schools and contact was maintained for several years. Interviews were conducted with approximately 1 in 4 of the housemasters, 1 in 4 of the matrons, and 1 in 7 of the school doctors. In order to explore the family life of the boarding school boy, the parents of a stratified random sample of 179 boys were interviewed for three hours in their own homes. The researchers were able to compare the boys' questionnaires (completed at school) with the data derived from the parent interviews with what they describe as 'fascinating results'.

Cell 3: King (4) *All Things Bright and Beautiful?*

Unlike Lambert and his associates whose structured approach to their boarding school enquiry derived from a particular model of the school as a social system, King (4) began his study of infant schools unfettered by preplanned questionnaires and interview schedules:

> I asked the headmistress of a large infants' school . . . if she would allow me to make observations in one of the classrooms. I was not able to give her any clear idea of what I was trying to do because I did not know exactly myself.

This is not to say, however, that King did not have a theoretical orientation. He had, so he says, a 'vaguely anthropological model of trying to understand life in classroom, the key word in that sentence being *understand*'. King's orientation towards *Verstehen* (the study of meanings) reveals that like Lambert, he too had a guiding model, in his case derived from Max Weber (14) and action theory rather than Talcott Parsons (15) and Ralph Dahrendorf (16). At the beginning of his research, King was anxious to follow some of the ideas of two American sociologists, Glaser and Strauss (17), who argue that sociological theories should be grounded in data that are generated by the act of research. In short, theory should follow from research, not precede it. This argument has a familiar ring; it is essentially the one made by Diesing (12) which we quoted in our outline of Wolcott's study of the school principal in Cell 1. Not unexpectedly, King's research strategy is very similar to that adopted by Wolcott.

How did King set about the task of observing and making sense of the kaleidoscope of activities that typifies the busy infant classroom? Quota sampling, snowball sampling and the search for exceptions are three commonly-used procedures in participant observation. King used all three.

Quota sampling involves interviewing certain individuals from particular categories that the researcher has delineated. In King's study, one such category, *infant teacher*, is self-evident. He was interested in the fact that most of the things that happened in the classes he observed were arranged to happen or allowed to happen by the teachers. Gradually, he began to discern the structure of infant teachers' ideologies which guided their classroom behaviour. We give the following examples from King's own account:

Developmentalism:
Small boy picks up work card from tray.
Teacher: You're too young to do those sums.

Individualism:
Teacher: If your approach doesn't suit a particular child then change it — the approach, not the child.

Play as learning:
Teacher: Most of what adults would regard as play is, in reality, of the deepest significance in the child's intellectual development.

Childhood innocence:
A girl complains to the teacher: 'Gary keeps flicking paint on my picture.'
Teacher: I'm sure he didn't mean it.

Snowball sampling involves recording a particular incident and then looking for another example of it, then another, and another, and so on (see Box 5.2). King used this technique in looking at the various methods of social control used by infant teachers in the three schools under study. Thus, he was able to interpret five distinct *teacher voices*:

'Now we are going to do something exciting' voice.
'Slightly aggrieved, sad' voice.
'I'm being very patient with you' voice.
'Oh, nevermind, don't let's have a fuss' voice.
'Listen to me, I'm saying something important' voice.

The *search for exceptions* (see Box 5.2) is a way of falsifying working hypotheses or reformulating them. King's search for the general rules governing the behaviour of infant teachers towards pupils led him to suspect the occasional incidence of certain children being permitted a special status by their teachers. His subsequent search for exceptions led him to delineate a group whom he termed, *'permitted eccentric children from professional homes'*.

One boy came to school for several days in a kilt. It was not his, he was not even Scottish.

Strange child — her father's a psychologist.

The Nature of Infant Education. King's methodology has much in common with the ethogenic approach that we outline in Chapter 10, and his final chapter is in the style of an *account of accounts* in which the researcher, having made explicit the methods he has applied in eliciting his information from informants and the processes he has employed in transforming his data, attempts to place his findings in a wider theoretical perspective. King argues as follows:

The child-centred ideologies which represent what is real about children and their learning to infants' teachers are social constructs; that is to say, there was a time when they did not exist nor are they accepted by everyone. With this in mind, it is possible to discuss and to evaluate classroom practices and ideologies independently of any claim for their being either the most appropriate or the truth.

This is what King proceeds to do, showing the consequences of teachers' insistence on 'play is learning' and 'childhood innocence' and their adherence to 'family-home background' theories of child deficiencies in learning. He concludes his analysis with the proposition that infant education can be viewed as a middle-class institution.

Cell 4: Adams and Biddle (18) *Realities of Teaching*

Adams and Biddle's (18) study of 16 classrooms involved making video-tape recordings of 32 lessons, half of which were in primary schools and half in secondary. The sample of lessons they recorded ranged across the curriculum — half the sessions consisted of social studies, the other half arithmetic (in primary classes) and mathematics in the secondary classes. Half of the teachers were male, and half female. Moreover, half the teachers were over 40 years of age, and half under 30. Clearly, the researchers had in mind controlling a number of variables they believed would affect the 'realities of teaching' that constituted the foci of their study. But why videotape? Adams and Biddle claim three major advantages of this method. First, it provides an extremely comprehensive record of classroom behaviour that can be preserved for subsequent analysis. Second, what they term the fidelity of the system is good, that is to say, the cameras can deal with conventional classroom settings, and microphones are able to pick up the greater proportion of the public utterances that take place. Third, the stop-rewind facility of the tape recorder permits sequences of behaviour to be viewed and reviewed at will during data-coding. Recorded data were analysed as follows. The coder identified a sought-for activity on the video screen, stopped the tape and rewound beyond the point at which the activity occurred. He then replayed the episode and on reaching the particular point, took a reading from a time counter and recorded it on coding sheets. The tape recorder was kept running until the end of the sought-for activity whereupon another reading was recorded from the time counter. In this way, two kinds of measurements were obtained: (1) an *incident* count, registering each instance when the different kinds of behaviour occurred; and (2) a *duration* count which registered the time-span of each particular incident. Computer analysis later provided data on the number of incidents and the total amount of time spent on each kind of behaviour. Thus a complete record was accumulated of all instances of particular activities in the 32 classrooms, showing the number of times that an activity occurred and how long it lasted. That record, the researchers propose, tells something of the story of *life in classrooms*, where typically a scene of rapid and frequent change is the order of the day involving some 371 activity episodes in the average lesson and some 4,500 episodes in the busiest classrooms in one school day. From this mass of data, Adams and Biddle develop *lesson profiles*, classifying incidents according to the *roles* that teachers and pupils adopt, the *location* and the *function* of various activities in which they are engaged, and whether the

Box 5.7

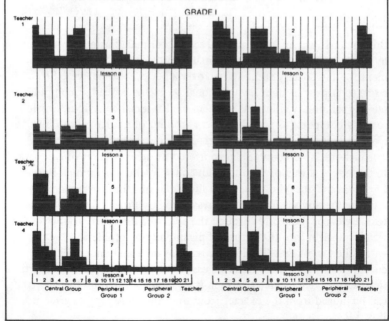

Lesson profiles in primary classrooms

Central Group

1. Role Allocation (who the emitter, target, audience, and residue members are)
2. Emitter Location (where the emitters are)
3. Target Location (where the targets are)
4. Audience Location (where the audience is)
5. Functional Code (what the educative process is about)
6. Role Structure (how many roles are operating at one time)
7. Communication Structure (what sorts of groups exist)

First Peripheral Group

8. Role Allocation (who the emitter, target, audience, and residue members are)
9. Emitter Location (where the emitters are)
10. Target Location (where the targets are)
11. Audience Location (where the audience is)
12. Functional Code (what the educative process is about)
13. Role Structure (how many roles are operating at one time)

Second Peripheral Group

14. Role Allocation (who the emitter, target, audience, and residue members are)
15. Emitter Location (where the emitters are)
16. Target Location (where the targets are)
17. Audience Location (where the audience is)
18. Functional Code (what the educative process is about)
19. Role Structure (how many roles are operating at one time)

Teacher

20. Teacher Role Assignment (whether the teacher is emitter, target, or audience member)
21. Teacher Location (where the teacher is)

GRADE I

Source: Adams and Biddle (18)

participants in the interpersonal exchanges are *emitters* or *targets*. Box 5.7 shows a series of lesson profiles developed from data gathered in the classrooms of younger children.

Each 'block' in the profiles shows how many instances occurred of a particular kind of activity. For example, Block 21 at the extreme right hand side of the profiles shows the number of teacher locations. Inspection of the profiles in Box 5.7 shows that whilst classroom activities differ from room to room, there is a common pattern discernible in the lessons that have been observed and analysed. Notice how the 'ends' of the profiles in each case are higher than the 'middles'. Notice, too, the height of teacher blocks 20 and 21. The higher the block, the more frequently the teacher changed roles from emitter to target, to audience and back. The profiles in Box 5.7 suggest that teachers of younger children initiate a great deal of role switching. The extent to which they diversify their teaching activities can be judged by comparison with the profiles of their secondary school colleagues teaching social studies and mathematics in classes of older students (Box 5.8).

Realities of Teaching is a good example of the type of case study in which the individual unit of analysis is the relatively natural setting of the classroom and the observational approach is highly structured, gathering data that are objective and capable of quantification.

Cell 5: Shields (19) A Cure of Delinquents

Bredinghurst was an experimental school for maladjusted boys set up by the then London County Council to provide a specialised environment for anti-social children who, over a period of time, were helped to come to grips with their own personal problems instead of compulsively seeking temporary solutions to them in anti-social behaviour. Shield's case study report (19) on Chris is an account of a three-month involvement in twice-weekly sessions with a severely disturbed adolescent. Throughout the therapy, Shields offered no structural set of categories to the boy as a way of mounting an active rescue programme. Rather, Chris was the one who structured the situations that governed the ongoing therapy sessions. In this way, the boy provided the therapist with a view of the world through the eyes of a disturbed youngster and thus, an insight into the nature of his underlying problems.

To the extent that the therapy sessions occurred under clinical conditions we have classified this case study as taking place in an artificial setting. The degree to which it was unstructured by the observer can be judged from the extract from the case study reports given in Box 5.9.

Box 5.8

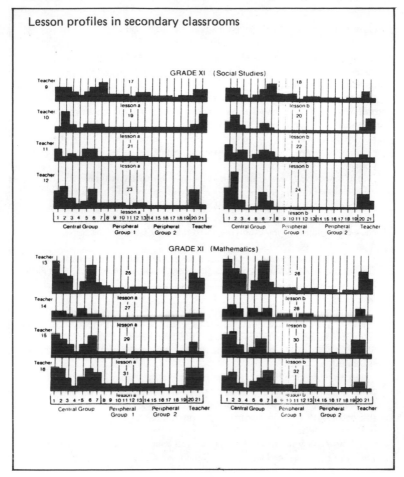

Lesson profiles in secondary classrooms

Source: Adams and Biddle (18)

Cell 6: Weinreich (in Verma and Bagley, eds (20)): Cross-ethnic identification and self-rejection in a black adolescent

Our final example of a case study was also undertaken in the artificial setting of a clinical laboratory but, as will become apparent, the account shows a considerable degree of structure in the observational techniques that were employed by the researcher. The study (20) was concerned with the problem of cross-ethnic identification in a 16-year-old West Indian adolescent boy. *Cross-ethnic identification* was

Box 5.9

Case study extract on Chris, a severely disturbed adolescent

Chris reported these things to me also, saying that in his nightmares he had repeatedly dreamt that he was about to die or be killed, and he asked many questions about death . . .

I arranged to see him again the next day, and he arrived in a furious mood. He stalked up and down my room swearing at me, accusing me of being a liar, an ignoramus, bad like the rest.

'I would like to kick your fire in', he said, and did in fact kick at the gas-fire. 'Why my fire?' I asked. 'All right, then', he yelled, 'I'd like to kick your f . . . . . g teeth in!'

His whole body was trembling as he went on to say what cruel and vicious things he would like to do to me, ending up, 'and cut out your guts and smear them all over the bleeding wall'.

He clenched his fists so that the nails cut into the flesh and he bit the back of his hand till the blood began to flow. By now he was trembling so much that he had to sit down . . .

Pulling up his trouser leg he drew a long sheath knife from his stocking and leapt at me holding the knife against my chest. His face contorted with fury, he shouted, 'I've only got to push this one inch further and you're dead . . .'

Facetiously I reminded him that a condemned man was allowed to smoke one last cigarette and asked if he would permit this indulgence. This infuriated him further but he agreed. Then he turned the knife against himself . . . finally he flung it at the door with such force that it stuck into the wood . . .

Suddenly all the fight went out of him and he slipped to the floor sobbing loudly and uncontrollably . . . Towards the end of this long session lasting nearly three hours, he said, 'I've never talked to anyone like this before. It's all been terribly frightening, but I'm glad now I told you everything I felt.'

'Why aren't you afraid of me? I've never met anyone like you before. Why don't you get mad with me? I could have killed you, you know.'

Source: Adapted from Shields (19)

defined as the extent to which John, the boy in question, identified with the indigenous white population but knew that he himself was black, that is, he did not mis-identify himself as white. The researcher elicited personal constructs (see Chapter 14) from the transcripts of interviews carried out with John. These constructs were presented to the boy, one at a time, on rating sheets on which he systematically construed aspects of his self-image alongside significant individuals and

groups from his own social world. The number of constructs entering
the analyses was about 15 to 20 whilst the number of social entities
was about 10 (see Box 5.10).

The following extracts from the interview data show the degree
of structure employed by the observer in his various lines of enquiry,
and at the same time demonstrate his ability to make use of focused
interview techniques (see Chapter 13) to get beneath John's initial
bland responses to certain key issues.

> *Questioner:* What do people respect you for?
> *John:* I goes around with whites, 'cos not many kids do that.
> *Questioner:* Do you think you'll get married to a white girl sometime?
> *John:* No, I don't think so. I'd like to, but I don't think so. Wouldn't
> be right for the children, would it? When they grow up, you
> know what would be said about them.

John is talking about his skin colour and his experience of prejudice:

> *John:* I don't like my own colour. I must admit that.
> *Questioner:* Why is that?

Box 5.10

Changes between John's past and current identifications with West Indian and English people			
Social entity	*Past identifica- tion*	*Current identifica- tion*	*Direction of change*
West Indian people	.27	.08	less current iden.
West Indian boys	.40	.38	less current iden.
West Indian girls	.20	.15	less current iden.
Black Power	.27	.15	less current iden.
That little group of blacks	.53	.08	less current iden.
English people	.27	.46	greater current iden.
White boys	.20	.31	greater current iden.
White girls	.27	.40	greater current iden.
Friendly whites	.33	.62	greater current iden.
Me as whites see me	.33	.54	greater current iden.

Source: Adapted from Verma and Bagley (20)

John: It seems to be bogging me down, fellows come up in the open
. . . I feel afraid.

Questioner: You feel afraid because of the reactions of white people?

John: Yes. But I prefer white to black . . . I would rather be white.
What they don't realize is that if they were in our position they
would know what it feels like, see. They would have to take it
then.

Box 5.10 shows the changes that have occurred between John's past
and current identifications with West Indian and English people. The
correlations are to be interpreted as 0.00 indicating a total absence of
identification while 1.00 represents maximum identification.

Weinreich draws two specific conclusions from his analysis of John's
identity structure. First, the process of identity diffusion resolution
does not necessarily mean that the person becomes better adapted to
his own situation as judged in mental health terms. It may even be
that the terminology of mental health is inappropriate in this case.
From one vantage point, Weinrich suggests, John has improved. His
self-evaluation is becoming more positive and his behaviour more controlled. From a different vantage point, however, things are far from
well. John dislikes his own skin colour and dissociates himself from his
own ethnic group. It is the understanding of John's identity structure,
the research suggests, which is an essential prerequisite to any therapeutic aid that might be undertaken by a black therapist.

To conclude, the very different strategies we have illustrated in our
six examples of educational case studies suggest that *participant
observation* is best thought of as a generic term that describes a
methodological approach rather than one specific method. What our
examples have shown is that the representativeness of a particular
sample often relates to the observational strategy open to the researcher.
Generally speaking, the larger the sample, the more representative it is,
and the more likely that the observer's role is of a participant nature.

References

1. Patrick J., *A Glasgow Gang Observed* (Eyre Methuen, London, 1973).
2. Parker, H.J., *View from the Boys* (David and Charles, Newton Abbot, 1974).
3. Young, J. *The Drugtakers* (Paladin, London, 1971).
4. King, R. *All Things Bright and Beautiful?* (John Wiley, Chichester, 1979);
    Sharp, R. and Green, A. *Education and Social Control* (Routledge and Kegan
    Paul, London. 1975); Hargreaves, D.H., *Social Relations in a Secondary*

School (Routledge and Kegan Paul, London, 1967); Lacey, C., *Hightown Grammar* (Manchester University Press, Manchester, 1970); Woods, P., *The Divided School* (Routledge and Kegan Paul, London, 1979).
5. Willis, P.E., *Learning to Labour* (Saxon House, London, 1977).
6. Bailey, K.D., *Methods of Social Research* (Collier-Macmillan, London, 1978).
7. Schutz, A., *Collected Papers* (Nijhoff, The Hague, 1962).
8. Denzin, N., *The Research Act in Sociology: A Theoretical Introduction to Sociological Methods* (The Butterworth Group, London, 1970).
9. Lofland, J., *Analysing Social Settings* (Wadsworth, Belmont, Ca., 1971).
10. Wolcott, H.F., *The Man in the Principal's Office* (Holt, Rinehart and Winston, New York, 1973).
11. Rutter, M., Maughan, B., Mortimore, P. and Ouston, J., *Fifteen Thousand Hours* (Open Books, London, 1979).
12. Diesing, P., *Patterns of Discovery in the Social Sciences* (Aldine, Chicago, 1971).
13. Lambert, R., Bullock, R. and Millham, S., *The Chance of a Lifetime?* (Weidenfeld and Nicholson, London, 1975); Lambert, R., Millham, S. and Bullock, R., *A Manual to the Sociology of the School* (Weidenfeld and Nicholson, London, 1970).
14. Weber, M., *Essays in Sociology* (Routledge and Kegan Paul, London, 1948); Weber, M., *The Theory of Social and Economic Organization* (Free Press, Glencoe, 1964).
15. Parsons, T., *The Social System* (Free Press, New York, 1951).
16. Dahrendorf, R., *Class and Class Conflict in Industrial Society* (Routledge and Kegan Paul, London, 1959).
17. Glaser, B.G. and Strauss, A.L., *The Discovery of Grounded Theory* (Aldine, Chicago, 1967).
18. Adams, R.S. and Biddle, B.J., *Realities of Teaching* (Holt, Rinehart and Winston, New York, 1970).
19. Shields, R.W., *A Cure of Delinquents* (Heinemann Educational Books, London, 1962).
20. Verma, G. and Bagley, C. (eds), *Race, Education and Equality* (Macmillan, London, 1979).

6   CORRELATIONAL RESEARCH

Introduction

Human behaviour at both the individual and social level is characterised by great complexity, a complexity about which we understand comparatively little, given the present state of social research. One approach to a fuller understanding of human behaviour is to begin by teasing out simple relationships between those factors and elements deemed to have some bearing on the phenomena in question. The value of correlational research is that it is able to achieve this end.

Before we attempt to examine correlational research as such, it might be useful if we begin by defining *correlation* and related terms and indicating the purposes they fulfil in statistical analysis. We saw in the introduction that one of the primary purposes of science as it is traditionally conceived is to discover relationships among phenomena with a view ultimately to predicting and, in some situations, controlling their occurrence. As we suggested above, much of social research in general, and educational research more particularly, is concerned at our present stage of development with the first step in this sequence — establishing interrelationships among variables. We may wish to know, for example, how delinquency is related to social class background; or whether an association exists between the number of years spent in full-time education and subsequent annual income; or whether there is a link between personality and achievement. Numerous techniques have been devised to provide us with numerical representations of such relationships and they are known as *measures of association*. We list the principal ones in Box 6.1. Three of them are of special interest to us in our examination of correlational research — Pearson's product-moment coefficient of correlation, multiple correlation and partial correlation.

Correlational techniques are generally intended to answer three questions about two variables or two sets of data (2): (a) is there a relationship between the two variables (or sets of data)? If the answer to this question is 'yes', then two other questions follow: (b) what is the direction of the relationship? and (c) what is the magnitude?

Relationship in this context refers to any tendency for the two variables (or sets of data) to vary consistently. Pearson's product-moment coefficient of correlation, one of the best known measures of association, is a statistical value ranging from -1.0 to $+1.0$ and expresses

Box 6.1

Common measures of relationship

Measure	Nature of Variables	Comment
Pearson product moment r	Two continuous variables; interval or ratio scale	Relationship linear
Rank order or Kendall's tau	Two continuous variables; ordinal scale	
Correlation ratio, η (eta)	One variable continuous, other either continuous or discrete	Relationship nonlinear
Intraclass	One variable continuous; other discrete; interval or ratio scale	Purpose: to determine within-group similarity
Biserial, r_{bis} Point biserial, $r_{pt.bis}$	One variable continuous; other (a) continuous but dichotomised, r_{bis}, or (b) true dichotomy, $r_{pt.bis}$	Index of item discrimination (used in item analysis)
Phi coefficient, ϕ	Two true dichotomies; nominal or ordinal series	
Partial correlation $r_{1\,2.3\,\ldots}$	Three or more continuous variables	Purpose: to determine relationship between two variables, with effect of third held constant
Multiple correlation $R_{1.234\,\ldots}$	Three or more continuous variables	Purpose: to predict one variable from a linear weighted combination of two or more independent variables
Kendall's coefficient of concordance, ω	Three or more continuous variables; ordinal series	Purpose: to determine the degree of (say, interrater) agreement

Source: Mouly (1)

this relationship in quantitative form. The coefficient is represented by the symbol r. Where the two variables (or sets of data) fluctuate in the same direction, i.e. as one increases so does the other or as one decreases so does the other, a *positive* relationship is said to exist. Correlations reflecting this pattern are prefaced with a plus sign to indicate the positive nature of the relationship. Thus, +1.0 would indicate perfect positive correlation between two factors, as with the radius and diameter of a circle, and +.80 a high positive correlation, as between academic achievement and intelligence, for example. Where the sign has been omitted, a plus sign is assumed.

A negative correlation or relationship, on the other hand, is to be found when an increase in one variable is accompanied by a decrease in the other variable. Negative correlations are prefaced with a minus sign. Thus, −1.0 would represent perfect negative correlation, as between the number of errors children make on a spelling test and their score on the test, and −0.20, a low negative correlation, as between absenteeism and intelligence, say. There is no other meaning to the signs used; they indicate nothing more than which pattern holds for any two variables (or sets of data).

Generally speaking, researchers tend to be more interested in the magnitude or size of an obtained correlation than they are in its direction. Correlational procedures have been developed so that no relationship whatever between two variables is represented by zero (or 0.00), as between body weight and intelligence, possibly. This means that a person's performance on one variable is totally unrelated to his performance on a second variable. If he is high on one, for example, he is just as likely to be high or low on the other. Perfect correlations of +1.00 or −1.00 are rarely found and, as we shall see, most coefficients of correlation in social research are around +0.50 or less. The correlation coefficient may be seen then as an indication of the predictability of one variable given the other: it is an indication of covariation. The relationship between two variables can be examined visually by plotting the paired measurements on graph paper with each pair of observations being represented by a point. The resulting arrangement of points is known as a *scatter diagram* and enables us to assess graphically the degree of relationship between the characteristics being measured. Box 6.2 gives some examples of scatter diagrams in the field of educational research.

The coefficient of correlation, then, tells us something about the relationship between *two variables*. Other measures exist, however, which allow us to specify relationships when more than two variables are involved. These are known as measures of *multiple correlation* and *partial correlation*.

Multiple correlation measures indicate the degree of association between three or more variables simultaneously. We may want to know, for example, the degree of association between delinquency, social class background and leisure facilities. Or we may be interested in finding

Box 6.2

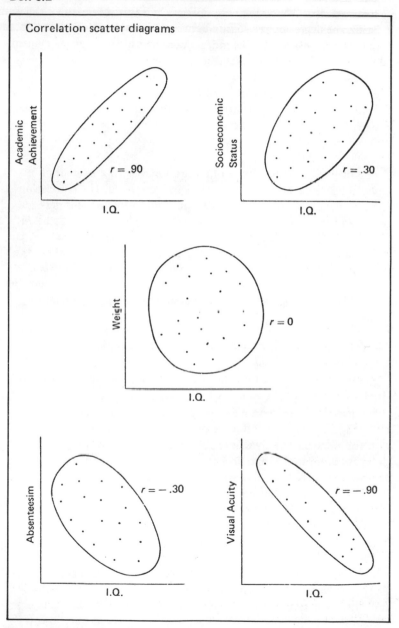

Correlation scatter diagrams

Source: Tuckman (4)

out the relationship between academic achievement, intelligence and neuroticism. Multiple correlation, or *regression* as it is sometimes called, indicates the degree of association between *n* variables. It is related not only to the correlations of the independent variable with the dependent variables, but also to the intercorrelations between the dependent variables.

Partial correlation aims at establishing the degree of association between two variables after the influence of a third has been controlled or partialled out. Guilford and Fruchter (3) define a partial correlation between two variables as

> one that nullifies the effects of a third variable (or a number of variables) upon both the variables being correlated. The correlation between height and weight of boys in a group where age is permitted to vary would be higher than the correlation between height and weight in a group at constant age. The reason is obvious. Because certain boys are older, they are both heavier and taller. Age is a factor that enhances the strength of correspondence between height and weight. With age held constant, the correlation would still be positive and significant because at any age, taller boys tend to be heavier.

Consider, too, the relationship between success in basketball and previous experience in the game. Suppose, also, that the presence of a third factor, the height of the players, was known to have an important influence on the other two factors. The use of partial correlation techniques would enable a measure of the two primary variables to be achieved freed from the influence of the secondary variable.

It follows from what we have said so far that *correlational research* embraces those studies and projects in which attempts are made to discover or clarify relationships through the use of correlation co-efficients. Relationships thus disclosed may simply indicate what goes with what in a given context, or else they may provide a basis on which to make predictions about the variables being studied. The basic design of correlational research is simple and involves collecting two or more scores on the same group of subjects and computing correlation coefficients. Many useful studies have been based on this simple design. Those involving more complex relationships, however, utilise multiple and partial correlations in order to provide a clearer picture of the relationships being investigated. One observer (5) points out, however, that the quality of correlation studies is determined not by the complexity of the design or the sophistication of the correlational techniques used but by the level of planning and the depth of the theoretical constructs going into the development of the hypotheses.

One final point: it is important to stress that correlations refer to measures of association and do not necessarily indicate causal relationships between variables. Mouly (1) puts it like this:

> The correlation simply implies concomitance; it is not synonymous with causation. It may suggest causation in the same sense that the variables involved are part of a cause and effect system, but the nature of the system and the direction in which the components operate is not specified in the correlation. The two variables are not necessarily (or perhaps even commonly) the 'cause' and 'effect' of each other. The correlation between X and Y is often nothing more than the reflection of the operation of a third factor.

Characteristics

We indicated above that correlational studies may be broadly classified as either *relational studies* or as *prediction studies*. We now look at each a little more closely.

In the case of the first of these two categories, correlational research is mainly concerned with achieving a fuller understanding of the complexity of phenomena or, in the matter of behavioural and educational research, behavioural patterns by studying the relationships between the variables which the researcher hypothesises as being related. As a method, it is particularly useful in exploratory studies into fields where little or no previous research has been undertaken. It is often a shot in the dark aimed at verifying hunches a researcher has about a presumed relationship between characteristics or variables. Take a complex notion like *teacher effectiveness*, for example. This is dependent upon a number of less complex factors operating singly or in combination. Factors such as intelligence, motivation, person perception, verbal skills and empathy come to mind as possibly having an effect on teaching outcomes. A review of the literature of research will confirm or reject these possibilities. Once an appropriate number have been identified in this way, suitable measures may then be chosen or developed to assess them. They are then given to a representative sample and the scores obtained are then correlated with a measure of the complex factor being investigated, namely, teacher effectiveness. As it is an exploratory undertaking, the analysis will consist of correlation coefficients only, though if it is designed carefully, we will begin to achieve some understanding of the particular behaviour being studied. The investigation and its outcomes may then be used as a basis for further research or as a source for additional hypotheses.

Exploratory relationship studies may also employ partial correlational techniques. Partial correlation is a particularly suitable approach when a researcher wishes to nullify the influence of one or more important factors upon behaviour in order to bring the effect of less important factors into greater prominence. If, for example, we wanted to understand more fully the determinants of academic achievement in a comprehensive school, we might begin by acknowledging the importance of the factor of intelligence and establishing a relationship between intelligence and academic achievement. The intelligence factor could then be held constant by partial correlation, thus enabling the investigator to clarify other, lesser factors such as motivation, parental encouragement or vocational aspiration. Clearly, motivation is related to academic achievement but if a pupil's motivation score is correlated with academic achievement without controlling the intelligence factor, it will be difficult to assess the true effect of motivation on achievement because the pupil with high intelligence but low motivation may possibly achieve more than pupils with lower intelligence but higher motivation. Once intelligence has been nullified, it is possible to see more clearly the relationship between motivation and achievement. The next stage might be to control the effects of both intelligence and motivation and then to seek a clearer idea of the effects of other selected factors — parental encouragement or vocational aspiration, for instance.

In contrast to exploratory relationship studies, prediction studies are usually undertaken in areas having a firmer and securer knowledge base. Prediction through the use of correlational techniques is based on the assumption that at least some of the factors that will lead to the behaviour to be predicted are present and measurable at the time the prediction is made (5). If, for example, we wanted to predict the probable success of a group of salesmen on an intensive training course, we would start with variables that have been found in previous research to be related to later success in saleswork. These might include: enterprise, verbal ability, achievement motivation, emotional maturity, sociability and so on. The extent to which these predictors correlate with the particular behaviour we wish to predict, namely, successful salesmanship, will determine the accuracy of our prediction. Clearly, variables crucial to success cannot be predicted if they are not present at the time of making the prediction. A salesman's ability to fit in with a team of fellow salesmen cannot be predicted where these future colleagues are unknown.

In order to be valuable in prediction, the magnitude of association between two variables must be substantial; and the greater the association, the more accurate the prediction it permits. In practice, this means that anything less than perfect correlation will permit errors in predicting one variable from a knowledge of the other. As Mouly (1) explains,

The correlation must, of course, represent a real relationship rather than simply the operation of chance. Beyond this, what constitutes an adequate correlation between two variables can be appraised only on the basis of what can logically be expected, and, of course, what accuracy of prediction is required to serve the purpose of the study. A coefficient of correlation of +0.35 between motivation and grades, for example, is perhaps all that can be expected from our presently crude measures of motivation and of grades.

Borg (5) recalls that much prediction research in the United States has been carried out in the field of scholastic success. Some studies in this connection have been aimed at short-term prediction of students' performance in specific courses of study, while other studies have been directed at long-term prediction of general academic success. Sometimes, short-term academic prediction is based upon a single predictor variable. Most efforts to predict future behaviours, however, are based upon scores on a number of predictor variables each of which is useful in predicting a specific aspect of future behaviour. In the prediction of college success, for example, a single variable such as academic achievement is less effective as a predictor than a combination of variables such as academic achievement together with, say, motivation, intelligence, study habits, etc. More complex studies of this kind, therefore, generally make use of multiple correlation and multiple regression equations.

Predicting behaviours or events likely to occur in the near future is easier and less hazardous than predicting behaviours likely to occur in the more distant future. The reason is that in short-term prediction, more of the factors leading to success in the predicted behaviour are likely to be present. In addition, short-term prediction allows less time for important predictor variables to change or for the individual to gain experience that would tend to change his likelihood of success in the predicted behaviour.

One further point: correlation, as Mouly observes, is a group concept, a generalised measure that is useful basically in predicting group performance. Whereas, for instance, it can be predicted that gifted children as a group will succeed at school, it cannot be predicted with certainty that one particular gifted child will excel. As to the relative value of the correlation coefficient he notes,

> Since most correlations between the variables of interest in the social sciences are of the order of 0.50, relatively little confidence can be placed in such prediction in the individual case. It is, there-fore, necessary to raise the correlation on the basis of which predictions are made in order to increase their precision. This can be done by refining the instruments used and/or the criterion being predicted, and . . . by combining a number of variables into a com-posite predictor of the criterion.

Occasions When Appropriate

From the preceding discussion, we may readily see that the techniques of correlational research are particularly useful in social and educational investigations. Abstracting from the main points of the arguments, then, we may say that correlational research is appropriate in the following *two* instances. *First*, it is appropriate when there is a need to *discover* or *clarify* relationships and where correlation coefficients will achieve these ends. It is especially useful in this connection in the initial stages of a project where a certain amount of basic groundwork has to be covered to get some idea of the structure of the relationships. In this way it gets at degrees of relationships rather than the all-or-nothing question posed by experimental design — is an effect present or absent? Beyond this stage, relationships may become the source of hypotheses and further research. The correlational approach is also valuable when variables are complex and do not lend themselves therefore to the experimental method and controlled manipulation. It also permits the measurement of several variables and their interrelationships simultaneously in realistic settings. Both of these latter instances will be characterised by the use of multiple and partial correlations.

Second, correlational research is appropriate where the objective, or one of a set of objectives, is to achieve some degree of prediction. Correlational techniques make up one of a range of alternative approaches in this regard. We have already identified a number of characteristics of prediction studies and it is sufficient at this point to note them as being occasions when a predictive approach may be fruitful. Thus, prediction studies are appropriate where a firm basis of previous knowledge is present, the assumption being that at least some of the factors will relate to the behaviour to be predicted. There needs, too, to be a reasonable chance of achieving a high or moderately high correlation coefficient. Low coefficients will have little predictive value. Further, for confident results prediction research is more appropriate for events likely to occur in the immediate future than at some point in the distant future. Finally, prediction studies are suitable where a group as opposed to an individual is the focus of a project. Only a high correlation can be regarded as valid for individual prediction.

Advantages and Disadvantages

Correlational research possesses a number of advantages and disadvantages which we will here briefly review. As regards its advantages, correlational research is particularly useful in tackling the problems of education and the social sciences because it allows for the measurement of a number of variables and their relationships simultaneously. The experimental approach, by contrast, is characterised by the manipulation of a single variable and is thus appropriate for dealing with problems where simple causal relationships exist. In educational and behavioural research, it is invariably the case that a number of variables contribute to a particular outcome. Experimental research thus introduces a note of unreality into research, whereas correlational approaches, while less rigorous, allow for the study of behaviour in more realistic settings. Where an element of control is required, however, partial correlation achieves this without changing the context in which the study takes place.

A second advantage of correlational research we have already noted: it yields information concerning the degree of relationship between the variables being studied. It thus provides the researcher with insights into the way variables operate that cannot be gained by other means. We may itemise the remaining strengths of the method in a few words: as a basis for prediction studies, it enables researchers to make estimates of the probable accuracy of their predictions; it is especially useful for lower-level ground work where it serves as a powerful exploratory tool; and it does not require large samples.

Among its limitations, correlational research only identifies what goes with what — it only implies concomitance and therefore does not necessarily establish cause-and-effect relationships; it is less rigorous than the experimental approach because it exercises less control over the independent variables; it is prone to identify spurious relational patterns; it adopts an atomistic approach; and the correlation index is relatively imprecise, being limited by the unreliability of the measurements of the variables.

Interpreting the Correlation Coefficient

Once a correlation coefficient has been computed, there remains the problem of interpreting it. A question often asked in this connection is how large should the coefficient be for it to be meaningful. The question may be approached in three ways: (1) by examining the strength of the relationship; (2) by examining the statistical significance of the relationship; and (3) by examining the square of the correlation coefficient.

Inspection of the numerical value of a correlation coefficient will yield clear indication of the *strength* of the relationship between the variables in question. Low or near zero values indicate weak relationships, while those nearer to +1 or −1 suggest stronger relationships. Imagine, for instance, that a measure of a teacher's success in the classroom after five years in the profession is correlated with his final school experience grade as a student and that it was found that r = 0.19. Suppose now that his score on classroom success is correlated with a measure of need for professional achievement and that this yielded a correlation of 0.65. It could be concluded that there is a stronger relationship between success and professional achievement scores than between success and final student grade.

Where a correlation coefficient has been derived from a sample and one wishes to use it as a basis for inference about the parent population, the *statistical significance* of the obtained correlation must be considered. Statistical significance when applied to a correlation coefficient indicates whether or not the correlation is different from zero at a given level of confidence. A statistically significant correlation is indicative of an actual relationship rather than one due entirely to chance. The level of statistical significance of a correlation is determined to a great extent by the number of cases upon which the correlation is based. Thus, the more cases, the smaller the correlation coefficient need be to be significant at a given level of confidence.

Exploratory relationship studies are generally interpreted with reference to their statistical significance, whereas prediction studies depend for their efficacy on the strength of the correlation coefficients. These need to be considerably higher than those found in exploratory relationship studies and for this reason rarely invoke the concept of significance.

The third approach to interpreting a coefficient is provided by examining the *square* of the coefficient of correlation, r^2. This shows the proportion of variance in one variable that can be attributed to its linear relationship with the second variable. In other words, it indicates the amount the two variables have in common. If, for example, two variables A and B have a correlation of 0.50, then $(0.50)^2$ or 0.25 of the variation shown by the B scores can be attributed to the tendency of B to vary linearly with A. Box 6.3 shows graphically the common variance between reading grade and arithmetic grade having a correlation of 0.65.

Box 6.3

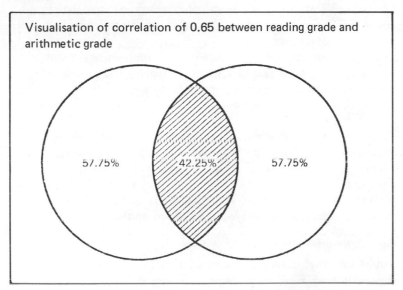

Visualisation of correlation of 0.65 between reading grade and arithmetic grade

57.75%   42.25%   57.75%

Source: Fox (2)

There are three cautions to be borne in mind when one is interpreting a correlation coefficient. First, a coefficient is a simple number and must not be interpreted as a percentage. A correlation of 0.50, for instance, does not mean 50 per cent relationship between the variables. Further, a correlation of 0.50 does *not* indicate twice as much relationship as that shown by a correlation of 0.25. A correlation of 0.50 actually indicates more than twice the relationship shown by a correlation of 0.25. In fact, as coefficients approach +1 or −1, a difference in the absolute values of the coefficients becomes more important than the same numerical difference between lower correlations would be.

Second, a correlation does not necessarily imply a cause-and-effect relationship between two factors, as we have previously indicated. It should not therefore be interpreted as meaning that one factor is causing the scores on the other to be as they are. There are invariably other factors influencing both variables under consideration. Suspected cause-and-effect relationships would have to be confirmed by subsequent experimental study.

Third, a correlation coefficient is not to be interpreted in any absolute sense. A correlational value for a given sample of a population may not necessarily be the same as that found in another sample from the same population. Many factors influence the value of a given correlation coefficient and if a researcher wishes to extrapolate to the population from which he drew his sample, he will then have to test the significance of the correlation.

We now offer some general guidelines for interpreting correlation coefficients. They are based on Borg's (5) analysis and assume that the correlations relate to a hundred or more subjects.

Correlations Ranging from 0.20 to 0.35

Correlations within this range show only very slight relationship between variables although they may be statistically significant. A correlation of 0.20 shows that only 4 per cent of the variance is common to the two measures. Whereas correlations at this level may have limited meaning in exploratory relationship research, they are of no value in either individual or group prediction studies.

Correlations Ranging from 0.35 to 0.65

Within this range, correlations are statistically significant beyond the 1 per cent level. When correlations are around 0.40, crude group prediction may be possible. As Borg notes, correlations within this range are useful, however, when combined with other correlations in a multiple regression equation. Combining several correlations in this range can in some cases yield individual predictions that are correct within an acceptable margin of error. Correlations at this level used singly are of little use for individual prediction because they yield only a few more correct predictions than could be accomplished by guessing or by using some chance selection procedure.

Correlations Ranging from 0.65 to 0.85

Correlations within this range make possible group predictions that are accurate enough for most purposes. Nearer the top of the range, group predictions can be made very accurately, usually predicting the proportion of successful candidates in selection problems within a very small margin of error. Near the top of this correlation range individual predictions can be made that are considerably more accurate than would occur if no such selection procedures were used.

Correlations Over 0.85

Correlations as high as this indicate a close relationship between the two variables correlated. A correlation of 0.85 indicates that the measure used for prediction has about 72 per cent variance in common with the performance being predicted. Prediction studies in education very rarely yield correlations this high. When correlations at this level are obtained, however, they are very useful for either individual or group prediction.

An Illustration of the Use of Correlation From the Research Literature

Correlational research has been one of the more popular kinds of research in both social and educational fields. That correlational studies in these areas are relatively easy to design and coefficients comparatively easy to compute have contributed to the popularity of the approach. To conclude this chapter, we illustrate the use of correlational coefficients in an exploratory relationship study drawn from the field of social research.

Suppose a researcher were interested in the alleged connection between watching violence on television and subsequent aggressive behaviour. After a little thought on the matter, he would probably come to the conclusion that there are four competing hypotheses accounting for the phenomenon: (1) that aggression is the independent variable and television violence the dependent variable; (2) that television violence is the independent variable and aggression the dependent variable; (3) that both aggression and television violence are independent variables; or (4) that both aggression and television violence are dependent variables and that some other, as yet unspecified, variable is their common cause.

A study by Eron, Huesman, Lefkowitz and Walder (6) has attempted to unravel just such a situation. Concerned about the increasing prominence of violence in society, the researchers followed up earlier studies in this area in which a definite relationship between overt aggression and television habits had been demonstrated by attempting to establish a causal link between the two. Their hypothesis posited, therefore, that a young adult's aggressiveness is positively related to his preference for violent television when he was eight or nine years of age and that his preference for violent television during this critical period is one cause for his aggressiveness.

The approach adopted by the researchers was to examine the correlations across the two variables over a period of time within the framework of a longitudinal design. The cross-lagged analysis which was used in this instance examined the temporal cross correlations of the variables, thus enabling the investigators to eliminate some of the rival hypotheses. Briefly, longitudinal data were collected on 427 teenagers of an original group of 875 children who had taken part in a study of third-grade children (8-9 years old) ten years earlier in 1960. Data on the 427 teenagers were therefore collected in 1970. Of this number, 211 were boys and it is the part of the study involving these that we are particularly interested in. Two measures were taken on both occasions — measures of the boys' aggressive behaviour and measures of their preference for watching violence on television programmes. In addition, other variables which may have contributed to either interest in television violence or aggressiveness were controlled by means of partial correlations.

The correlations between a preference for violent television and aggression for the 211 boys over the ten-year period are illustrated in Box 6.4. In examining the 'outer' correlations, we notice a small but positive relationship between the preference for violent television and aggression among the third graders (0.21), but only a tiny, negative relationship between the same variables when the boys were in the thirteenth grade (19 years old) (−0.05). Further, there is little relationship between the boys' viewing habits in childhood and their television preferences as adolescents (0.05), but a higher correlation between aggression in the third grade and aggression in the thirteenth grade, which seems to suggest that the pattern of aggression persists once learnt.

If we now inspect the cross-lagged correlations, we see a negligible correlation of 0.01 between aggression in the third grade and a preference for violent television in the thirteenth grade and this would seem to rule out the possibility that aggression was a determinant of the boys' subsequent television habits. If we now examine the correlation between preference for television violence in the third grade and aggression in the thirteenth grade, we see a highly significant relationship. This effect was not apparent for the girls in the group. As the researchers themselves explain:

Box 6.4 The correlations between a preference for violent television and peer-rated aggression for 211 boys over a 10-year lag

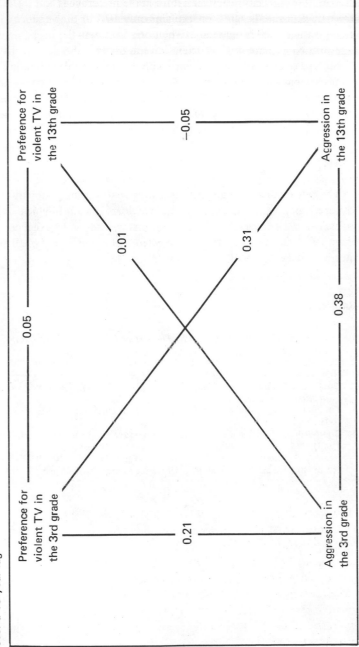

Preference for violent TV in the 13th grade

Preference for violent TV in the 3rd grade

Aggression in the 13th grade

Aggression in the 3rd grade

−0.05

0.01

0.31

0.05

0.38

0.21

Source: Eron *et al.* (6)

While the correlation between third-grade preferences and thirteenth-grade peer-rated aggression explains only 10% of the variance in aggression, 10% is impressive when one considers the probable limitations on the size of the correlation imposed by the skewed distributions of the variables, the large number of variables affecting aggression, the comparatively small explanatory power of these other variables, and the 10-year lag between measurement times. The extremely low likelihood of achieving such a correlation by chance is a good indicator of the strength of the relation between preference for violent television at age 8 years and peer-rated aggression at age 19.

The researchers conclude by suggesting that watching violent television programmes in the early formative years has a probable causative influence on later aggression. This interesting study is an excellent example of the use of correlation in relational research and of the sophisticated ends to which it can be put.

References

1. Mouly, G.J., *Educational Research: The Art and Science of Investigation* (Allyn and Bacon, Boston, 1978).
2. Fox, D.J., *The Research Process in Education* (Holt, Rinehart and Winston, New York, 1969).
3. Guilford, J.P. and Fruchter, B. *Fundamental Statistics in Psychology and Education* (McGraw Hill, New York, 1973).
4. Tuckman, B.W., *Conducting Educational Research* (Harcourt Brace Jovanovich, New York, 1972).
5. Borg, W.R., *Educational Research: An Introduction* (Longmans, London, 1963).
6. Eron, L.D., Huesman, L.R., Lefkowitz, M.M. and Walder, L.O., 'Does television violence cause aggression?', *American Psychologist* (April 1972) 253-63.

7 *EX POST FACTO* RESEARCH

Introduction

When translated literally, *ex post facto* means 'from what is done afterwards'. In the context of social and educational research the phrase means 'after the fact' or 'retrospectively' and refers to those studies which investigate possible cause-and-effect relationships by observing an existing condition or state of affairs and searching back in time for plausible causal factors. In effect, the researcher asks himself what factors seem to be associated with certain occurrences, or conditions, or aspects of behaviour. *Ex post facto* research, then, is a method of teasing out possible antecedents of events that have happened and cannot, because of this fact, be engineered or manipulated by the investigator. The following example will illustrate the basic idea. Imagine a situation in which there has been a dramatic increase in the number of fatal road accidents in a particular locality. An expert is called in to investigate. Naturally, there is no way in which he can study the actual accidents because they have happened; nor can he turn to technology for a video replay of the incidents. What he can do, however, is attempt to reconstruct what happened by studying the statistics, examining the accident spots, and taking note of the statements given by victims and witnesses. In this way the expert will be in a position to identify possible determinants of the accidents. These may include excessive speed, poor road conditions, careless driving, frustration, inefficient vehicles, the effects of drugs or alcohol and so on. On the basis of his examination, he can formulate hypotheses as to the likely causes and submit them to the appropriate authority in the form of recommendations. These may include improving road conditions, or lowering the speed limit, or increasing police surveillance, for instance. The point of interest to us is that in identifying the causes *retrospectively*, the expert adopts an *ex post facto* perspective.

Kerlinger (1) has defined *ex post facto* research more formally as that in which the independent variable or variables have already occurred and in which the researcher starts with the observation of a dependent variable or variables. He then studies the independent variable or variables in retrospect for their possible relationship to, and effects on, the dependent variable or variables. The researcher is thus examining retrospectively the effects of a naturally occurring event on a subsequent outcome with a view to establishing a causal link between

143

them. Interestingly, some instances of *ex post facto* designs correspond to experimental research in reverse, for instead of taking groups that are equivalent and subjecting them to different treatments so as to bring about differences in the dependent variables to be measured, an *ex post facto* experiment begins with groups that are already different in some respect and searches in retrospect for the factor that brought about the difference.

Two kinds of design may be identified in *ex post facto* research — the *co-relational study* and the *criterion group study*. The former is sometimes termed *causal research* and the latter, *causal-comparative research*. A co-relational (or causal) study is concerned with identifying the antecedents of a present condition. As its name suggests, it involves the collection of two sets of data, one of which will be retrospective, with a view to determining the relationship between them. The basic design of such an experiment may be represented thus:*

A study by Borkowsky (3) was based upon this kind of design. He attempted to show a relationship between the quality of a music teacher's undergraduate training (X) and his subsequent effectiveness as a teacher of his subject (O). Measures of the quality of a music teacher's college training can include grades in specific courses, overall grade average and self-ratings, etc. Teacher effectiveness can be assessed by indices of pupil performance, pupil knowledge, pupil attitudes and judgement of experts, etc. Correlations between all measures were obtained to determine the relationship. At most, this study could show that a relationship existed, after the fact, between the quality of teacher preparation and subsequent teacher effectiveness. Where a strong relationship is found between the independent and dependent variables, three possible interpretations are open to the researcher:

1. that the variable X has caused O;
2. that the variable O has caused X; or
3. that some third unidentified, and therefore unmeasured, variable has caused X and O.

It is often the case that a researcher cannot tell which of these is correct.

---

* In Chapters 7 and 8, we adopt the symbols and conventions used by Campbell and Stanley (2). These are presented fully on p. 159.

The value of co-relational or causal studies lies chiefly in their exploratory or suggestive character for, as we have seen, while they are not always adequate in themselves for establishing causal relationships among variables, they are a useful first step in this direction in that they do yield measures of association.

In the criterion-group (or causal-comparative) approach, the investigator sets out to discover possible causes for a phenomenon being studied by comparing the subjects in which the variable is present with similar subjects in whom it is absent. The basic design in this kind of study may be represented thus:

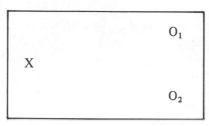

If, for example, a researcher chose such a design to investigate factors contributing to teacher effectiveness, the criterion group O_1, the effective teachers, and its counterpart O_2, a group *not* showing the characteristics of the criterion group, are identified by measuring the differential effects of the groups on classes of children. The researcher may then examine X, some variable or event, i.e. the background,

Box 7.1

Factors associated with failure at university

Out of 802 students who began their studies at the University of Bradford in 1966, 102 dropped out at the end of their first year. On entry to the university the whole freshman intake had provided academic and personal information about their backgrounds, their interests, their motivations and values.

In an *ex post facto* research design, comparisons were made between dropouts and non-dropouts in an attempt to discover factors associated with university failure.

In line with previous studies, university failure was found to relate (1) to inferior educational qualifications on entry; (2) to less certainty about choice of career; (3) to a greater degree of worry over abilities to pursue a university course of study; and (4) to feelings of being overwhelmed by the academic work demanded.

Source: Adapted from Cohen and Child (4).

training, skills and personality of the groups to discover what might 'cause' only some teachers to be effective.

Criterion-group or causal comparative studies may be seen as bridging the gap between descriptive research methods on the one hand and true experimental research on the other. In Box 7.1 we give a brief summary of an example of the use of the causal comparative design in an investigation into university failure.

Characteristics of Ex Post Facto Research

The most distinctive feature of both causal and causal-comparative research we have already established. That they are *ex post facto* indicates that data are collected after the presumed cause or causes have occurred. The researcher takes the effect (or dependent variable) and examines the data retrospectively to establish causes, relationships or associations, and their meanings.

Other characteristics of *ex post facto* research become apparent when it is contrasted with true experimental research. Kerlinger describes the *modus operandi* of the experimental researcher. ('If x, then y' in Kerlinger's usage. We have substituted X for x and O for y to fit in with Campbell and Stanley's conventions throughout the chapter.) He hypothesises: if X, then O; if frustration, then aggression. Depending on circumstances and his own predilections in research design, he uses some method to manipulate X. He then observes O to see if concomitant variation, the variation expected or predicted from the variation in X, occurs. If it does, this is evidence for the validity of the proposition, X − O, meaning 'If X, then O'. Note that the scientist here predicts from a controlled X to O. To help him achieve control, he can use the principle of randomisation and active manipulation of X and can assume, other things being equal, that O is varying as a result of the manipulation of X.

In *ex post facto* designs, on the other hand, O is observed. Then a retrospective search for X ensues. An X is found that is plausible and agrees with the hypothesis. Due to lack of control of X and other possible Xs, the truth of the hypothesised relation between X and O cannot be asserted with the confidence of the experimental researcher. Basically, then, *ex post facto* investigations have, so to speak, a built-in weakness: lack of control of the independent variable or variables.

This brief comparison highlights the most important difference between the two designs − control. In the experimental situation, the investigator at least has manipulative control: he has as a minimum one active variable. If an experiment is a 'true' experiment, he can also exercise control by randomisation. He can assign subjects to groups randomly; or, at the very least, he can assign treatments to groups at random. In the *ex post facto* research situation, this control of the independent variable is not possible, and what is perhaps more important, neither is randomisation. The investigator must take things as they are and try to disentangle them, though having said this, we must point out that he can make use of selected procedures that will give him an element of control in this research. These we shall touch upon shortly.

By their very nature, *ex post facto* experiments can provide support for any number of different, perhaps even contradictory, hypotheses; they are so completely flexible that it is largely a matter of postulating hypotheses according to one's personal preference. The investigator begins with certain data and looks for an interpretation consistent with them; often, however, a number of interpretations may be at hand. Consider again the hypothetical increase in road accidents in a given town. A retrospective search for causes will disclose half a dozen plausible ones. Experimental studies, by contrast, begin with a specific interpretation and then determine whether it is congruent with externally derived data. Frequently, causal relationships seem to be established on nothing more substantial than the premiss that any related event occurring prior to the phenomenon under study is assumed to be its cause — the classical *post hoc ergo propter hoc* fallacy. Overlooked is the fact that even when we do find a relationship between two variables, we must recognise the possibility that both are individual results of a common third factor rather than the first being necessarily the cause of the second. And as we have seen earlier, there is also the real possibility of reverse causation, e.g. that a heart condition promotes obesity rather than the other way around, or that they encourage each other. The point is that the evidence simply illustrates the hypothesis; it does not test it, since hypotheses cannot be tested on the same data from which they were derived. The relationship noted may actually exist, but it is not necessarily the only relationship, or perhaps the crucial one. Before we can accept that smoking is the primary cause of lung cancer, we have to rule out alternative hypotheses.

We must not conclude from what has just been said that *ex post facto* studies are of little value; many of our important investigations in education and psychology are *ex post facto* designs. There is often no choice in the matter: an investigator cannot cause one group to become failures, delinquent, suicidal, brain-damaged or dropouts. He must of necessity rely on existing groups. On the other hand, the inability of *ex post facto* designs to incorporate the basic need for control (e.g. through manipulation or randomisation) makes them vulnerable from a scientific point of view and the possibility of their being misleading should be clearly acknowledged. *Ex post facto* designs are probably better conceived more circumspectly, not as experiments with the greater certainty that these denote, but more as surveys, useful as sources of hypotheses to be tested by more conventional experimental means at a later date.

Occasions When Appropriate

It would follow from what we have said in the preceding section that *ex post facto* designs are appropriate in circumstances where the more powerful experimental method is not possible. These would arise when, for example, it is not always possible to select, control and manipulate the factors necessary to study cause-and-effect relationships directly; or when the control of all variables except a single independent variable may be unrealistic and artificial, preventing the normal interaction with other influential variables; or when laboratory controls for many research purposes would be impractical, costly or ethically undesirable.

Ex post facto research is particularly suitable in social, educational and — to a lesser extent — psychological contexts where the independent variable or variables lie outside the researcher's control. Examples of the method abound in these areas: the research on cigarette-smoking and lung cancer, for instance; or studies of teacher characteristics; or studies examining the relationship between political and religious affiliation and attitudes; or investigations into the relationship between school achievement and independent variables such as social class, race, sex and intelligence. Many of these may be divided into large- or small-scale *ex post facto* studies.

In the former category, for example, Kerlinger refers to a study by Caldwell and Courtis (5), *Then and Now in Education*, which attempted to compared the results of twentieth-century education with nineteenth-century education. It is a classic example of *ex post facto* research. The investigators compared the achievements of Boston High School children in history, geography, arithmetic, grammar and so on in 1845 with those of high school children all over the United States in 1919. Actually, the 'selected best' of the 1845 pupils were compared with the unselected lower 40 per cent of the 1919 pupils. The same tests that were given to the 1845 pupils were administered to the 1919 pupils.

It was found, among other things, that the 1919 pupils tended to make lower scores on memory and abstract skill questions and higher scores on thought questions. The results were consistent throughout the United States. The authors concluded that the pupils today were much like those of 1845: they tended to achieve the same successes and make the same errors.

The lack of control in this study is of course obvious; and though the findings are of little scientific value, the study within its limits is an interesting one.

Kerlinger also refers to a good example of small-scale *ex post facto* research in the field of education. It is a cross-cultural study of school children's anxiety by Sarnoff and his colleagues (6). The researchers here used the English eleven-plus examination system in which the outcomes of a group of tests determined the direction of a child's educational future. The investigators reasoned that, since the eleven-plus examination was so crucial to British children, it would probably produce *test anxiety*. They further reasoned that American children would probably not have as high test anxiety because of the difference in their educational system. The basic hypothesis, therefore, was that a difference would be found between English and American children in the degree of test anxiety and that there would be no difference between the groups in *general anxiety* if comparable English and American groups were studied.

The study skilfully used an existing independent variable, test examinations, to test a hypothesis on *presumed* existing differences between national groups. Because the researchers seemingly predicted from X to O, and because they matched their samples so carefully, some students of research might say that this is not an *ex post facto* study at all. In fact, however, it is a characteristic example because it was *not* experimental; experimental manipulation and randomisation were lacking, so that the basic approach was the same as that of the cigarette-smoking and lung cancer study. What is particularly noteworthy is that the investigators tested a 'control hypothesis' — that there would be a difference between the two groups on *test anxiety* but not on *general anxiety*.

Advantages and Disadvantages

We have already touched incidentally on some of the strengths and weaknesses of *ex post facto* research. We will now look at them more systematically. Among the advantages of the approach we may identify the following: (1) *ex post facto* research meets an important need of the researcher where the more rigorous experimental approach is not possible. In the case of the alleged relationship between smoking and lung cancer, for instance, this cannot be tested experimentally (at least as far as human beings are concerned); (2) the method yields useful information concerning the nature of phenomena — what goes with what, and under what conditions. In this way, *ex post facto* research is a valuable exploratory tool; (3) improvements in statistical techniques and general methodology have made *ex post facto* designs more defensible; (4) in some ways and in certain situations the method is more useful than the experimental method, especially where the setting up of the latter would introduce a note of artificiality into research proceedings; (5) *ex post facto* research is particularly appropriate when simple cause-and-effect relationships are being explored; and (6) the method can give a sense of direction and provide a fruitful source of hypotheses that can be tested by the more rigorous experimental method subsequently.

Among the limitations and weaknesses of *ex post facto* designs the following may be mentioned: (1) there is the problem of lack of control in that the researcher is unable to manipulate the independent variable or to randomise his subjects; (2) one cannot know for certain whether the causative factor has been included or even identified; (3) it may be that no one single factor is the cause; (4) a particular outcome may result from different causes on different occasions; (5) when a relationship has been discovered, there is the problem of deciding which is the cause and which the effect: the possibility of reverse causation has to be considered; (6) that two factors are related does not establish cause and effect; (7) classifying into dichotomous groups can be problematic; (8) there is the difficulty of interpretation and the danger of the *post hoc* assumption being made, that is, believing that because X precedes O, X causes O; (9) it often bases its conclusions on too limited a sample or number of occurrences; (10) it frequently fails to single out the really significant factor or factors, and fails to recognise that events have multiple rather than single causes; (11) as a method it is regarded by some as too flexible; and (12) it lacks nullifiability and confirmation.

Designing an Ex Post Facto Investigation

We earlier referred to the two basic designs embraced by *ex post facto* research — the co-relational (or causal) model and the criterion group (or causal-comparative) model. We return to them again here in order to consider designing both types of investigation. As we saw, the causal model attempts to identify the antecedent of a present condition and may be represented thus:

	Independent variable	Dependent variable
	X	O

Although one variable in an *ex post facto* study cannot be confidently said to depend upon the other as would be the case in a truly experimental investigation, it is nevertheless usual to designate one of the variables as independent (X) and the other as dependent (O). The left to right dimension indicates the temporal order, though having established this, we must not overlook the possibility of reverse causality.

In a typical investigation of this kind, then, two sets of data relating to the independent and dependent variables respectively will be gathered. As indicated earlier in the chapter, the data on the independent variable (X) will be retrospective in character and as such will be prone to the kinds of weakness, limitations and distortions to which all historical evidence is subject. Let us now translate the design into a hypothetical situation. Imagine a secondary school in which it is hypothesised that low staff morale (O) has come about as a direct result of comprehensive reorganisation some two years earlier, say. A number of key factors distinguishing the new organisation from the previous one can be readily identified. Collectively these could represent or contain the independent variable X and data on them could be accumulated retrospectively. They could include, for example, the introduction of mixed ability and team teaching, curricular innovation, loss of teacher status, decline in pupil motivation, modifications to the school catchment area, or the appointment of a new headmaster. These could then be checked against a measure of prevailing teachers' attitudes (O), thus providing the researcher with some leads at least as to possible causes of current discontent.

The second model, the causal-comparative, may be represented schematically as shown:

Group	Independent variable	Dependent variable
E	X	O_1
C		O_2

Using this model, the investigator hypothesises the independent variable and then compares two groups, an experimental group (E) which has been exposed to the presumed independent variable X and a control group (C) which has not. (The dashed line in the model shows that the comparison groups E and C are not equated by random assignment. See p. 161).

See p. 161

Alternatively, he may examine two groups that are different in some way or ways and then try to account for the difference or differences by investigating possible antecedents. These two examples reflect two types of approach to causal-comparative research: the 'cause-to-effect' kind and the 'effect-to-cause' kind (7).

The basic design of causal-comparative investigations is similar to an experimentally designed study. The chief difference resides in the nature of the independent variable, X. In a truly experimental situation, this will be under the control of the investigator and may therefore be described as manipulable. In the causal-comparative model (and also the causal model), however, the independent variable is beyond his control, having already occurred. It may therefore be described in this design as non-manipulable.

Two brief examples will underscore these two types of research design: the 'cause-to-effect' kind and the 'effect-to-cause' kind. A researcher may study the influence of school reorganisation on low staff morale and then compare staff attitudes with those of teachers in a comparable school, though not having undergone reorganisation. Or a researcher may investigate the problems of the college dropout by comparing personality characteristics of the dropouts with those of students who stay the course. He may thereby be able to identify the antecedents of failure to stay the course on the part of the dropouts.

Procedures in Ex Post Facto Research

Ex post facto research is concerned with discovering relationships among variables in one's data; and we have seen how this may be accomplished by using either a causal or causal-comparative model. We now examine the steps involved in implementing a piece of *ex post facto* research. We may begin by identifying the problem area to be investigated. This stage will be followed by a clear and precise statement of the hypothesis to be tested or questions to be answered. The next step will be to make explicit the assumptions on which the hypothesis and subsequent procedures will be based. A review of the research literature will follow. This will enable the investigator to ascertain the kinds of issues, problems, obstacles and findings disclosed by previous studies in the area. There will then follow the planning of the actual investigation and will consist of three broad stages —

identification of the population and samples; the selection and construction of techniques for collecting data; and the establishment of categories for classifying the data. The final stage will involve the description, analysis and interpretation of the findings.

It was noted earlier that the principal weakness of *ex post facto* research is the absence of control over the independent variable influencing the dependent variable in the case of causal designs or affecting observed differences between dependent variables in the case of causal-comparative designs. (We take up the question of *control* in experimental research in greater detail in the next chapter.) Although the *ex post facto* researcher is denied not only this kind of control but also the principle of randomisation, he can nevertheless utilise procedures that will give him some measure of control in his investigation. And it is to some of these that we now turn.

One of the commonest means of introducing control into this type of research is that of matching the subjects in the experimental and control groups where the design is causal-comparative. One group of writers (8) explain it thus:

> The matching is usually done on a subject-to-subject basis to form matched pairs. For example, if one were interested in the relationship between scouting experiences and delinquency, he could locate two groups of boys classified as delinquent and non-delinquent according to specified criteria. It would be wise in such a study to select pairs from these groups matched on the basis of socioeconomic status, family structure, and other variables known to be related to both scouting experience and delinquency. Analysis of the data from the matched samples could be made to determine whether or not scouting characterized the non-delinquent and was absent in the background of the delinquent.

There are difficulties with this procedure, however, for it assumes that the investigator knows what the relevant factors are, that is, the factors that may be related to the dependent variable. Further, there is the possibility of losing those subjects which cannot be matched, thus reducing one's sample.

As an alternative procedure for introducing a degree of control into *ex post facto* research, Ary and his colleagues (8) suggest building the extraneous independent variables into the design and using an analysis of variance technique. They explain:

Assume that intelligence is a relevant extraneous variable and it is not feasible to control it through matching or other means. In this case, intelligence could be added to the design as another independent variable and the subjects of the study classified in terms of intelligence levels. The dependent variable measures would then be analysed through an analysis of variance and the main and interaction effects of intelligence might be determined. Such a procedure would reveal any significant differences among the groups on the dependent variable, but no causal relationship between intelligence and the dependent variable could be assumed. Other extraneous variables could be operating to produce both the main effect and any interaction effects.

Yet another procedure which may be adopted for introducing a measure of control into *ex post facto* designs is that of selecting samples that are as homogeneous as possible on a given variable. The writers quoted above illustrate the procedure with the following example.

If intelligence were a relevant extraneous variable, its effects could be controlled by using subjects from only one intelligence level. This procedure serves the purpose of disentangling the independent variable in which the investigator may be interested from other variables with which it is commonly associated, so that any effects that are found can justifiably be associated with the independent variable.

Finally, control may be introduced into an *ex post facto* investigation by stating and testing any alternative hypotheses that might be plausible explanations for the empirical outcomes of the study (8). A researcher has thus to beware of accepting the first likely explanation of relationships in an *ex post facto* study as necessarily the only or final one. A well-known recent instance is the presumed relationship between cigarette-smoking and lung cancer. Government health officials have been quick to seize on the explanation that smoking causes lung cancer. Tobacco firms, however, have put forward an alternative hypothesis — that both smoking and lung cancer are possibly the result of a third, as yet unspecified, factor. In other words, the possibility that both the independent and dependent variables are simply two separate results of a single common cause cannot be ignored.

And, of course, in some situations there is the possibility of reverse causality. Thus, instead of claiming that A causes B, it might be that B is the cause of A. A researcher might, for instance, hypothesise that aggressive behaviour is the result of watching violent television programmes. Reverse causality, however, would posit that some people choose to watch violent television programmes because they are aggressive in the first place. Box 7.2 summarises the procedures just reviewed.

Box 7.2

> Some procedures for introducing measures of control into ex post facto research designs
>
> 1. Matching of the subjects in the experimental and control groups where the design of the study is causal-comparative.
> 2. Building extraneous independent variables into the design and using an analysis of variable technique.
> 3. Using, where possible, homogeneous samples on a given variable.
> 4. The testing of rival hypotheses offering alternative explanations.

An Example of Ex Post Facto Research

In a period marked by fundamental changes in the organisation of education, the question may be asked: what effects do such changes have on educational outcomes? Can a relationship be shown to exist between the way a school is organised in certain respects and pupil achievement? Such a question was posed by two British researchers, Christie and Oliver (9), working in the 1960s, who investigated the academic performance of 18-year-olds as related to school organisation. The study is a good example of *ex post facto* research using a causal model: the dependent variable (O) was represented by pupil achievement in A-level examinations and the independent variable (X), by school organisation. The latter related particularly to the organisation of school time and staffing.

The sample consisted of 73 boys' maintained grammar schools drawn roughly from the northern half of England. Although all were local authority schools, there was considerable fluctuation in the total number of hours available for sixth-form work, the range varying from 1,525 to 1,975 hours, a difference of the order of nine 40-minute periods a week.

Box 7.3

Relationship Between Mean A-Level Attainment and Number of Timetable Hours' Instruction in Twelve Subject Matter Areas

	Number of schools	Mean A-level grade (1)		Mean O-level grade (2)		Number of hours' instruction (3)		Correlations with mean A-level grade		
								Mean O-level grade (2)	Number of hours (3)	O-level held constant r 13.2 hours
		mean	s.d.	mean	s.d.	mean	s.d.			
Art	26	3.29	1.04	49.55	6.04	303.94	80.52	0.33	0.22	0.25
French	34	2.78	0.98	54.27	3.94	350.74	40.73	0.58**	−0.25	−0.11
German	22	2.63	1.27	56.55	6.22	343.01	40.65	0.63**	−0.34	−0.09
Latin	24	2.97	1.24	57.83	5.27	350.71	49.11	0.64**	−0.07	0.06
English	36	2.78	0.93	52.32	4.46	349.89	39.50	0.29	0.14	0.19
History	36	2.85	0.79	52.19	4.08	351.86	32.28	0.27	0.21	0.29
Geography	36	3.46	0.97	51.97	4.75	351.50	38.47	0.00	−0.16	
Economics	16	3.01	1.20	50.46	4.04	359.75	44.88	0.13	0.08	
Mathematics	38	3.00	0.79	55.43	4.04	386.11	60.78	0.41*	−0.07	−0.03
Physics	38	3.16	0.67	55.51	3.21	383.00	47.87	0.25	0.00	
Chemistry	38	3.03	0.76	55.46	3.74	382.42	43.28	0.51**	0.33	0.45**
Biology	26	2.46	0.92	54.88	4.58	365.38	55.17	0.37	−0.27	−0.30

* Significant beyond the 5 per cent level.
** Significant beyond the 1 per cent level.

Source: Christie and Oliver (9)

It was found that within this framework, time was allocated to four major purposes: (1) a quasi-statutory allocation of time to physical education, games and religious instruction; (2) time set aside to counteract the effects of specialisation (minority time); (3) the major allocation of time for A-level specialisation; and (4) time for private study. Box 7.3 indicates the relationship between mean A-level attainment and the number of timetabled hours' instruction in twelve subject matter areas.

An interesting conclusion arising from an analysis of A-level grades in relation to the number of hours of A-level teaching was that, beyond a certain point, about 300 hours of A-level teaching or about four hours a week on average, additional teaching time does not, with the exception of chemistry, lead to higher A-level grades. The researchers inferred that more time could be devoted to other purposes such as minority time courses or general studies without jeopardising achievement in A-level subjects.

References

1. Kerlinger, F.N., *Foundations of Behavioural Research* (Holt, Rinehart and Winston, New York, 1979).
2. Campbell, D.T. and Stanley, J.C., 'Experimental and quasi-experimental designs for research on teaching' in N.L. Gage (ed.), *Handbook of Research on Teaching* (Rand McNally, Chicago, 1963).
3. Borkowsky, F.T., 'The relationship of work quality in undergraduate music curricula to effectiveness in instrumental music teaching in the public schools', *J. Exp. Educ.*, 39 (1970) 14-19.
4. Cohen, L. and Child, D., 'Some sociological and psychological factors in university failure', *Durham Research Review*, 22 (1969) 365-72.
5. Caldwell, O. and Courtis, S., *Then and Now in Education* (Harcourt, New York, 1925).
6. Sarnoff, I. *et al.*, 'A cross-cultural study of anxiety among American and English school children', *J. Educ. Psychol.*, 49 (1958) 129-36.
7. Chapin, F.S., *Experimental Designs in Sociological Research* (Harper and Row, New York, 1947).
8. Ary, D., Jacobs, L.C. and Razavieh, A., *Introduction to Research in Education* (Holt, Rinehart and Winston, New York, 1972).
9. Christie, T. and Oliver, R.A.C., 'Academic performance at age 18+ as related to school organization', *Research in Education*, 2 (November 1969) 13-31.

8 EXPERIMENTS AND QUASI-EXPERIMENTS

Introduction

In Chapter 7, we described *ex post facto* research as experimentation in reverse in that *ex post facto* studies start with groups that are already different with regard to certain characteristics and then proceed to search, in retrospect, for the factors that brought about those differences. We then went on to cite Kerlinger's (1) description of the experimental researcher's approach:

> If x, then y; if frustration, then aggression . . . the researcher uses some method to measure x and then observes y to see if concomitant variation occurs.

The essential feature of experimental research is that the investigator deliberately controls and manipulates the conditions which determine the events in which he is interested. At its simplest, an experiment involves making a change in the value of one variable — called the independent variable — and observing the effect of that change on another variable — called the dependent variable. Frequently in learning experiments in classroom settings the independent variable is a stimulus of some kind, a new method in arithmetical computation for example, and the dependent variable is a response, the time taken to do 20 sums using the new method. Most empirical studies in educational settings, however, are quasi-experimental rather than experimental. The single most important difference between the quasi-experiment and the true experiment is that in the former case, the researcher undertakes his study with groups that are *intact*, that is to say, the groups have been constituted by means other than random selection. Later in the chapter we present an example of a quasi-experimental design in an ongoing education study specifically undertaken to improve upon an earlier research project employing a pre-experimental methodology.

First however, we begin by identifying the essential features of pre-experimental, true experimental and quasi-experimental designs, our intention being to introduce the reader to the meaning and purpose of *control* in educational experimentation.

Designs in Educational Experimentation

In the outline of research designs that follows we use symbols and conventions from Campbell and Stanley (2):

1. X represents the exposure of a group to an experimental variable or event, the effects of which are to be measured.
2. O refers to the process of observation or measurement.
3. Xs and Os in a given row are applied to the same persons.
4. Left to right order indicates temporal sequence.
5. Xs and Os vertical to one another are simultaneous.
6. R indicates random assignment to separate treatment groups.
7. Parallel rows unseparated by dashes represent comparison groups equated by randomisation while those separated by a dashed line represent groups not equated by random assignment.

A Pre-experimental Design: the One Group Pretest-Post-test

Very often, reports about the value of a new teaching method or the interest aroused by some curriculum innovation or other reveal that a researcher has measured a group on a dependent variable (O_1), for example, attitudes towards minority groups, and then introduced an experimental manipulation (X), perhaps a ten week curriculum project designed to increase tolerance of ethnic minorities. Following the experimental treatment, the researcher has again measured group attitudes (O_2) and proceeded to account for differences between pre-test and post-test scores by reference to the effects of X.

The one group pretest-post-test design can be represented as:

(Experimental) | O_1 | X | O_2

Suppose that just such a project has been undertaken and that the researcher finds that O_2 scores indicate greater tolerance of ethnic minorities than O_1 scores. How justified is he in attributing the cause of $O_1 - O_2$ differences to the experimental treatment (X), that is, the term's project work? At first glance the assumption of causality seems reasonable enough. The situation is not that simple, however. Compare for a moment the circumstances represented in our hypothetical educational example with those which typically obtain in experiments in the physical sciences. A physicist who applies heat to a metal bar can confidently attribute the observed expansion to the rise in temperature that he has introduced because within the confines of his laboratory he has excluded (i.e. *controlled*) all other extraneous sources of variation (this example is suggested by Pilliner (4)).

The same degree of control can never be attained in educational experimentation. At this point the reader may care to reflect upon some possible influences other than the ten-week curriculum project that might account for the $O_1 - O_2$ differences in our hypothetical educational example.

He may conclude that factors to do with the pupils, the teacher, the school, the classroom organisation, the curriculum materials and the their presentation, the way that the subjects' attitudes were measured, to say nothing of the thousand and one other events that occurred in and about the school during the course of the term's work, might all have exerted some influence upon the observed differences in attitude. These kind of extraneous variables which are outside of an experimenter's *control* in a one-group pretest-post-test design threaten to invalidate his research efforts. We later identify a number of such threats to the validity of educational experimentation.

The problems arising out of the use of pre-experimental designs are graphically illustrated in the comments of a researcher who employed a pretest-post-test design in six secondary schools in an evaluation of the use of archive materials in the teaching of history (3).

The pretests were taken by 158 children in six schools . . . not all the children who had taken the pretests either used the Unit [farming in Leicestershire] or took the posttests, which were completed by only 72 children. Without the backing of a national body like the Schools Council, one's status and purpose are suspect and offers of assistance are not readily forthcoming . . . The six schools used were the only ones to offer assistance after a request had been sent to most secondary schools in [the county]. This had two main results. In the first place, the need to work with any school classes whose teachers offered to co-operate in order to obtain a sample of adequate size meant that variables such as age, intelligence, previous learning experiences, etc. could not be controlled . . . Secondly, although all classes used the same materials, it was impossible to insist on common teaching patterns, equal provision of additional resources, similar periods of time devoted to each section of the materials or the use of control groups. Drop out during the use of the materials due to natural causes such as illness or a teacher's practice of allowing unrestricted choice of work patterns also reduced the size of the sample, resulting in different sample sizes for pre- and posttests.

A 'True' Experimental Design: the Pretest-Post-test Control Group Design

A complete exposition of experimental designs is beyond the scope of the present chapter. In the brief outline that follows, we have selected one design from the comprehensive treatment of the subject by Campbell and Stanley (2) in order to identify the essential features of what they term a 'true experimental' and what Kerlinger (1) refers to as a 'good' design. Along with its variants, the chosen design is commonly used in educational experimentation.

The pretest-post-test control group design can be represented as:

(Experimental)	RO_1	X	O_2
(Control)	RO_3		O_4

It differs from the pre-experimental design that we have just described in that it involves the use of two groups which have been constituted by *randomisation*. As Kerlinger (1) observes, *in theory*, random assignment to E and C conditions controls *all* possible independent variables. *In practice*, of course, it is only when enough subjects are included in the experiment that the principle of randomisation has a chance to operate as a powerful control. However, the effects of randomisation even with a small number of subjects is well illustrated in Box 8.1.

Randomisation, then, ensures the greater likelihood of equivalence, that is, the apportioning* out between the experimental and control groups of any other factors or characteristics of the subjects which might conceivably affect the experimental variables in which the researcher is interested. It is, as Kerlinger notes, the addition of the *control group* in our present example and the random assignment of subjects to E and C groups that radically alters the situation from that which obtains in the pre-experimental design outlined earlier. For if the groups are made equivalent, then any so-called 'clouding' effects should be present in both groups.

---

* *Randomisation* is one way of apportioning out or controlling for extraneous variables. Alternatively, the experimenter may use *matched cases*, that is, subjects are matched in pairs in terms of some other variable thought likely to affect scores on the dependent variable and pairs are then allocated randomly to E and C conditions in such a way that the means and variances of the two groups are as nearly equal as possible. Finally, *analysis of covariance* is a powerful statistical procedure which uses pretest mean scores as covariates to control for initial differences between E and C groups on a number of independent variables.

Box 8.1

The effects of randomisation

Select twenty cards from a pack, ten red and ten black. Shuffle and deal into two ten-card piles. Now count the number of red cards and black cards in either pile and record the results. Repeat the whole sequence many times, recording the results each time.

You will soon convince yourself that the most likely distribution of reds and blacks in a pile is five in each; the next most likely, six red (or black) and four black (or red); and so on. You will be lucky (or unlucky for the purpose of the demonstration!) to achieve one pile of red and the other entirely of black cards. The probability of this happening is 1 in 92,378! On the other hand, the probability of obtaining a 'mix' not more than 6 of one colour and 4 of the other is about 82 in 100.

If you now imagine the red cards to stand for the 'better' ten children and the black cards for the 'poorer' ten children in a class of twenty, you will conclude that the operation of the laws of chance alone will almost probably give you close equivalent 'mixes' of 'better' and 'poorer' children in the experimental and control groups.

Source: Adapted from Pilliner (4).

If the mental ages of the children of the experimental group increase, so should the mental ages of the children of the control group . . . If something happens to affect the experimental subjects between the pretest and the posttest, this something should also affect the subjects of the control groups (1).

So strong is this simple and elegant true experimental design, that all the threats to internal validity identified below are, according to Campbell and Stanley (2), controlled in the pretest-post-test control group design.

One problem that has been identified with this particular experimental design is the *interaction effect of testing*. Good (5) explains the interaction effect weakness in the pretest-post-test control group design as follows:

Whereas the various threats to the validity of the experiment that we have listed below can be thought of as *main effects*, manifesting themselves in mean differences independently of the presence of other variables, interaction effects, as their name implies, are *joint effects* and may occur even when no main effects are present. For example, an interaction effect may occur as a result of the pretest measure sensitising the subjects to the experimental variable. Interaction effects can be controlled for by adding to the pretest-post-test control group design two more groups that do not experience the pretest measures. The result is a *four-group design* as suggested by Solomon (6). Later in the chapter, we describe an educational study which built into a pretest-post-test group design a further control group to take account of the possibility of pretest sensitisation.

A Quasi-experimental Design: the Non-equivalent Control Group Design

Often in educational research, it is simply not possible for investigators to undertake true experiments. At best, they may be able to employ something approaching a true experimental design in which they have control over what Campbell and Stanley (2) refer to as '*the who and to whom of measurement*' but lack control over '*the when and to whom of exposure*', or the randomisation of exposures — essential if true experimentation is to take place. These situations are quasi-experimental and the methodologies employed by researchers are termed quasi-experimental designs. (Kerlinger refers to quasi-experimental situations as '*compromise designs*', an apt description when applied to much educational research where the random selection or random assignment of schools and classrooms is quite impracticable.)

One of the most commonly used quasi-experimental designs in educational research can be represented as:

(Experimental)	O_1	X	O_2
(Control)	O_3		O_4

The dashed line separating the parallel rows in the diagram of the non-equivalent control group design indicates that the experimental and control groups have not been equated by randomisation — hence the term 'non-equivalent'. The addition of a control group makes the present design a decided improvement over the one group pretest-post-test design, for to the degree that the experimenter can make E and C groups as equivalent as possible, he can avoid the equivocality of interpretations that plague the pre-experimental design discussed earlier. The equivalence of groups can be strengthened by matching, followed by random assignment to E and C treatments. Later in the chapter, we illustrate the use of matching on such key variables as socio-economic background of pupils, school size, organisation and teaching methods in an ongoing study of reading in middle schools. Where matching is not possible, the researcher is advised (1) to use samples from the same population or samples that are as alike as possible. Where intact groups differ substantially, however, matching is unsatisfactory due to regression effects which lead to different group means on post-test measures. Campbell and Stanley (2) put it this way:

> If [in the non-equivalent control group design] the means of the groups are substantially different, then the process of matching not only fails to provide the intended equation but in addition insures the occurrence of unwanted regression effects. It becomes predictably certain that the two groups will differ on their posttest scores altogether independently of any effects of X, and that this difference will vary directly with the difference between the total populations from which the selection was made and inversely with the test-retest correlation.

The Validity of Experiments

As we have seen, the fundamental purpose of experimental design is to impose control over conditions that would otherwise cloud the true effects of the independent variables upon the dependent variables.

Clouding conditions that threaten to jeopardise the validity of experiments have been identified by Campbell and Stanley (2) and by Bracht and Glass (7), conditions incidentally that are of greater consequence to the validity of quasi-experiments (more typical in educational research) than to true experiments in which random assignment to treatments occurs and where both treatment and measurement can be more adequately controlled by the researcher. The following summaries adapted from Campbell and Stanley (2) and Bracht and Glass (7) distinguish between *internal validity* and *external validity*.

Internal validity is concerned with the question, do the experimental treatments, in fact, make a difference in the specific experiments under scrutiny?

External validity, on the other hand, asks the question, given these demonstrable effects, to what populations or settings can they be generalised?

Threats to Internal Validity

1. History

Frequently in educational research, events other than the experimental treatments occur during the time between pretest and post-test observations. Such events produce effects that can mistakenly be attributed to differences in treatment.

2. Maturation

Between any two observations subjects change in a variety of ways. Such changes can produce differences that are independent of the experimental treatments. The problem of maturation is more acute in protracted educational studies than in brief laboratory experiments.

3. Statistical Regression

Like maturation effects, regression effects increase systematically with the time interval between pre- and post-tests. Statistical regression occurs in educational (and other) research due to the unreliability of measuring instruments and to extraneous factors unique to each experimental group. Regression means, simply, that subjects scoring highest on a pretest are likely to score relatively lower on a post-test; conversely, those scoring lowest on a pretest are likely to score relatively higher on a post-test. In a word, in pretest-post-test situations, there is regression to the mean. Regression effects can lead the educational researcher mistakenly to attribute post-test gains and losses to low scoring and high scoring respectively.

4. Testing

Pretests at the beginning of experiments can produce effects other than those due to the experimental treatments. Such effects can include sensitising subjects to the true purposes of the experiment and practice effects which produce higher scores on post-test measures.

5. Instrumentation

Unreliable tests or instruments can introduce serious errors into experiments. With human observers or judges, error can result from changes in their skills and levels of concentration over the course of the experiment.

6. Selection

Bias may be introduced as a result of differences in the selection of subjects for the comparison groups or when intact classes are employed as experimental or control groups. Selection bias, moreover, may interact with other factors (history, maturation, etc.) to cloud even further the effects of the comparative treatments.

7. Experimental Mortality

The loss of subjects through dropout often occurs in long-running experiments and may result in confounding the effects of the experimental variables, for whereas initially the groups may have been randomly selected, the residue that stays the course is likely to be different from the unbiased sample that began it.

Threats to External Validity

Threats to external validity are likely to limit the degree to which generalisations can be made from the particular experimental conditions to other populations or settings. Below, we summarise a number of factors (adapted from Campbell and Stanley (2) and Bracht and Glass (7)) that jeopardise external validity.

1. Failure to Describe Independent Variables Explicitly

Unless independent variables are adequately described by the researcher, future replications of the experimental conditions are virtually impossible.

2. Lack of Representativeness of Available and Target Populations

Whilst those participating in the experiment may be representative of an available population, they may not be representative of the population to which the experimenter seeks to generalise his findings.

3. Hawthorne Effect

Medical research has long recognised the psychological effects that arise out of mere participation in drug experiments, and placebos and double-blind designs are commonly employed to counteract the biasing effects of participation. Similarly, so-called Hawthorne effects threaten to contaminate experimental treatments in educational research when subjects realise their role as guinea pigs.

4. Inadequate Operationalising of Dependent Variables

Dependent variables that the experimenter operationalises must have validity in the non-experimental setting to which he wishes to generalise his findings. A paper and pencil questionnaire on career choice, for example, may have little validity in respect of the actual employment decisions made by undergraduates on leaving university.

5. Sensitisation to Experimental Conditions

As with threats to internal validity, pretests may cause changes in the subjects' sensitivity to the experimental variables and thus cloud the true effects of the experimental treatment.

6. Interaction Effects of Extraneous Factors and Experimental Treatments

All of the above threats to external validity represent interactions of various clouding factors with treatments. As well as these, interaction effects may also arise as a result of any or all of those factors identified under the section on Threats to Internal Validity above.

By way of summary, we have seen that an experiment can be said to be *internally* valid to the extent that *within its own confines*, its results are credible (4); but for those results to be useful, they must be generalisable beyond the confines of the particular experiment; in a word, they must be *externally* valid also. Pilliner (4) points to a lopsided relationship between internal and external validity. Without internal validity an experiment cannot possibly be externally valid. But the converse does not necessarily follow: an internally valid experiment may or may not have external validity. Thus, the most carefully designed experiment involving a sample of Welsh-speaking children is not necessarily generalisable to a target population which includes non-Welsh-speaking subjects.

It follows, then, that the way to good experimentation in schools and classrooms lies in maximising both internal and external validity.

Procedures in Conducting Experimental Research

In Chapter 7, we identified a sequence of steps in carrying out an *ex post facto* study. An experimental investigation must also follow a set of logical procedures. Those that we now enumerate, however, should be treated with some circumspection. It is extraordinarily difficult (and indeed, foolhardy) to lay down clear-cut rules as guides to experimental research. At best, we can identify an ideal route to be followed, knowing full well that educational research rarely proceeds in such a systematic fashion. (For a detailed discussion of the practical problems in educational experimentation, see Evans (8), Chapter 4, 'Planning experimental work'.)

First, the researcher must identify and define the research problem as precisely as possible, always supposing that the problem is amenable to experimental methods.

Second, he must formulate hypotheses that he wishes to test. This involves making predictions about relationships between specific variables and at the same time, making decisions about other variables that are to be excluded from the experiment by means of controls. Formulating hypotheses leads directly to a consideration of experimental design.

Third, in planning the design of the experiment the researcher must take account of the population to which he wishes to generalise his results. This involves him in decisions over sample sizes and sampling methods. Sampling decisions are also bound up with questions of finance, manpower and the amount of time available for experimentation.

Fourth, with problems of validity in mind, the researcher must select instruments, choose tests and decide upon appropriate methods of analysis.

Fifth, before embarking upon the actual experiment the researcher must pilot test the experimental procedures to identify possible snags in connection with any aspect of the investigation.

Sixth, during the experiment itself, the researcher must endeavour to follow tested and agreed-on procedures to the letter. The standardisation of instructions, the exact timing of experimental sequences, the meticulous recording and checking of observations — these are the hallmarks of the competent researcher.

Finally, with his data collected, the researcher faces the most important part of the whole enterprise. Processing data, analysing results and drafting reports are all extremely demanding activities both in intellectual effort and time. Often this last part of the experimental research is given too little time in the overall planning of the investigation. Experienced researchers rarely make such a mistake: card 'wrecks', programme faults, and a dozen more unanticipated disasters teach the hard lesson of leaving ample time for the analysis and interpretation of experimental findings.

Examples From Educational Research

Example 1   A Pre-experimental Design

A pre-experimental design was employed in a study undertaken for the New Zealand Book Council. In 1973, the New Zealand Council for

Educational Research began work on a research project concerned with the effects of a 'book flood' on the reading habits, tastes and abilities of school children. Two schools with an intake aged from 5 years to 11 years were involved in the study. Over half of their intake were Maori children many of whom were said to have 'limited access to books'. Suitable books were selected by a committee of teachers and librarians and introduced into the schools over a period two terms. To assess the impact of the flood of books, a series of baseline assessments of reading skills and attitudes was obtained between March and May 1976 before the books arrived and then again six months after the initial influx of books had taken place. The pretest battery included tests of reading comprehension, vocabulary and listening, and scales to assess children's interests in books, attitudes to school, to reading and to themselves. The amount of reading undertaken in a two-week period was recorded by the children themselves and teachers' ratings of interest in reading were also obtained. Case studies were made of five children in each class and information was obtained about the books the children owned and had read, their home background, parental interest, library borrowing and TV viewing. Finally, informal reading inventories were used to study the children's reading behaviour.

The effects of the book flood were analysed in terms of the amount of reading undertaken by the children during the course of the project, their reading skills, reading interests and their attitudes toward reading in general.

Using the symbols and conventions adopted earlier (p. 159) to represent research designs, we can illustrate the New Zealand study* as:

(Experimental) O_1 X O_2

The briefest consideration reveals inadequacies in the design. Indeed, Campbell and Stanley (2) describe *the one group pretest-post-test design* as 'a "bad example" to illustrate several of the confounded extraneous variables than can jeopardize internal validity. These variables offer plausible hypotheses explaining an $O_1 - O_2$ difference, rival to the hypothesis that caused the difference'.

Nevertheless, the New Zealand researchers confidently report that the first six months of the book flood produced significant changes in the

---

* Despite the fact that two schools were employed, thus offering the possibility of replication, the New Zealand study is essentially a *one group pretest-post-test design*.

amount of their subjects' voluntary reading, and improvements in their reading abilities, attitudes and interests. The reader may care to formulate alternative explanations of the incremental gains reported in the study after consulting the various threats to internal validity which we detailed on p. 165.

Example 2   A Quasi-experimental Design

The Bradford Book Flood Experiment (9) began in 1976 with two aims in view. First, to study the effects of a book flood on children's reading abilities and interests. Second, to improve upon the research design used in the New Zealand study within the limits imposed by funding and the requests that could be made for changes in the timetabling and day-to-day organisation of the participating schools. The design finally adopted by the Bradford research team after considerable discussion may be represented thus:

(Experimental)	O_1	X	O_2
(Control)	O_3		O_4

It is, of course, the *non-equivalent control group design* outlined earlier in the chapter in which the parallel rows separated by the dashed line represent groups that have not been equated by random assignment.

Four middle schools took part in the Bradford study, two serving as experimental and two as control schools. Two schools forming a matched pair were situated on council estates, the second matched pair being located in inner city areas. Allocation to experiment or control treatments was made on the flip of a coin.

The schools were selected by a senior educational adviser who attempted to choose schools of similar size, background, organisation, teaching methods and catering for children of a similar range of abilities. Unlike the New Zealand study, the Bradford research followed one particular year group (second year pupils) through the school.

Pretest and post-test measures of reading skills, attitudes and interests were supplemented by classroom observation and interviews with selected children, the analysis of diaries and reading record forms, and the use of teachers' assessments. In the light of the problems of *instrumentation* to which we referred earlier, particular care was taken to select reading tests that: (1) had been recently constructed or recently restandardised; (2) had British norms; (3) were reliable and valid; (4) were suitable for the age group under study; and (5) were appropriate over the two-year testing sessions. Unlike the New Zealand study, the Bradford design attempted to use both matching and random allocation (of a sort) to obtain equivalent groups at the outset of the research. Despite this, the study remains firmly quasi-experimental rather than experimental since random allocation to experimental and control groups at the level of individual pupils was clearly impossible and what random allocation did take place at the level of institutions was of little consequence because of the small number of schools involved. Although the Bradford investigators attempted to exercise control over extraneous variables, it is not difficult to criticise the study in respect of each of the threats to internal and external validity that we identified earlier. For example, the matching of schools that was undertaken was relatively crude and did not take account of the important variations in the intrasessional histories of the schools that participated. Of equal import, it does not appear that a precise, unequivocal description of the experimental treatment was ever undertaken. What exactly constitutes a book flood? One could go on raising aspects of design weakness which jeopardise the validity of the Bradford research project, but such criticisms would serve only to reinforce the point that true experimentation in education is rarely, if ever, achieved.

Example 3   A 'True' Experimental Design

We have chosen a study (10) of children's understanding of a scientific concept to illustrate a stronger design than the pretest-post-test control group design that was discussed earlier in the chapter. The experimental design adopted by the researchers owes its origins to Solomon (6) and can be represented as:

(Experimental)	RO_1	X	O_2
(1st Control)	RO_3		O_4
(2nd Control)		X	O_5

This three-group design provides all that the *pretest-post-test control group design* does by the way of control, but in addition, it enables the researcher to test whether the pretest exercises any significant influence on the performance in the post-test situation. Suppose, for example, that it is found that the average score of the experimental group (top line in the diagram) is significantly greater than that of the first control group. Can it be concluded that this effect is entirely due to the experimental treatment X or could it possibly have resulted from an increased sensitisation among the experimental subjects as a result of the pretest? The average score of the second control group (bottom line) enables us to test our suspicion. If the average score of the second control group is also significantly greater than that of the first control group, then it is safe to conclude that the pretest itself does not exercise any sensitising effect upon the experimental subjects. In the actual research study, Harvey and Cooper tested for a pretest sensitisation effect in second, third and fourth year junior school pupils randomly assigned to experimental and control groups in a *Solomon three-group design*. Their results provided conclusive proof of a lack of pretest sensitisation.

| | Mean post-test scores | | |
	Experimental	1st Control	2nd Control
4th year groups	8.78	3.25	7.52
3rd year groups	6.65	2.38	7.56
2nd year groups	6.56	2.25	5.38

Source: Adapted from Harvey and Cooper (10)

Inter alia, the experiment provided evidence that a teaching programme to do with basic electricity, presented over a two-week period in four 30-minute lessons, could produce a significant incremental effect in the performance of children on a hierarchically structured concept-formation test. Of particular interest was the discovery that children of the youngest age group showed increased understanding of the concepts at all levels despite differences in reading ability when compared with older age groups.

References

1.   Kerlinger, F.N., *Foundations of Behavioural Research* (Holt, Rinehart and Winston, New York, 1970).
2.   Campbell, D.T. and Stanley, J.C., 'Experimental and quasi-experimental designs for research on teaching' in N.L. Gage (ed.), *Handbook of Research on Teaching* (Rand McNally, Chicago, 1963).
3.   Palmer, M., 'An experimental study of the use of archive materials in the secondary school history curriculum', PhD dissertation (University of Leicester, 1976).
4.   Pilliner, A., *Experiment in Education Research*, E341 Block 5. (The Open

University Press, Bletchley, 1973).
5. Good, C.V., *Introduction to Educational Research* (Appleton Century Crofts, New York, 1963).
6. Solomon, R.L., 'An extension of control group design', *Psychol. Bull.*, 46 (1949) 137-50.
7. Bracht, G.H. and Glass, G.V., 'The external validity of experiments', *Amer. Educ. Res. Journ.*, 4, 5 (1968) 437-74.
8. Evans, K.M., *Planning Small Scale Research* (NFER Publishing Co., Windsor, 1978).
9. Beard, R., Cohen, L. and Verma, G., *The Bradford Book Flood Experiment* (School of Research in Education, University of Bradford, 1978).
10. Harvey, T.J. and Cooper, C.J., 'An investigation into some possible factors affecting children's understanding of the concept of an electric circuit in the age range 8-11 years old', *Educational Studies*, 4, 2 (1978) 149-55.

9 ACTION RESEARCH

Introduction

We come now to a style of research that has received rather more publicity over the years than most other methods in the social sciences. This may indeed stem from the implied tension in its name, *action research*, for *action* and *research* as separate activities in whatever context each have their own ideology and modus operandi and when conjoined in this way, lie as uneasy bedfellows. To give a comprehensive definition of the term at this stage is difficult because usage varies with time, place and setting. None the less, we may offer a conventional definition and use this as a starting point: *action research is small-scale intervention in the functioning of the real world and a close examination of the effects of such intervention* (1). By looking at a few examples of the use of the method in the research literature, we may further identify other tangible features: action research is *situational* — it is concerned with diagnosing a problem in a specific context and attempting to solve it in that context; it is usually (though not inevitably) *collaborative* — teams of researchers and practitioners work together on a project; it is *participatory* — team members themselves take part directly or indirectly in implementing the research; and it is *self-evaluative* — modifications are continuously evaluated within the ongoing situation, the ultimate objective being to improve practice in some way or other. According to Blum (2), the use of action research in the social sciences can be resolved into two stages: a *diagnostic stage* in which the problems are analysed and the hypotheses developed; and a *therapeutic stage* in which the hypotheses are tested by a consciously directed change experiment, preferably in a social life situation.

The scope of action research as a method is impressive. Its usage may range at one extreme from a teacher trying out a novel way of teaching social studies with his class to, at another, a sophisticated study of organisational change in industry using a large research team and backed by government sponsors. Whatever the situation, however, the method's evaluative frame of reference remains the same, namely, to add to the practitioner's *functional knowledge* of the phenomena he deals with. This type of research is therefore usually considered in conjunction with social or educational aims (3).

It will be useful here if we distinguish *action research* from *applied research*, for although they are similar in some ways, there are important differences between them which need to be made explicit, for confusion between the two does sometimes arise. Both utilise the scientific method. Since applied research is concerned mainly with establishing relationships and testing theories, it is quite rigorous in its application of the conditions of this method. To this end, therefore, it insists on: studying a large number of cases; establishing as much control as possible over variables; precise sampling techniques; and a serious concern to generalise its findings to comparable situations. It does not claim to contribute directly to the solution of problems. Action research, by contrast, interprets the scientific method much more loosely, chiefly because its focus is a specific problem in a specific setting. The emphasis is not so much on obtaining generalisable scientific knowledge as on precise knowledge for a particular situation and purpose. The conditions imposed on applied research, therefore, are normally relaxed with action research. Of course, as action research projects become more extensive in their coverage, the boundary between the two methods becomes less easy to define. A curriculum project involving 100 schools, say, or a community action programme embracing a number of major conurbations, will tend to yield rather more generalisable knowledge and information than purely localised undertakings.

Having drawn this distinction between action research and applied research, we are now free to concentrate on the former and ask ourselves the question: what kinds of intervention programme are featured in action research? The following examples, while by no means exhaustive, give some idea of the contexts in which the method may be used. They are not mutually exclusive so there may be considerable overlap between some of them. There is the kind: (1) which acts as *a spur to action*, its objective being to get something done more expeditiously than would be the case with alternative means; (2) which addresses itself to *personal functioning, human relations and morale* and is thus concerned with people's job efficiency, their motivations, relationships and general well-being; (3) which focuses on *job analysis* and aims at improving professional functioning and efficiency; (4) which is concerned with *organisational change* in so far as it results in improved functioning in business or industry; (5) which is concerned with *planning and policy-making*, generally in the field of social administration; (6) which is concerned with *innovation and change* and the ways in which these may be implemented in ongoing systems; (7) which concentrates on *problem-solving* virtually in any context in which a specific problem needs solving; and (8) which provides the opportunity to develop *theoretical knowledge*, the emphasis here being more on the research element of the method.

Equally diverse are the situations in which these different kinds of intervention may be used – almost any setting, in fact, where a problem involving people, tasks and procedures cries out for solution, or where some change of feature results in a more desirable outcome. Notable instances of the use of action research may be found in such starkly contrasting worlds as insurance, prisons, social administration, ships, hospitals, community projects, education, industry, coal-mining and business management. Examination of the work of the Tavistock Institute of Human Relations which has done so much to develop action research as a methodology will illustrate how the method may be applied in these diverse areas (4). For our own purposes, however, we shall now restrict our discussion chiefly to the use of action research in the field of education.

Although the action research movement in education was initiated in the United States in the 1940s, the scene for its appearance began to be set in that country in the 1920s with the application of the scientific method to the study of educational problems, growing interest in group interaction and group processes, and the emerging progressive movement. Indeed, the latter is seen by some as the principal causal agent for subsequent developments in action research. One writer (5) says: 'Action research . . . is a direct and logical outcome of the progressive position. After showing children how to work together to solve their problems, the next step was for teachers to adopt the methods they had been teaching their children, and learn to solve their own problems co-operatively.' Reaching its peak in the 1960s, the movement had multi-farious aims of a decidedly practical nature which were often embellished with ideological, even political, counterpoints. Some, for instance, saw it as a necessary corrective to the failure of official bodies to implement traditional research findings; others, as a means of improving the quality of life. Action research in Britain has enjoyed something of a revival since the establishment of the Schools Council in 1964 under whose aegis it has been used to implement curriculum research and development. The purposes of action research in school and classroom fall broadly into five categories: (1) it is a means of remedying problems diagnosed in specific situations, or of improving in some way a given set of circumstances; (2) it is a means of in-service training, thereby equipping the teacher with new skills and methods, sharpening his analytical powers and heightening his self-awareness; (3) it is a

Box 9.1

Humanities Curriculum Project — Aim and Premisses

Aim:
To develop an understanding of social situations and human acts and of the controversial value issues which they raise.

Premisses:
1. that controversial issues should be handled in the classroom.

2. that the teacher should accept the need to submit his teaching in controversial areas to the criterion of neutrality at this stage of education, i.e. that he should regard it as part of his responsibility not to promote his own view.

3. that the mode of enquiry in controversial areas should have discussion, rather than instruction, as its core.

4. that the discussion should protect divergence of view among participants, rather than attempt to achieve consensus.

5. that the teacher as chairman of the discussion should have responsibility for quality and standards of learning.

Source: Butcher and Pont (6)

means of injecting additional or innovatory approaches to teaching and learning into an ongoing system which normally inhibits innovation and change; (4) it is a means of improving the normally poor communications between the practising teacher and the academic researcher, and of remedying the failure of traditional research to give clear prescriptions; and (5) although lacking the rigour of true scientific research, it is a means of providing a preferable alternative to the more subjective, impressionistic approach to problem-solving in the classroom.

We close our introduction by asking: who actually undertakes action research in schools? Three possibilities present themselves. First, there is the single teacher operating on his own with his class. He will feel the need for some kind of change or improvement in teaching, learning or organisation, for example, and will be in a position to translate his ideas into action in his own classroom. He is, as it were, both practitioner and researcher in one and will integrate the practical and theoretical orientations within himself. Second, action research may be pursued by a group of teachers working co-operatively within one school, though of necessity functioning against a bigger backdrop than the teacher working solo. They may or may not be advised by an outside researcher. And third, there is the occasion — perhaps the most characteristic in recent years — where a team of teachers work along-side a team of researchers in a sustained relationship, possibly with other interested parties, like advisers, university departments and sponsors, on the periphery. This third possibility, though potentially the most promising, may also be the most problematic, at least initially, because of rival characterisations of action and research by the teachers and researchers respectively. We shall return to this point at the end of the chapter. Advocates of action research believe that little can be achieved if only one person is involved in changing his ideas and practices. For this reason, co-operative research tends to be emphasised and encouraged. One commentator (7) notes:

> Action research functions best when it is co-operative action research. This method of research incorporates the ideas and expectations of all persons involved in the situation. Co-operative action research has the concomitants of beneficial effects for workers, and the improvement of the services, conditions, and functions of the situation. In education this activity translates into more practice in research and problem-solving by teachers, administrators, pupils, and certain community personnel, while the quality of teaching and learning is in the process of being improved.

Characteristics

The principal characteristics of action research which we hereupon describe are more or less present in all instances of its usage (those having an experimental slant need to be considered in a somewhat different category). We have already referred to its prime feature — that it is essentially an on-the-spot procedure designed to deal with a concrete problem located in an immediate situation. This means that the step-by-step process is constantly monitored (ideally, that is) over varying periods of time and by a variety of mechanisms (questionnaires, diaries, interviews and case studies, for example) so that the ensuing feedback may be translated into modifications, adjustments, directional changes, re-definitions, as necessary, so as to bring about lasting benefit to the ongoing process itself rather than to some future occasion, as is the purpose of more traditionally oriented research. Unlike other methods, no attempt is made to identify one particular factor and study it in isolation, divorced from the context giving it meaning. That the findings are applied immediately, then, or in the short term is another important characteristic, although having made this point we need to qualify it to the extent that members of research teams —

especially in curriculum projects — frequently have a more long-term perspective. The following extract from Stenhouse's (8) account of the Humanities Curriculum Project illustrates how some of the points we have just made appear 'in the field':

> During the session 1968-9 the schools worked on collections on war, education, and the family. Feedback on materials was by questionnaire supported by interviews with the schools officer or other team members when they visited schools. Information was sought on coverage of the collection, accessibility of the material to the students (readability and sophistication of ideas), and the extent to which materials provoked or supported discussion. Most schools used only a small proportion of materials (as was intended) so that feedback on any one piece was not extensive. It was also frequently contradictory, particularly as to readability. Collections were radically re-edited as a result of experience in schools; often only half the trial pack survived.

The principal justification for the use of action research in the context of the school is improvement of practice. This can be achieved only if teachers are able to change their attitudes and behaviour. One of the best means of bringing about these kind of changes is pressure from the group with which one works. As we have seen, because the problems of teachers are often shared with other teachers in the same school, action research has tended to become co-operative involving many or all of the teachers in the school. Group interaction is frequently another characteristic, therefore.

A feature which makes action research a very suitable procedure for work in classrooms and schools (as well as other field settings) is its flexibility and adaptability. These qualities are revealed in the changes that may take place during its implementation and in the course of on-the-spot experimentation and innovation characterising the approach. They come out particularly strongly when set against the usual background of constraints in schools — those to do with organisation, resources, timetabling, staff deployment and teachers' attitudes, for example, as well as pressures from other agencies involved and from competing interests.

Action research relies chiefly on observation and behavioural data. That it is therefore empirical is another distinguishing feature of the method. This implies that over the period of a project information is collected, shared, discussed, recorded in some way, evaluated and acted

Box 9.2

The ideal teacher for an integrated studies project

The ideal teacher for an Integrated Studies Project would be one willing to
maintain his subject discipline within a team and to engage in planning
integrated work through discussions with other specialist colleagues. This
teacher would be an active producer of new materials, teaching methods
and ideas for integrated subject work. He would keep accounts of his
innovatory work, fill in the questionnaires sent him by the project team
and feed his experience back to them. He would organize his work so that
children would not only come to see and use the concepts within separate
subject disciplines, but would learn the skills of those subjects through
enquiry-based programmes.

Source: Adapted from Shipman (9)

upon; and that from time to time, this sequence of events forms the
basis of reviews of progress. In this one respect at least it is superior to
the more usual subjective, impressionistic methods we have already
alluded to. Where an experimental note is introduced into a project, it
is generally achieved through the use of control groups with a view to
testing specific hypotheses and arriving at more generalisable knowledge.

In our earlier comparison with applied research, we said that action
research took a much more relaxed view of the scientific method. We
return to this point here because it is a characteristic which forms the
basis of persistent criticisms of the method by its opponents. Travers
(10), for example, in reviewing a number of action research projects
writes:

> The writer's evaluation of the last fifty studies which have been
> undertaken which compare the outcomes of one teaching method-
> ology with another is that they have contributed almost nothing to
> our knowledge of the factors that influence the learning process in
> the classroom. Many of them do not even identify what the experi-
> mentally controlled variables are and indicate only that the study
> compares the outcomes of educational practices in the community
> where the study originates with educational practices elsewhere.

That the method should be lacking in scientific rigour, however, is
not surprising since the very factors which make it distinctively what
it is — and therefore of value in certain contexts — are the antithesis
of true experimental research. The points usually made are: that its

objective is situational and specific (unlike the scientific method which goes beyond the solution of practical problems); its sample is restricted and unrepresentative; it has little or no control over independent variables; and its findings are not generalisable but generally restricted to the environment in which the research is carried out. While these criticisms hold in most cases, it is important that we refer again to the qualification made earlier: that as action research programmes become more extensive and use more schools, that is, become more standardised, less personalised and more 'open', some of these strictures at least will become less valid.

Occasions When Action Research as a Method is Appropriate

We come now to a brief consideration of the occasions when the use of action research is fitting and appropriate. The answer in short is this: that action research is appropriate whenever specific knowledge is required for a specific problem in a specific situation; or when a new approach is to be grafted on to an existing system. More than this, however, suitable mechanisms must be available for monitoring progress and for translating feedback into the ongoing system. This means that, other things being equal, the action research method may be applied to any classroom or school situation where these conditions apply. We have already referred to the suitability of the approach to curriculum research and development. Let us now take this further by identifying other areas in school life where action research could be used and illustrating each area with a concrete example: (1) *teaching methods* – perhaps replacing a traditional method by a discovery method; (2) *learning strategies* – adopting an integrated approach to learning in preference to a single subject style of teaching and learning; (3) *evaluative procedures* – improving one's methods of continuous assessment, say; (4) the realm of *attitudes and values* – possibly encouraging more positive attitudes to work, for instance, or modifying pupils' value systems with regard to some aspect of life; (5) the personal *in-service development* of teachers – improving teaching skills, developing new methods of learning, increasing powers of analysis, or heightening self-awareness, for example; (6) *management and control* – the gradual introduction of the techniques of behaviour modification; and (7) *administration* – increasing the efficiency of some aspect of the administrative side of school life.

Of course, it would be naive of us simply to select a problem area *in vacuo*, so to speak. We have also to consider the context in which the project is to be undertaken. More specifically this means bearing in mind factors that will directly affect the outcomes. One of these concerns the teachers themselves and the extent to which they are favourably disposed towards the project, particularly when they are part of a collectivity working with outside agencies for, as we shall see in our final section, this very factor on its own can be a source of intense friction. It is important, therefore, that the teachers taking part in the project are truly involved, that they know what the objectives are, what these imply, and that they are adequately motivated — or at least sufficiently open-minded for motivation to be induced. Another important factor concerns the organisational aspect of the school so that there is a reasonable amount of congruence between the setting and the programme to be initiated. This can be achieved without too much discord when a programme is internally organised by the school itself. When outside parties are involved, however, who themselves are working concurrently in other schools, difficulties may arise over such matters as implementing a new style of teaching, for example, or use of project materials, and so on. One further factor concerns resources: are there enough sufficiently competent researchers at hand? And has the school got reasonable access to college and university libraries to consult appropriate professional and research journals should this need arise? Some or all of these factors need to be reviewed as part of the planning stage of an action research programme.

Box 9.3

Metaphors reflecting teachers' perceptions of a curriculum project

1. *The exchange of gifts*: The project as reciprocal obligation.

2. *The other drummer*: The project as unselected affinity.

3. *Troubled waters*: The project as agitation or distress.

4. *The gift of grace*: The project as salvation.

5. *New props for identity*: The project as theatre.

6. *Free sample*: The project as commercialism.

7. *Ground bait*: The project as exploitation.

8. *Taking issue*: The project as management consultancy.

9. *Cargo cult*: The project as overwhelming technology.

Source: Shipman (9)

Some Issues

We have already seen that the participants in a change situation may be either a teacher, a group of teachers working internally, or else teachers and researchers working on a collaborative basis. It is this latter category, where action research brings together two professional bodies each with its own objectives and values, that we shall consider further at this point because of its inherent problematic nature. Both parties share the same interest in an educational problem, yet their respective orientations to it differ. It has been observed (1), for instance, that research values *precision*, *control*, *replication* and attempts to generalise from specific events. Teaching, on the other hand, is concerned with *action*, with *doing things*, and translates generalisations into specific acts. The incompatibility between action and research in these respects, therefore, can be a source of problems. Marris and Rein (11), for example, on reviewing the relationship between the two in a number of American community action programmes concluded that the principles of *action* and *experienced research* are so different and so often mutually exclusive that attempts to link them into a single process are likely to produce internal conflict and the subordination of one element to another. They express it thus:

> Research requires a clear and constant purpose, which both defines and precedes the choice of means; that the means be exactly and consistently followed; and that no revision takes place until the sequence of steps is completed. Action is tentative, non-commital and adaptive. It concentrates upon the next step, breaking the sequence into discrete, manageable decisions. It casts events in a fundamentally different perspective, evolving the future out of present opportunities, where research perceives the present in the context of the final outcomes. Research cannot interpret the present until it knows the answers to its ultimate questions. Action cannot foresee what questions to ask until it has interpreted the present. Action attempts to comprehend all the factors relevant to an immediate problem whose nature continually changes as events proceed, where research abstracts one or two factors for attention, and holds to a constant definition of the problem until the experiment is concluded.

Those who are not quite as pessimistic about the viability of the action/research coupling would question whether the characterisation of *action* and *research* as put forward by Marris and Rein necessarily holds in all contexts. They would advocate a more flexible approach to the relationship. Some researchers (1), for instance, suggest that projects could vary along a number of dimensions such as the degree of control exercised by the action and research components, the amount of knowledge about the means of achieving the desired outcomes, and the level of co-operation between action and research. Such a classification could be linked to different kinds of action research (see p. 175) and suggest what combinations of action and research were most appropriate for particular conditions. In short, what seems to be needed is a clear and unambiguous statement of the project's objectives such that all participants understand them and their implications; and a careful analysis of the context(s) in which the programme is to be mounted to determine the precise, but flexible, relationship between the two components. This would help to ensure that the positive contributions of both are maximised and that the constraints of each on the other are kept to a minimum.

Procedures

We now trace the possible stages and procedures that may be followed in an action research programme, or from which a suitable selection may be made. As we have already seen, projects may vary along a number of dimensions — whether they are to be conducted by teachers only, or by teachers in collaboration with researchers, whether small or large samples of schools are involved, whether they tackle specific problems or more diffuse ones, for example. Given the particular set of circumstances, an appropriate model may be selected to guide procedures, one that will be tailor-made to meet the needs of the change situation in question. As we are here concerned with a review of procedures in general terms, however, and not with a specific instance, we offer a basic, flexible framework by way of illustration: it will need to be intepreted or adjusted in the light of the particular undertaking.

The *first stage* will involve the identification, evaluation and formulation of the problem perceived as critical in an everyday teaching situation. 'Problem' should be interpreted loosely here so that it could refer to the need to introduce innovation into some aspect of a school's established programme. The *second stage* involves preliminary discussion and negotiations among the interested parties — teachers, researchers, advisers, sponsors, possibly — which may culminate in a draft proposal. This may include a statement of the questions to be answered (e.g. Under what conditions can curriculum change be best effected? What are the limiting factors in bringing about effective curriculum change? What strong points of action research can be employed to bring about curriculum change?). The researchers in their capacity as consultants (or sometimes as programme initiators) may draw upon their expertise to bring the problem more into focus, possibly determining causal factors or recommending alternative lines of approach to established ones. This is often the crucial stage for the venture as it is at this point that the seeds of success or failure are planted, for unless the objectives, purposes and assumptions are made perfectly clear to all concerned, and unless the role of key concepts is stressed (e.g. feedback), the enterprise can easily miscarry. The *third stage* may in some circumstances involve a review of the research literature to find out what can be learned from comparable studies, their objectives, procedures and problems encountered. The *fourth stage* may involve a modification or redefinition of the initial statement of the problem at stage one. It may now emerge in the form of a testable hypothesis; or as a set of guiding objectives. In Box 9.1 we give an example of an aim and accompanying premises which were used in this connection in the Humanities Curriculum Project. Sometimes change agents deliberately decide against the use of objectives on the grounds that they have a constraining effect on the process itself. It is also at this stage that assumptions underlying the project are made explicit (e.g. in order to effect curriculum changes, the attitudes, values, skills and objectives of the teachers involved must be changed). The *fifth stage* may be concerned with the selection of research procedures — sampling, administration, choice of materials, methods of teaching and learning, allocation of resources and tasks, deployment of staff and so on.

The *sixth stage* will be concerned with the choice of the evaluation procedures to be used and will need to take into consideration that evaluation in this context will be continuous. Box 9.4 provides a set of evaluation objectives from the Humanities Project by way of example. The *seventh stage* embraces the implementation of the project itself (over varying periods of time). It will include the conditions and methods of data collection (e.g. bi-weekly meetings, the keeping of records, interim reports, final reports, the submission of self-evaluation and group-evaluation reports, etc.); the monitoring of tasks and the transmission of feedback to the research team; and the classification and analysis of data. The *eighth and final stage* will involve the interpretation of the data; inferences to be drawn; and overall evaluation of the project. Discussions on the findings will take place in the light of previously agreed evaluative criteria. Errors, mistakes and problems will

Box 9.4

The objectives of the Evaluation Unit in the Humanities
Curriculum Project

1. To ascertain the effects of the Project, document the circumstances in
   which they occur, and present this information in a form which will
   help educational decision-makers to evaluate the likely consequences
   of adopting the programme.

2. To describe the present situation and operations of the schools we study
   so that decision-makers can understand more fully what it is they are
   trying to change.

3. To describe the work of the project team in terms which will help the
   sponsors and planners of such a venture to weigh the value of this form
   of investment, and to determine more precisely the framework of
   support, guidance and control which are appropriate.

4. To make a contribution to evaluation theory by articulating our
   problems clearly, recording our experiences, and perhaps most
   importantly, by publicising our errors.

5. To contribute to the understanding of the problems of curriculum
   innovation generally.

Source: Butcher and Pont (8)

be considered. A general summing up may follow this in which the
outcomes of the project are reviewed, recommendations made, and
arrangements for dissemination of results to interested parties decided.

As we stressed, this is a basic framework: much activity of an
incidental and possibly *ad hoc* nature will take place in and around it.
This may comprise discussions among teachers, researchers and pupils;
regular meetings among teachers or schools to discuss progress and
problems, and to exchange information; possibly regional conferences;
and related activities, all enhanced by the range of current hardware —
tapes, video-recordings and transcripts.

Conclusion: Examples of Action Research in the Field of Curriculum Development

So far in our review of action research as a method, we have touched
upon its principal characteristics, occasions when it may be used, conceptual issues and the stages of its implementation. Another important
feature which we have only mentioned in passing concerns the problems
and difficulties encountered in mounting this kind of project, especially
when on a fairly ambitious scale. It is these problems and difficulties

which help to give this particular methodology its special flavour. Often unforeseen, and therefore not prepared for, they are as valuable for what can be learned from them as are the planned aspects of a project. We conclude this chapter, then, with a problem-oriented look at two action-research-based projects of some magnitude which have been undertaken in the field of curriculum research and development in recent years — the Humanities Curriculum Project and the Keele Integrated Studies Project.

The first of these, the Humanities Curriculum Project, was set up in 1967 under the joint sponsorship of the Schools Council and the Nuffield Foundation. Its aim and premisses we have listed in Box 9.1. The overall task of the project was to discover a teaching strategy which would implement these premisses in the classroom, to report this strategy, and to support teachers who wished to develop it with training and if necessary with materials.

The problems and difficulties in mounting this project appear to have stemmed in the main from mistaken or incongruent attitudes and expectations on the part of the teachers in the experimental schools. Thus, their initial outlook tended to be coloured by earlier, more traditional approaches to the curriculum based on single-subject specialisms with the emphasis on improving teaching methods in these fields. They failed to appreciate that the venture had a social science basis and that they would need to adopt a suitably detached stance in keeping with its experimental nature. Having this kind of basis, the project was seen by the researchers as a means of testing hypotheses; many of the teachers, however, in awe of the presumed authority of the Schools Council, its sponsors, felt that they themselves were on trial. As a result, some of the experimental feedback was distorted. Misunderstandings with respect to the researchers' time perspective was another source of difficulty. The research team was concerned with long-term development; yet they were often perceived as attempting an instant and easy solution to problems. Finally, the teachers in the experimental schools tended to harbour feelings that the project would in some way help to solve problems of discipline and control. As it was, 'It made them more acute [and] opened them up instead of containing them' (8).

The second example of the use of action research is that of the Keele Integrated Studies Project initiated in 1969. Notwithstanding the success of the project and the value of the accrued experience in implementing it, we here again restrict ourselves to some of the more problematic aspects. Difficulties arose once more from the way the project was perceived or misperceived by the teachers in the experimental schools, as well as from the ambiguous relationship they had with it (we refer you to Box 9.3, which lists the metaphors selected by one of the parties involved to describe the teachers' perceptions of the project). We will, however, focus our remarks on the problem of communication between teachers and researchers which seemed to persist throughout the undertaking.

Efforts on the part of the research team to inform the schools at the outset of the project's objectives by means of meetings, conferences and circulars met with sustained complaints from the teachers about jargon and the lack of specific advice. The latter at this stage were indifferent to the researchers' attempts to explain the principles of integration and theories of curriculum development. This bears out the point we made earlier about rival characterisations of teaching and research. Subsequently, however, after having experienced the practical difficulties of implementing integrated studies, the teachers reversed their complaint, demanding explanation and theoretical reasoning for what they were doing. The discrepancy between what they requested and what they were prepared to do resulted in a lasting tension. As Shipman (9) points out, they wanted 'both academic rigour and easy-bake recipes from the same source'.

A further serious problem, yet another aspect of the communication gap, arose from the low priority given by the teachers to feedback. To this may be added their general reluctance to seek advice. In spite of the provision made by the researchers, only two out of the thirty-eight schools involved provided regular feedback to the research team. As Shipman again observes, this omission may be traced to the fact that the definitions of the project team and of the teachers were at different levels: 'The teachers were involved with their own problems and defined the project out of their own experience in their own classrooms. As a consequence the basic principles behind the project were usually misunderstood and often unconsidered.'

We see from all this that what is involved is group process and that this is not easy to handle. Favourable conditions for action research include the following: a willingness on the part of the teachers to admit limitations and to make themselves familiar with the basic techniques of research; the provision of opportunities to invent; the encouragement of new ideas; the provision of time for experimentation; a mutual trust of those involved; and a knowledge on the part of the participants of the fundamentals of group processes. Additionally, it must be realised that many minds working on the same problem will increase the number of ways of looking at it. There will be more suggested solutions and more effective criticisms of each proposed solution. It must also be recognised that action research involves a re-education of teachers; that their attitudes and values will need to change; that the longer they have been in the job, the more difficult this will be; and that in all probability, it will be more difficult for secondary teachers (as opposed to primary teachers) because they are less used to working together.

In conclusion it might be added that in a representative sample of action research studies conducted in the United States, it was found (5) that the teachers taking part were generally enthusiastic. They seemed to feel that the staff worked more as a unit than before the research, that staff members were drawn closer together with the knowledge that they shared problems and goals, and that respect for individuals, both teachers and pupils, had increased.

References

1. Halsey, A.H. (ed.), *Educational Priority: Volume 1: E.P.A. Problems and Policies* (HMSO, London, 1972).
2. *Association for Supervision and Curriculum Development. Learning about Learning from Action Research* (National Educational Association of the United States, Washington, DC, 1959).
3. Corey, S.M., *Action Research to Improve School Practices* (Bureau of Publications, Teachers College, Columbia University, New York, 1953).
4. See, for example: Brown, R.K., 'Research and consultancy in industrial enterprises: a review of the contribution of the Tavistock Institute of Human Relations to the development of Industrial Sociology', *Sociology*, 1, 1 (1967) 33-60.
5. Hodgkinson, H.L., 'Action research – a critique', *J. Educ. Sociol.*, 31, 4 (1957) 137-53.
6. Butcher, H.J. and Pont, H.B. (eds), *Educational Research in Britain 3* (University of London Press, London, 1973).
7. Hill, J.E. and Kerber, A., *Models, Methods, and Analytical Procedures in Educational Research* (Wayne State University Press, Detroit, 1967).
8. Stenhouse, L., 'The Humanities Curriculum Project' in Butcher and Pont, *Educational Research in Britain 3*.
9. Shipman, M.D., *Inside a Curriculum Project* (Methuen, London, 1974).
10. Travers, R.M.W., Extract quoted in Halsey (ed.), *Educational Priority*.
11. Marris, P. and Rein, M. *Dilemmas of Social Reform: Poverty and Community Action in the United States* (Routledge and Kegan Paul, London, 1967).

10 ACCOUNTS

Introduction

Although each of us sees the world from our own point of view, we have a way of speaking about our experiences which we share with those around us. Explaining our behaviour towards one another can be thought of as accounting for our actions in order to make them intelligible and justifiable to our fellowmen. Thus, saying 'I'm terribly sorry, I didn't mean to bump into you', is a simple case of the explication of social meaning, for by locating the bump outside any planned sequence and neutralising it by making it intelligible in such a way that it is not warrantable, it ceases to be offensive in that situation (1).

Accounting for actions in those larger slices of life called social episodes is the central concern of a new participatory psychology which focuses upon an actor's intentions, his beliefs about what sorts of behaviour will enable him to reach his goals, and his awareness of the rules that govern those behaviours. Studies carried out within this new framework have been termed *ethogenic*, an adjective which expresses a view of the human being *as a person*, that is, a plan-making, self-monitoring agent, aware of goals and deliberately considering the best ways to achieve them (2). Ethogenic studies represent a new approach to the study of social behaviour and their methods stand in bold contrast to those commonly employed in much of the educational research which we described in Chapter 8. Before discussing the elicitation and analysis of accounts we need to outline the ethogenic approach in more detail. This we do by reference to the work of one of its foremost British exponents.

The Ethogenic Approach

Harré (3) identifies five main principles in the ethogenic approach:

1. An explicit distinction is drawn between *synchronic analysis*, that is, the analysis of social practices and institutions as they exist at any one time, and *diachronic analysis*, the study of the stages and the processes by which social practices and institutions are created and abandoned, change and are changed. Neither type of analysis can be expected to lead directly to the discovery of universal social psychological principles or laws.

190

2. In social interaction, it is assumed that action takes place through endowing intersubjective entities with meaning; the ethogenic approach therefore concentrates upon the *meaning system*, that is, the whole sequence by which a social act is achieved in an episode. Consider, for example, the action of a kiss in the particular episodes of (a) leaving a friend's house; (b) the passing-out parade at St Cyr; and (c) the meeting in the garden of Gethsemane.
3. The ethogenic approach is concerned with speech which accompanies action. That speech is intended to make the action intelligible and justifiable in occurring at the time and the place it did in the whole sequence of unfolding and co-ordinated action. Such speech is *accounting*. In so far as accounts are socially meaningful, it is possible to derive *accounts of accounts*.
4. The ethogenic approach is founded upon the belief that a human being tends to be the kind of person his language, his traditions, his tacit and explicit knowledge tell him he is.
5. The skills that are employed in ethogenic studies therefore make use of common-sense understandings of the social world. As such the activities of the poet and the playwright offer the ethogenic researcher a better model than those of the physical scientist.

Characteristics of Accounts and Episodes

The discussion of accounts and episodes that now follows develops some of the ideas contained in the principles of the ethogenic approach outlined above.

We have already noted that accounts must be seen within the context of social episodes. The idea of an episode is a fairly general one. The concept itself may be defined as any coherent fragment of social life. Being a natural division of life, an episode will often have a recognisable beginning and end, and the sequence of actions that constitute it will have some meaning for the participants. Episodes may thus vary in duration and reflect innumerable aspects of life. A pupil entering primary school at seven and leaving at eleven would be an extended episode. A two-minute television interview with a political celebrity would be another. And, as we shall shortly illustrate, prospective house buyers recounting their experiences of negotiating a purchase, yet another. The contents of an episode which interest the ethogenic researcher include not only the perceived behaviour such as gesture and speech, but also the thoughts, the feelings and the intentions of those taking part. And the 'speech' that accounts for those thoughts, feelings and intentions must be conceived of in the widest connotation of the word. Thus, accounts may be personal records of the events we experience in our day-to-day lives, our conversations with neighbours, our letters to friends, our entries in diaries. Accounts serve to explain our past, present and future-oriented actions.

Providing that accounts are authentic, it is argued, there is no reason why they should not be used as scientific tools in explaining people's actions. Just how accounts can be authenticated will become clear in the following example of how an account may be elicited and analysed (see p. 220 for a discussion of triangulation methods in analysing accounts). The study is to do with an experience familiar to many readers — the processes involved in buying a house (4).

Procedures in Eliciting, Analysing and Authenticating Accounts: an Example

From the outset of this research project, prime importance was placed upon the authority of each informant to account for his own actions. This meant that leading questions and excessive guidance were avoided by the research team although they established the format of the interview in pilot work before the main research endeavour. Care was taken to select informants who were representative of various house buyer needs (newly-weds, large families, divorcees, etc.) and of a range of house styles and prices. The researchers were concerned with the degree to which respondents were actually involved in the house purchase, the recency of the experience, their reasons for participating in the study, and their articulateness and competence in providing information.

These early stages of the research, involving selection and collection activities, serve as checks on the authenticity of the accounts provided by those from whom it was possible to obtain adequate information. Further ways of establishing authenticity involved: (1) checking with respondents through a process of negotiation during the account-gathering stage about their perceptions of the events they described; (2) using secondary evidence such as expert corroboration from solicitors and estate agents, that is, comparing objective and subjective realities; and (3) comparing the separate accounts of other participants in the same event, that is, looking at various subjective realities. We illustrate this latter aspect in Box 10.1.

Once accounts had been gathered from informants, the researchers' task was to transform them into working documents which could be coded and analysed. Checks on the authenticity of the accounts were again incorporated at this stage of the research as well as standard checks on the intercoder reliability of those engaged in the

Box 10.1

Accounts of a social episode: house purchase

Mrs Y: 'Agents put us in touch with three people who were interested. Couple X seemed to be the absolutely perfect customer. They gave us the offer we wanted, bought some brand new carpets over and above the asking price. Some problems followed and things were delayed.

'I don't think the X's were quite aware of the urgency. We got the impression from the agents that they were cash buyers. But it turned out they weren't and it was a bit naughty to give us this impression.

'We didn't get on so well with Mr X and Mrs X was a bit of a tough cookie. My husband had words with her and he got a bit ruffled.'

Mrs X: 'It started off a very amicable relationship. We came over here and agreed to buy carpets and curtains. But the whole situation deteriorated which made the whole thing unpleasant. Mr Y would call every night sometimes he would call twice and harangue and harangue. They seemed to think we were cash buyers, the agents having told them so. So I said we are cash buyers only in the sense that we don't have anything to sell.

'It all became more and more abusive, finally I got so upset that I refused any more calls and anything that had to be said should go via a solicitor. Every time the 'phone goes I would just cringe.'

Source: Adapted from Brown and Sime (4).

transformation of the materials. Depending on the nature of the research problem and the objectives of the enquiry, the analyses that then followed could either be qualitative or quantitative. The final stage in the research was the production of an *account of the accounts*. Here, the researchers made explicit the controls that they had applied in eliciting accounts from informants and in the transformation process itself. Having satisfied the demands of authenticity in respect of their own account, the final product was then ready to be evaluated. Only when accounts were subjected to these periodic stringent checks for authenticity were they considered as scientific data.

Problems of eliciting, analysing and authenticating accounts are further illustrated in the following outlines of two educational studies. The first is concerned with valuing among older boys and girls; the second is to do with teachers' judgements about their own competence as classroom practitioners.

**Qualitative Analysis of Accounts of Social Episodes:
Further Examples**

In a study of adolescent values, Kitwood (5) developed an *experience-sampling method*, that is, a qualitative technique for gathering and analysing accounts based upon tape-recorded interviews that were themselves prompted by the 15 situations listed in Box 10.2.

Because the experience-sampling method avoids interrogation, the material which emerges is less organised than that obtained from a tightly structured interview. Successful handling of individual accounts therefore requires the researcher to know the interview content extremely well and to work toward the gradual emergence of tentative interpretive schemata which he then modifies, confirms or falsifies as the research continues. Kitwood identifies eight methods for dealing with the tape-recorded accounts. Methods 1-4 are fairly close to the approach adopted in handling questionnaires; and methods 5-8 are more in tune with the ethogenic principles that we identified earlier.

Method 1: The Total Pattern of Choice

The frequency of choice of various items permits some surface general-isations about the participants, taken as a group. The most revealing analyses may be those of the least and most popular items.

Method 2: Similarities and Differences

Using the same technique as in Method 1, it is possible to investigate similarities and differences within the total sample of accounts accord-ing to some characteristic(s) of the participants such as age, sex, level of educational attainment etc.

Method 3: Grouping Items Together

It may be convenient for some purposes to fuse together categories that cover similar subject matter. For example, items 1, 5 and 14 in Box 10.2 relate to conflict; items 4, 7 and 15, to personal growth and change.

Method 4: Categorisation of Content

The content of a particular item is inspected for the total sample and an attempt is then made to develop some categories into which all the material will fit. The analysis is most effective when two or more researchers work in collaboration, each initially proposing a category system independently and then exchanging views to negotiate a final

Box 10.2

Below are listed 15 types of situation which most people have been in at
some time. Try to think of something that has happened in your life in
the last year or so, or perhaps something that keeps on happening, which
fits into each of the descriptions. Then choose the ten of them which
deal with the things that seem to you to be most important, which cover
your main interests and concerns, and the different parts of your life.
When we meet we will talk together about the situations you have
chosen. Try beforehand to remember as clearly as you can what happened,
what you and others did, and how you yourself felt and thought. Be as
definite as you can. If you like, write a few notes to help you keep the
situation in mind.

1. When there was a misunderstanding between you and someone else
   (or several others) . . .
2. When you got on really well with people . . .
3. When you had to make an important decision . . .
4. When you discovered something new about yourself . . .
5. When you felt angry, annoyed or resentful . . .
6. When you did what was expected of you . . .
7. When your life changed direction in some way . . .
8. When you felt you had done something well . . .
9. When you were right on your own, with hardly anyone taking
   your side . . .
10. When you 'got away with it', or were not found out . . .
11. When you made a serious mistake . . .
12. When you felt afterwards that you had done right . . .
13. When you were disappointed with yourself . . .
14. When you had a serious clash or disagreement with another
    person . . .
15. When you began to take seriously something that had not
    mattered much to you before . . .

Source: Adapted from Kitwood (5).

category system.

Method 5: Tracing a Theme

This type of analysis transcends the rather artificial boundaries which
the items themselves imply. It aims to collect as much data as possible
relevant to a particular topic regardless of where it occurs in the interview material. The method is exacting because it requires very detailed
knowledge of content and may entail going through taped interviews

several times. Data so collected may be further analysed along the lines suggested in Method 4 above.

Method 6: The Study of Omissions

The researcher may well have expectations about the kind of issues likely to occur in the interviews. When some of these are absent, that fact may be highly significant. The absence of an anticipated topic should be explored to discover the correct explanation of its omission.

Method 7: Reconstruction of a Social Life-world

This method can be applied to the accounts of a number of people who have part of their lives in common, for example, a group of friends who go around together. The aim is to attempt some kind of reconstruction of the world which the participants share in analysing the fragmentary material obtained in an interview. The researcher seeks to understand the dominant modes or orienting to reality, the conceptions of purpose and the limits to what is perceived.

Method 8: Generating and Testing Hypotheses

New hypotheses may occur to the researcher during the analysis of the tape-recordings. It is possible to do more than simply advance these as a result of tentative impressions; one can loosely apply the hypothetico-deductive method to the data. This involves putting the hypothesis forward as clearly as possible, working out what the verifiable inferences from it would logically be, and testing these against the account data. Where these data are too fragmentary, the researcher may then consider what kind of evidence and method of obtaining it would be necessary for a more thorough hypothesis testing. Subsequent sets of interviews forming part of the same piece of research might then be used to obtain relevant data.

The experience sampling method used by Kitwood led him to identify three key second-order concepts by which to explore the nature of adolescent values. The first he called *conflict in personal relationships*, having found a general theme of interpersonal conflict running strongly through the interviews. The second, he identified as *decision-making* on the evidence of a deep concern and realism among the adolescents interviewed about what might lie ahead of them. The third he termed *standing alone*, a major preoccupation among his subjects and a second-order concept of some complexity which was further broken down into five subcategories for more detailed analysis.

In the light of the weaknesses in account gathering and analysis to which we refer on p. 204, Kitwood's suggestions of safeguards are worth mentioning. First he calls for *cross-checking* between researchers as a precaution against consistent but unrecognised bias in the interviews themselves. Second he recommends *member tests*, that is, taking hypotheses and unresolved problems back to the participants themselves or to persons in similar situations to them for their comments. Only in this way can the researcher be sure that he understands the participants' *own* grounds for action. Since there is always the possibility that an obliging participant will readily confirm the researcher's own speculations, every effort should be made to convey to the participant that one wants to know the truth as he or she sees it, and that one is as glad to be proved wrong as right.

Denscombe's (6) study of teaching as a practical activity approached the problem of authentication from a similar direction to that proposed by Kitwood. Denscombe's tape-recorded interviews with some 67 comprehensive school teachers *followed* a series of observations of the teachers' classroom activities. He used his observations as checks on the validity of the taped accounts. More importantly however, he provided opportunities for his participants to explain why a lesson had taken a particular course and why pupils had reacted in a particular way. In a word, teachers had a chance to *justify* their actions to the researcher.

As a further precaution against social desirability responses, Denscombe adopted a trainee identity, that is, as one seeking advice and needing the help of experienced teachers. That identity greatly facilitated the normalising of the researcher's presence in classrooms both from the point of view of teachers and of pupils. Some of Denscombe's findings are reported in Box 10.3.

Quantitative Analysis of Judgemental Ratings of Social Episodes

A major problem in the investigation of that natural unit of social behaviour, the *social episode*, has been the ambiguity that surrounds the concept itself and the lack of an acceptable taxonomy by which to classify an interaction sequence on the basis of empirically quantifiable characteristics (7). In this section we describe a number of quantitative approaches to the study of social episodes in educational settings.

Examples of Studies Using Factor Analysis and Linkage Analysis

The use of factor analysis and linkage analysis in studies of children's judgements of educational situations is illustrated in the work of

Box 10.3

> ### 'Competence' in the comprehensive classroom
>
> Competence is regarded as a shared method for interpreting events; teacher competence appears to owe more to control in the classroom than to the inculcation of knowledge *per se*.
>
> Competent teachers are expected to achieve control without the aid of others and are considered responsible for the control of their own classrooms.
>
> Classroom teaching, however, rarely becomes observable to colleagues. To assess the control of others therefore, teachers have to rely on publicly available indicators which transcend the isolation of setting, principally, *noise*. Control, then, is a socially organised phenomenon which is inferred rather than observed.

Source: Denscombe (6).

Magnusson (8) and Ekehammar and Magnusson (9). In the latter study, pupils were required to rate descriptions of various educational episodes on a scale of perceived similarity ranging from *0 = not at all similar* to *4 = identical*. Twenty different situations were presented two at a time in the same randomised order for all subjects. For example, 'listening to a lecture but do not understand a thing' would be judged against 'sitting at home writing an essay'. Product-moment correlation coefficients between pairs of similarity matrices calculated for all subjects varied between 0.57 and 0.79, with a median value of 0.71. No individual matrix deviated markedly from any of the others. A factor analysis of the total correlation matrix showed that the descriptions of situations had very clear structures for the children involved. Moreover, judgements of perceived similarity between situations had a considerable degree of consistency over time. Ekehammar and Magnusson compared their dimensional analysis with a categorical approach to the data using elementary linkage analysis (McQuitty (10)). They reported that this latter approach gave a result which was entirely in agreement with the result of the dimensional analysis. Five categories of situations were obtained with the same situations distributed in categories in the same way as they were distributed in factors in the dimensional analysis.

Examples of Studies using Multidimensional Scaling and Cluster Analysis

Forgas (7) studied housewives' and students' perceptions of typical social episodes in their lives, the episodes having been elicited from the respective groups by means of a diary technique. Subjects were required to supply two adjectives to describe each of the social episodes they had recorded as having occurred during the previous 24 hours. From a pool of some 146 adjectives thus generated, 10 (together with their antonyms) were selected on the basis of their salience, their diversity of usage and their independence of one another. Two more scales from speculative taxonomies were added to give 12 undimensional scales purporting to describe the underlying episode structures. These scales were used in the second part of the study to rate 25 social episodes in each group, the episodes being chosen as follows: an *index of relatedness* was computed on the basis of the number of times a pair of episodes was placed in the same category by respective housewife and student judges. Data were aggregated over the total number of subjects in each of the two groups. The 25 'top' social episodes in each group were retained. Forgas's analysis is based upon the ratings of 26 housewives and 25 students of their respective 25 episodes on each of the 12 undimensional scales. Box 10.4 shows a three-dimensional configuration of 25 social episodes rated by the student group on three of the scales. For illustrative purposes some of the social episodes numbered in Box 10.4 are identified by specific content.

In another study, Forgas (11) examined the social environment of a university department consisting of tutors, students and secretarial staff all of whom had interacted both inside and outside the department for at least six months prior to the research and thought of themselves as an intensive and cohesive social unit. Forgas's interest was in the relationship between two aspects of the social environment of the department — the perceived structure of the group and the perceptions that were held of specific social episodes. Participants were required to rate the similarity between each possible pairing of group members on a scale ranging from (1) extremely similar to (9) extremely dissimilar. An individual differences multidimensional scaling procedure (INDSCAL) produced an optimal three-dimensional configuration of group structure accounting for 68 per cent of the variance, group members being differentiated along the dimensions of *sociability, creativity* and *competence*.

A semi-structured procedure requiring participants to list typical and characteristic interaction situations was used to identify a number

Box 10.4

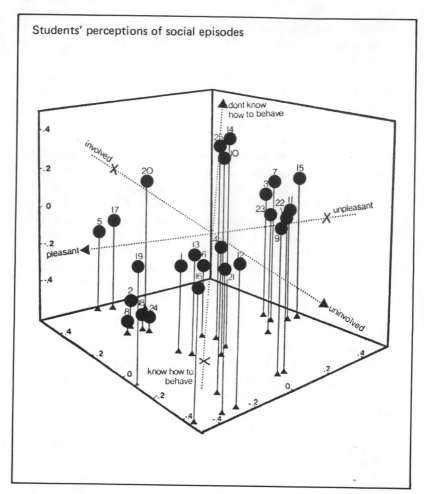

Students' perceptions of social episodes

Episodes

{
  14   Meeting new people at a sherry party in college
  25   Play chess
  10   Getting acquainted with a new person during dinner at hall.

{
  2   Having a drink with some friends in a pub
  18   Going to see a play at the theatre with friends
  24   Watching TV with some friends
  8   Going to the pictures with some friends

Source: Adapted from Forgas (7).

of social episodes. These in turn were validated by participant observation of the ongoing activities of the department. The most commonly occurring social episodes (those mentioned by nine or more members) served as the stimuli in the second stage of the study. Bi-polar scales similar to those reported by Forgas (7) above and elicited in like manner were used to obtain group members' judgements of social episodes.

An interesting finding reported by Forgas was that formal status differences exercised no significant effect upon the perception of the group by its members, the absence of differences being attributed to the strength of the department's cohesiveness and intimacy. In Forgas's analysis of the group's perceptions of social episodes, the INDSCAL scaling procedure produced an optimal four-dimensional solution accounting for 62 per cent of the variance, group members perceiving social episodes in terms of *anxiety, involvement, evaluation* and *socio-emotional versus task orientation.*

Box 10.5 illustrates how an average group member would see the characteristics of various social episodes in terms of the dimensions by which the group commonly judged them.

Finally we outline a classificatory system that has been developed to process materials elicited in a rather structured form of account-gathering.

Peevers and Secord's (12) study of developmental changes in children's use of descriptive concepts of persons illustrates the application of quantitative techniques to the analysis of one form of account.

In individual interviews, children of varying ages were asked to describe three friends and one person whom they disliked, all four persons being of the same sex as the interviewee. Interviews were tape-recorded and transcribed. A person concept coding system was developed, the categories of which are illustrated in Box 10.6. Each person-description was divided into items, each item consisting of one discrete piece of information. Each item was then coded on each of four major dimensions. Detailed coding procedures are set out in Peevers and Secord (12).

Tests of interjudge agreement on descriptiveness, personal involvement and evaluative consistency in which two judges worked independently on the interview transcripts of 21 boys and girls aged between 5 and 16 years resulted in interjudge agreement on those three dimensions of 87 per cent, 79 per cent and 97 per cent respectively.

Peevers and Secord also obtained evidence of the degree to which the participants themselves were consistent from one session to

Box 10.5

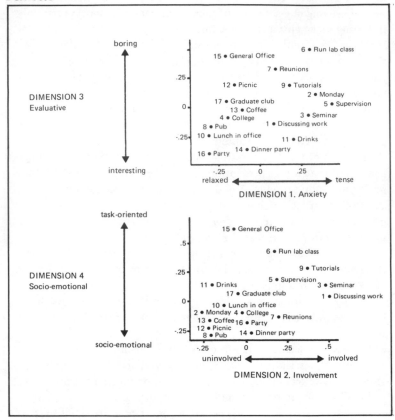

Source: Adapted from Forgas (11).

another in their use of concepts to describe other persons. Children were re-interviewed between one week and one month after the first session on the pretext of problems with the original recordings. Indices of test-retest reliability were computed for each of the major coding dimensions. Separate correlation coefficients (eta) were obtained for younger and older children in respect of their descriptive concepts of liked and disliked peers. Reliability coefficients are as set out on p. 204.

Peevers and Secord (13) conclude that their approach offers the possibility of an exciting line of enquiry into the depth of insight that an individual has into the personality of his acquaintances. Their 'free

Box 10.6

Person concept coding system	
Dimension	*Levels of descriptiveness*
	1. *Undifferentiating* . . . (person not differentiated from his environment)
	2. *Simple differentiating* . . . (person differentiated in simple global terms)
DESCRIPTIVENESS	3. *Differentiating* . . . (person differentiated in specific characteristics)
	4. *Dispositional* . . . (person differentiated in terms of traits)
	Degrees of involvement
	1. *Egocentric* . . . (other person described in self-oriented terms)
PERSONAL INVOLVEMENT	2. *Mutual* . . . (other person described in terms of his relationship to perceiver)
	3. *Other oriented* . . . (no personal involvement expressed by perceiver)
	Amount of consistency
	1. *Consistent* . . . (nothing favourable about 'disliked', nothing unfavourable about 'liked')
EVALUATIVE CONSISTENCY	2. *Inconsistent* . . . (some mixture of favourableness and unfavourableness)
	Levels of depth
	Level 1 (includes all undifferentiated and simple differentiated descriptions)
DEPTH	*Level 2* (includes differentiated and some dispositional descriptions)
	Level 3 (includes explanation-type differentiated and dispositional descriptions)

Source: Adapted from Peevers and Secord (12).

Dimension	Liked peers		Disliked peers	
	Younger subjects	Older subjects	Younger subjects	Older subjects
Descriptiveness	0.83	0.91	0.80	0.84
Personal involvement	0.76	0.80	0.84	0.77
Depth	0.65	0.71	0.65	0.75
Evaluative consistency	0.69	0.92	0.76	0.69

commentary' method is a modification of the more structured interview, requiring the interviewer to probe for explanations of why a person behaves the way he does or why a person is the kind of person he is. Peevers and Secord found that older children in their sample readily volunteered this sort of information. Harré (14) observes that this approach could also be extended to elicit commentary upon children's friends and enemies and the ritual actions associated with the creation and maintenance of these categories.

Problems in Gathering and Analysing Accounts

The importance of the meaning of events and actions to those who are involved is now generally recognised in social research. The implications of the ethogenic stance in terms of actual research techniques, however, remains problematic. Menzel (15) discusses a number of ambiguities and shortcomings in the ethogenic approach arising out of the multiplicity of meanings that may be held for the same behaviour. Most behaviour, Menzel observes, can be assigned meanings and more than one of these may very well be valid simultaneously. It is fallacious therefore, Menzel argues, to insist upon determining *the* meaning of an act. Nor can it be said that the task of interpreting an act is done when one has identified one meaning of it, or the one meaning that the researcher is pleased to designate as the true one.

A second problem that Menzel raises is to do with actors' meanings as sources of bias. How central a place, he asks, ought to be given to actors' meanings in formulating explanations of events? Should the researcher exclusively and invariably be guided by these considerations? To do so would be to ignore a whole range of potential explanations which few researchers would wish to see excluded from consideration.

These are far-reaching, difficult issues though by no means intractable. What solutions does Menzel propose?

First we must specify 'to whom' when asking what acts and situations mean. Second, researchers must make choices and take responsibility in the assignment of meanings to acts; moreover, problem formulations must respect the meaning of the act to us, the researchers. And third, explanations should respect the meanings of acts to the actors themselves but need not invariably be centred around these meanings.

Menzel's plea is for the usefulness of an outside observer's account of a social episode alongside the explanations that participants themselves may give of that event. A similar argument is implicit in McIntyre and McLeod's (16) justification of objective, systematic observation in classroom settings. Their case is set out in Box 10.7.

Box 10.7

Justification of objective systematic observation in classroom settings.

. . . When Smith looks at Jones and says, 'Jones, why does the blue substance spread through the liquid?' (probably with a particular kind of voice inflection), and then silently looks at Jones (probably with a particular kind of facial expression), the observer can unambiguously categorize the event as 'Smith asks Jones a question seeking an explanation of diffusion in a liquid.' Now Smith might describe the event as 'giving Jones a chance to show he knows something', and Jones might describe the event as 'Smith trying to get at me'; but if either of them denied the validity of the observer's description, they would be simply wrong, because the observer would be describing at least part of what the behaviour which occurred means in English in Britain. No assumptions are made here about the effectiveness of classroom communication; but the assumption is made that . . . communication is dependent on the system of conventional meanings available within the wider culture. More fundamentally, this interpretation implies that the systematic observer is concerned with an objective reality (or, if one prefers, a shared inter-subjective reality) of classroom events. This is not to suggest that the subjective meanings of events to participants are not important, but only that these are not accessible to the observer and that *there is an objective reality to classroom activity which does not depend on these meanings* [our emphasis].

Source: McAleese and Hamilton (16).

Strengths of the Ethogenic Approach

The advantages of the ethogenic approach to the educational researcher lie in the distinctive insights that are made available to him through the analysis of accounts of social episodes. The benefits to be derived from the exploration of accounts are best seen by contrasting (17) the ethogenic approach with a more traditional educational technique such as the survey which we discussed in Chapter 4.

There is a good deal of truth in the assertion of the ethogenically-oriented researcher that approaches which employ survey techniques such as the questionnaire take for granted the very things that should be treated as problematic in an educational study. Too often, the phenomena that ought to be the focus of attention are taken as given, that is, they are treated as the starting point of the research rather than becoming the centre of the researcher's interest and effort to discover how the phenomena arose or came to be important in the first place. Numerous educational studies, for example, have identified the incidence and the duration of disciplinary infractions in school; only very recently, however, has the *meaning* of classroom disorder, as opposed to its frequency and type, been subjected to intensive investigation (18). Unlike the survey, which is a cross-sectional technique that takes its data at a single point in time, the ethogenic study employs an on-going observational approach that focuses upon *processes* rather than *products*. Thus it is the process of becoming deviant in school which would capture the attention of the ethogenic researcher rather than the frequency and type of misbehaviour among k types of ability in children located in n kinds of school.

References

1. Harré, R., 'The ethogenic approach: theory and practice' in L. Berkowitz (ed.), *Advances in Experimental Social Psychology*, vol. 10 (Academic Press, New York, 1977).
2. Harré, R., 'Some remarks on "rule" as a scientific concept' in T. Mischel (ed.), *On Understanding Persons* (Basil Blackwell, Oxford, 1974).
3. Harré, R., 'Accounts, actions and meanings – the practice of participatory psychology' in M. Brenner, P. Marsh and M. Brenner (eds), *The Social Context of Method* (Croom Helm, London, 1978).
4. Brown, J. and Sime, J.D., 'Accounts as general methodology', paper presented to the British Psychological Society Conference (University of Exeter, 1977).
5. Kitwood, T.M., 'Values in adolescent life: towards a critical description', unpublished PhD dissertation, School of Research in Education (University of Bradford, 1977).
6. Denscombe, M., 'The social organization of teaching: a study of teaching

as a practical activity in two London comprehensive schools', unpublished PhD dissertation (University of Leicester, 1977).

7. Forgas, J.P., 'The perception of social episodes: categoric and dimensional representations in two different social milieux', *J. Pers. & Soc. Psychol.*, 34, 2 (1976) 199-209.

8. Magnusson, D., 'An analysis of situational dimensions', *Perceptual and Motor Skills*, 32 (1971) 851-67.

9. Ekehammar, B. and Magnusson, D., 'A method to study stressful situations', *J. pers. & soc. Psychol.*, 27, 2 (1973) 176-9.

10. McQuitty, L.L., 'Elementary linkage analysis for isolating orthogonal and oblique types and relevancies', *Educ. & psychol. Meas.*, 17 (1957) 207-29.

11. Forgas, J.P., 'Social episodes and social structure in an academic setting: the social environment of an intact group', *J. exp. soc. Psychol.*, 14 (1978) 434-48.

12. Peevers, B.H. and Secord, P.F., 'Developmental changes in attribution of descriptive concepts to persons', *J. pers. & soc. Psychol.*, 27, 1 (1973) 120-8.

13. Secord, P.F. and Peevers, B.H., 'The development and attribution of person concepts' in T. Mischel (ed.), *On Understanding Persons* (Basil Blackwell, Oxford, 1974).

14. Harré, R., 'Friendship as an accomplishment' in S. Duck (ed.), *Theory and Practice in Interpersonal Attraction* (Academic Press, London, 1977).

15. Menzel, H., 'Meaning – who needs it?' in M. Brenner, P. Marsh and M. Brenner (eds), *The Social Context of Method* (Croom Helm, London, 1978).

16. McIntyre, D. and MacLeod, G., 'The characteristics and uses of systematic classroom observation' in R. McAleese and D. Hamilton (eds), *Understanding Classroom Life* (NFER, Windsor, 1978), pp. 102-31.

17. The discussion at this point draws on that in K.D. Bailey, *Methods of Social Research* (Collier-Macmillan, London, 1978), p. 261.

18. See, for example: Hargreaves, D.H., Hester, S.K. and Mellor, F.J., *Deviance in Classrooms* (Routledge and Kegan Paul, London, 1975); Marsh, P., Rosser, E. and Harré, R., *The Rules of Disorder* (Routledge and Kegan Paul, London, 1978).

11 TRIANGULATION

Introduction

Triangulation may be defined as the use of two or more methods of data collection in the study of some aspect of human behaviour. It is a technique of research to which many subscribe in principle, but which only a minority use in practice. The use of multiple methods, or the multimethod approach as it is sometimes called, contrasts with the ubiquitous but generally more vulnerable single-method approach that characterises so much of research in the social sciences. In its original and literal sense, triangulation is a technique of physical measurement: maritime navigators, military strategists and surveyors, for example, use (or used to use) several locational markers in their endeavours to pinpoint a single spot or objective. By analogy, triangular techniques in the social sciences attempt to map out, or explain more fully, the richness and complexity of human behaviour by studying it from more than one standpoint and, in so doing, by making use of both quantitative and qualitative data.

The advantages of the multimethod approach in social research are manifold and we examine two of them. First, whereas the single observation in fields such as medicine, chemistry and physics normally yields sufficient and unambiguous information on selected phenomena, it provides only a limited view of the complexity of human behaviour and of situations in which human beings interact. It has been observed that as research methods act as filters through which the environment is selectively experienced, they are never atheoretical or neutral in representing the world of experience (1). Exclusive reliance on one method, therefore, may bias or distort the researcher's picture of the particular slice of reality he is investigating. He needs to be confident that the data generated are not simply artefacts of one specific method of collection (2). And this confidence can only be achieved as far as normative research is concerned when different methods of data collection yield substantially the same results. (Where triangulation is used in interpretive research to investigate different actors' viewpoints, the same method, e.g. accounts, will naturally produce different sets of data.) Further, the more the methods contrast with each other, the greater the researcher's confidence. If, for example, the outcomes of a questionnaire survey correspond to those of an observational study of the same phenomena, the more the researcher will be confident about the findings. Or, more extreme, where the results of a rigorous experimental investigation are replicated in, say, a role-playing exercise, the researcher will experience even greater assurance. If findings are artefacts of method, then the use of contrasting methods considerably reduces the chances that any consistent findings are attributable to similarities of method (2).

We come now to a second advantage: some theorists have been sharply critical of the limited use to which existing methods of enquiry in the social sciences have been put. One writer (1), for example, comments, 'Much research has employed particular methods or techniques out of methodological parochialism or ethnocentrism. Methodologists often push particular pet methods either because those are the only ones they have familiarity with, or because they believe their method is superior to all others.' The use of triangular techniques, it is argued, will help to overcome the problem of 'method-boundedness', as it has been termed. One of the earliest scientists to predict such a condition was Boring (3), who wrote:

> as long as a new construct has only the single operational definition that it received at birth, it is just a construct. When it gets two alternative operational definitions, it is beginning to be validated. When the defining operations, because of proven correlations, are many, then it becomes reified.

The following typify the kinds of current problems that critics point to (4): attitude scales are often selected for their convenience and accessibility rather than for their psychological criteria; many studies are culture-bound, that is, they are limited to one country; the vast majority are also time-bound, that is, they are limited to one point in time and do not take into consideration the fact of social change; sociological studies, which by definition imply a macro level of analysis, make excessive use of individuals; and rarely are studies replicated. Criticisms of this sort can be met by taking a more extended view of triangulation which we will consider shortly.

The principle of triangulation is illustrated at its most simple in a typical attitude scale. If you examine the example in Box 11.1, you will find ten items making up an attitude scale measuring a teacher's view of his role. One item, or 'locational marker', by itself will tell us very little about a teacher's attitude in this respect. But ten such related items, or 'locational markers', will give a much fuller picture. Imagine

Box 11.1

A teacher's attitude to his role

The scale below measures the extent to which a teacher interprets his role in either 'educational' or 'academic' terms. In using different 'locational markers', it gives a more representative picture of the respondent's orientation to his role and in so doing illustrates the principle of triangulation in simple form.

1. A teacher should teach informally most of the time.
2. A teacher should be emotionally involved with his pupils.
3. A teacher should use many and varied materials.
4. He should regard scholarly attitudes to be of primary importance for his pupils.
5. He should develop most of the work done in class from the children's own interests.
6. A teacher should get to know children as individuals.
7. A teacher should use corporal punishment.
8. A teacher should look out for children with serious personal problems.
9. A teacher should maintain discipline at all times.
10. A teacher should get his chief satisfaction from interest in his subject or from administrative work in the school, rather than from classroom teaching.

Source: Constructed by David Marsland

now a detailed study of a class of pupils in a secondary school which involves teachers' ratings of pupils, school records, psychometric data, sociometric data, case studies, questionnaires and observation. Add to this the findings of investigations of similar classes in ten other secondary schools and we then have an illustration of the principle of triangulation at a more complex level.

In its use of multiple methods, triangulation may utilise either normative or interpretive techniques; or it may draw on methods from both these approaches and use them in combination.

Types of Triangulation and Their Characteristics

We have just seen how triangulation is characterised by a multimethod approach to a problem in contrast to a single-method approach. Denzin (4) has, however, extended this view of triangulation to take in several other types as well as the multimethod kind which he terms 'methodological triangulation'. These he designates *time triangulation, space triangulation, combined levels of triangulation, theoretical triangulation, investigator triangulation* and — as already noted — *methodological triangulation*. The use of these several types of triangulation goes some way to meet the kinds of methodological criticisms we have already referred to. We now briefly identify the characteristics of each type and refer you to Box 11.2 for a summary of their purpose.

Box 11.2

The principal types of triangulation used in research

1. *Time triangulation*: this type attempts to take into consideration the factors of change and process by utilising cross-sectional and longitudinal designs.

2. *Space triangulation*: this type attempts to overcome the parochialism of studies conducted in the same country or within the same subculture by making use of cross-cultural techniques.

3. *Combined levels of triangulation*: this type uses more than one level of analysis from the three principal levels used in the social sciences, namely, the individual level, the interactive level (groups), and the level of collectivities (organisational, cultural or societal).

4. *Theoretical triangulation*: this type draws upon alternative or competing theories in preference to utilising one viewpoint only.

5. *Investigator triangulation*: this type engages more than one observer.

6. *Methodological triangulation*: this type uses either (a) the same method on different occasions, or (b) different methods on the same object of study.

Source: Based on Denzin's (4) typology

The vast majority of studies in the social sciences are conducted at one point only in time, thereby ignoring the effects of social change and process. *Time triangulation* goes some way to rectifying these omissions by making use of cross-sectional and longitudinal approaches. Cross-sectional studies collect data concerned with time-related processes from different groups at one point in time; longitudinal studies collect data from the same group at different points in the time sequence. The use of panel studies and trend studies may also be mentioned in this connection. The former compare the *same* measurements for the *same* individuals in a sample at several *different* points in time; and the latter examine selected processes continually over time. The weaknesses of each of these methods can be strengthened by using a combined approach to a given problem (see p. 50).

Space triangulation attempts to overcome the limitations of studies conducted within one culture or subculture. As one writer (1) says, 'Not only are the behavioural sciences culture-bound, they are sub-culture-bound. Yet many such scholarly works are written as if basic principles have been discovered which would hold true as tendencies in any society, anywhere, anytime.' Cross-cultural studies may involve the testing of theories among different people, as in recent cross-cultural studies in Piagetian and Freudian psychology; or they may measure differences between populations by using several different measuring instruments. Levine (5) describes how he used this strategy of convergent validation in his comparative studies:

> I have studied differences of achievement motivation among three Nigerian ethnic groups by the analysis of dream reports, written expressions of values, and public opinion survey data. The convergence of findings from the diverse set of data (and samples) strengthens my conviction . . . that the differences among the groups are not artifacts produced by measuring instruments.

Social scientists are concerned in their research with the individual, the group and society. These reflect the *three levels of analysis* adopted by researchers in their work. Those who are critical of much present-day research argue that some of it uses the wrong level of analysis — individual when it should be societal, for instance — or limits itself to one level only when a more meaningful picture would emerge by using more than one level. Smith (1) extends this analysis and identifies seven possible levels: the aggregative or individual level and six levels that are more global in that 'they characterize the collective as a whole, and do not derive from an accumulation of individual characteristics'.

The six include: (1) group analysis (the interaction patterns of individuals and groups); (2) organisational units of analysis (units which have qualities not possessed by the individuals making them up); (3) institutional analysis (relationships within and across the legal, political, economic and familial institutions of society); (4) ecological analysis (concerned with spatial explanation); (5) cultural analysis (concerned with the norms, values, practices, traditions and ideologies of a culture); and (6) societal analysis (concerned with gross factors such as urbanisation, industrialisation, education, wealth, etc.).

Where possible, studies combining *several* levels of analysis are to be preferred.

Researchers are sometimes taken to task for their rigid adherence to one particular theory or theoretical orientation to the exclusion of competing theories. Thus, advocates of Piaget's developmental theory of cognition rarely take into consideration Freud's psychoanalytic theory of development in their work; and Gestaltists work without reference to S–R theorists. Few published works, as Smith (1) points out, even go as far as to discuss alternative theories after a study in the light of methods used, much less consider alternatives prior to the research. As he recommends, 'The investigator should be more active in designing his research so that competing theories can be tested. Research which tests competing theories will normally call for a wider range of research techniques than has historically been the case; this virtually assures more confidence in the data analysis since it is more oriented towards the testing of rival hypotheses.'

Investigator triangulation refers to the use of more than one observer (or participant) in a research setting. Observers and participants working on their own each have their own observational styles and this is reflected in the resulting data. The careful use of two or more observers or participants independently, therefore, can lead to more valid and reliable data. Smith comments:

> Perhaps the greatest use of investigator triangulation centres around validity rather than reliability checks. More to the point, investigators with differing perspectives or paradigmatic biases may be used to check out the extent of divergence in the data each collects. Under such conditions if data divergence is minimal then one may feel more confident in the data's validity. On the other hand, if their data is significantly different, then one has an idea as to possible sources of biased measurement which should be further investigated.

We have already considered methodological triangulation in our introduction. Denzin identifies two categories in his typology: *within methods* triangulation and *between methods* triangulation. Triangulation *within methods* concerns the *replication* of a study as a check on reliability and theory confirmation (1). Triangulation *between methods*, as we have seen, involves the use of more than one method in the pursuit of a given objective. As a check on validity, the *between methods* approach embraces the notion of convergence between independent measures of the same objective as has been defined by Campbell and Fiske (6).

Occasions When Triangulation is Particularly Appropriate

Having outlined the principle of triangulation and described the types and their characteristics, we now consider the occasions when the technique is particularly appropriate and in so doing will be mainly concerned with the field of education. So complex and involved is the teaching–learning process in the context of the school that the single-method approach yields only limited and sometimes misleading data. Yet, ironically, this is the method that figures most in educational research. It is only comparatively recently that the utility of the multiple-method approach has come to be appreciated. Of the six categories of triangulation in Denzin's typology, something like four have been used in education. These are: time triangulation with its longitudinal and cross-sectional studies; space triangulation as on the occasions when a number of schools in an area or across the country are investigated in some way (7); investigator triangulation as when a team of inspectors visits and reports on a school or sample of schools (8); and methodological triangulation. Of these four, methodological triangulation is the one used most frequently and the one that possibly has the most to offer. All four approaches, however, present practical and financial obstacles to researchers and sponsors.

The following are instances of where the multiple-method approach in educational settings is appropriate:

1. Triangular techniques are suitable when a more holistic view of *educational outcomes* is sought. Isaac and Michael (9), for example, quote a study by Cronbach which investigated the effects of praise and blame on the outcomes of reading instruction. No significant differences were found among the various groups on the criterion of *gain in reading*. It was suggested that had a second criterion been used, such as *attitudes towards reading*, a significant treatment difference might have been found. The authors comment, 'Most research of this kind looks at an achievement or skill outcome rather than the development of attitudes. The failure of people to choose to read following their formal educa-tion, or to choose mathematics in their higher education, given the skill development to do both, strongly suggests that a counter-current of *negative attitudes* to avoid these experiences lies hidden underneath.'

2. Triangulation has special relevance where a *complex phenomena* requires elucidation. Imagine a comparative study of a formal and an informal classroom. Because of the contrasting philosophies, objectives and practices in the two classes, a single-method approach — say a measure of achievement in basic skills — would provide data of very limited value in that it would in no way reflect the more subtle,

intangible features and the non-academic factors distinguishing the two classrooms. The adoption of the multimethod approach would give a very different picture. Box 11.3 gives some suggested methods for tackling this kind of problem. The combination of academic criteria (achievement tests, record cards, assessment of class work) and non-academic factors (attitudes of children and teachers, relationships, interview data and observation by a researcher) will generate a fuller and more realistic view of the respective classes and thus enable the investigators to talk about them on a comparative basis.

Box 11.3

A multimethod approach to the study of two top-junior classes: one taught formally; the other, informally

Objective: To investigate the practices, interactions, climates and out-comes of a formal and informal classroom in two junior schools over the period of one term.

Methods:
1. Measures of achievement in reading, written language and maths.
2. Analysis and classification of children's written and practical work.
3. Classroom observation.
4. Examination of records.
5. Tests of attitudes of children to school and school work.
6. Tests of attitudes of teachers to respective teaching methods.
7. Interviews with samples of children
8. Interviews with teachers.

3. Triangulation is also appropriate when *different methods of teaching* are to be evaluated. Isaac and Michael also quote a study by Brownell comparing four methods of teaching subtraction. He found only small differences both on a *skill criterion* and on a *retention criterion* but clearly superior results favouring one method over all others when he measured transfer to a new process. Had he limited himself to a skill or retention criterion only, this valuable transfer criterion would have remained undisclosed.

4. Multiple methods are suitable where a *controversial aspect of education* needs to be evaluated more fully. The issue of comprehensive schools, for example, has been hotly debated since their inception; yet even at this point there has been little serious research investigating

these institutions as totalities. It is not sufficient to judge these schools solely on the grounds of academic achievement with 'league tables' based on O- and A-level results, important as these are. A much more rounded portrayal of these institutions is required and here is a clear case for the advocacy of multiple methods. These could measure and investigate factors such as academic achievement, teaching methods, practical skills, cultural interests, social skills, interpersonal relationships, community spirit and so on. Validity could then be greatly increased by researching a large sample of schools (space triangulation) for, say, once a year over a period of five years (time triangulation).

5. Triangulation is useful when an established approach yields a limited and frequently distorted picture. We are reminded here of the traditional dichotomies — normative v. interpretive, nomothetic v. ideographic, statistical v. clinical. The first of each pairing is associated with groups and more objective scientific data; the second, with individuals and subjective data. Again, by using, or drawing from, each of these usually mutually exclusive categories, contrasting perspectives are disclosed.

Some Issues and Problems

Three broad questions confront the researcher contemplating a multimethod approach to a problem: Which methods are to be selected? How are they to be combined? And how are the data to be used?

As far as the first question is concerned — which methods are to be selected — we take it as axiomatic that any one method can be efficient, less efficient or inefficient depending on the kind of information desired and the context of the research. Where a researcher seeks information from which his inferences can be generalised to wider populations, methods yielding statistical data will be most efficient. Where he looks for information representing a personal or phenomenological perspective, or process rather than product, accounts or interviews will meet his need more successfully. If he wants to integrate objective and subjective perspectives, he will use contrasting methods. The first task, therefore, will be to decide *what kinds* of information the researcher wants and, further, what he is to do with it. Perhaps he might want to raise educational standards, introduce correctives, make modifications, or merely acquire a fuller understanding of some situation. The next stage is to decide the most appropriate methods (or sources) for providing this information. To make all this more comprehensible, we have given a hypothetical example in Box 11.4. Imagine a researcher wanting to compare a formal and an informal classroom in two junior schools with particular reference to academic and non-academic factors, children's personality characteristics, social behaviour and classroom climates. The left-hand vertical column itemises the *kinds* of information he wants from each classroom — knowledge of the class's academic skills, children's personality characteristics and so on. The top horizontal row identifies the total number of methods (or sources) in respect of the information sought. Broadly speaking, the first four methods itemised yield quantifiable data (1–4); and the remaining four, non-quantifiable data (5–8). The system of double and single crosses illustrates the methods most efficient and the methods most supportive of these respectively so that, for example, the perspective of the individual pupil will best be expressed through an attitude questionnaire, a taped account of his view of classroom life, and an interview. So to return to our original question, the researcher will combine those methods (or sources) that will, in complementing each other, build up as full a picture of the areas he is investigating as time and facilities permit. You will notice that the combined methods approach may break down the traditional barriers between the normative and the interpretive approaches, the ideographic and the nomothetic, and the statistical and clinical.

No simple directive can be given for the question, how are the methods to be combined, for the answer will depend to a great extent on the objectives of the study, the particular situation, and the relative *weightings* which the researcher considers desirable to assign to the methods providing him with data. To take the issue of weightings further, in some schools, for example, teachers' assessments of pupil achievement (Box 11.4, column 8) will serve merely as glosses on formal examinations of academic achievement. In others, by contrast, teachers' opinions may play a much more decisive part in such assessments. These are the kinds of factors affecting a researcher's weightings. The crucial factor when it comes to integrating or contrasting the data and drawing inferences from them is the researcher's own judgement.

The third question, how are the data to be used, will depend on the researcher's original objectives in undertaking the study, his choice of methods and the kinds of data he accumulates. He will attempt, for instance, to impose some kind of meaning on *normative* or *quantifiable* data, possibly in line with a favoured theory or hypothesis. With *interpretive* or *qualitative* data, however, he will endeavour to draw meanings or explanations from the data themselves or, where appropriate, negotiate meanings with the subjects who are their source. Two kinds of problems face him here: (1) those stemming from inconsistencies

Box 11.4 Kinds of information sought and methods for obtaining them

Kinds of information	Methods used	1 Achievement tests	2 Personality tests	3 Attitude tests	4 Sociometric tests	5 Participant observation	6 Interviewing	7 Accounts	8 Teachers' assessments
1 Academic skills		xx							xx
2 Personality characteristics			xx			x	x		xx
3 Social skills				x		xx	x		xx
4 Social relationships				x	xx	xx	x		xx
5 Individual pupil viewpoint				xx			x	xx	
6 Classroom climate						xx			x

xx = most efficient means;
x = supportive means.

between quantified measures because of weaknesses in available measuring instruments; and (2) differences between quantifiable and qualitative data, or between different sets of qualitative data. The first calls for more refined and valid instrumentation; the second, an imaginative leap. The lurking danger in the case of the second problem is that of presenting discrepant sets of data in the form of a collage. Naturally enough, it is not to be expected that complete consensus among data can or should be achieved. Indeed, the very burden of the interpretive approach is that different actors in a situation will have different meanings and that each meaning is equally valid. What is required, however, is that some attempt be made to relate incongruent sets of data in some way or other. Accounting for differences would be one way; using them as a basis for further hypotheses, another.

Procedures

We now outline a possible sequence of procedures for implementing a multimethod approach to a chosen problem. The first stage is to select an area of interest and then to formulate a specific *research problem* or a *set of research objectives* within this general framework so as to reduce the scope of the project to manageable proportions. The second stage will be concerned with the more practical aspects of the research — choosing a school or setting, administrative or organisational factors, financial requirements and procedural problems. The third stage will involve decisions concerning the extent and range of information required so as to meet the research objectives or to solve the problems stated. The aim here will be to provide a balanced framework within which to operate. The fourth stage will be concerned with the choice of methods or sources necessary to provide the information desired. This will involve listing the possibilities and setting them against the kinds of information required so as to get a total picture of which ones will be efficient, which supportive and which unsuitable. It is at this point that the researcher will need to decide the extent to which he will seek quantifiable and/or non-quantifiable data, or use individual and/or group responses, for example. This stage will also be a suitable point in the sequence of procedures to consider the respective weightings that are to be given to the chosen methods. The fifth stage will involve implementing the research, and this will include collecting and analysing the data. The sixth and final stage will be the point where the data are interpreted and inferences drawn.

Examples of the Use of Triangular Techniques in Educational Research

In conclusion, we refer to two instances of the use of triangulation in educational research. The first is a literal application of the technique at its simplest; and the second, an excellent example of the multiple method approach.

In the first example, triangulation was used as part of the Ford Teaching Project one of the purposes of which was to make explicit from the teachers' and pupils' viewpoints the problems inherent in attempting enquiry/discovery methods of learning. The method was applied to episodes of classroom interaction between pupils and teachers. The procedure was to collect and analyse viewpoints on the episodes from three participants — the teachers, the pupils and the participant observer. As Walker and MacDonald (10) have explained in this connection:

> The process of gathering accounts from three distinct standpoints has an epistemological justification. Each point of the triangle stands in a unique epistemological position with respect to access to relevant data about a teaching situation. The teacher is in the best position to gain access via introspection to his own intentions and aims in the situation. The students are in the best position to explain how the teacher's actions influence the way they respond to the situation. The participant-observer is in the best position to collect data about the observable features of the interaction between teachers and pupils. By comparing his own account with accounts from the other two standpoints a person at one point of the triangle has an opportunity to test and perhaps revise it on the basis of more sufficient data.

The procedure consisted of three stages: (1) recording the original activity or episode; (2) playing back the recordings to the teachers and pupils in turn and eliciting their comments and explanations of what took place. To these interviews were added the observer's interpretation for further comment and discussion; and (3) eliciting teachers' views on playbacks of the pupils' accounts. The researchers themselves (11) say:

> As the project attempted to encourage teachers to monitor their own actions, the choice of triangulation seemed appropriate. The teachers or pupils may intend an action (including talk) to have a particular meaning, but how the recipient interprets the action is

Box 11.5

Extract from the researcher's interview with pupils

Pupil   But he wouldn't ask you what you think your conclusions were,
             he'll put his own conclusion up on the board, and you have to
             write it. He says do you agree, not always but he don't want to
             rub it off so you just say yes to keep him quiet.

Observer   You say yes to keep him quiet?

Pupil   Keep him happy . . .

Observer   There was a time when he said he was making a guess and he
             asked you if you agreed whether it was a reasonable guess. I
             don't know if you remember that?

Pupils   Yes.

Observer   And one person said yes and everybody else kept quiet. Now
             what I want to know is whether the person who said yes really
             did agree with him or just said yes because they thought he
             wanted them to say yes, and why everybody else kept quiet?

Pupil   Well he would have liked us to say yes, really, 'cause I mean you
             could see it.

Pupil   If you'd said no you waste time arguing wouldn't you.

Pupil   Yeh, if you ever say no he'll stand there and just keep on and on.

Pupil   He'll keep on till you come to his way of thinking.

Pupil   So it's best to say yes to start with.

Observer   So even if you did disagree when he said 'Do you all agree?' you
             wouldn't.

Pupil   If you said no he'd keep on to you until you said yes.

Pupil   If you said no he's going to say why not.

Pupil   And if you argued with him he'd come round to the same point
             where you left off.

Pupil   Back to his way of thinking.

Source: Quoted, along with other extracts, in Walker and MacDonald (10)

another matter. In spite of miscommunication, the classroom
inhabitants have a remarkable ability to 'remedy' or 'fill-in' the
action so that it makes sense to them. Through recording lessons,
selecting portions and playing them back to pupils with questions
like 'what did you understand the teacher to mean?', and playing
these back to the teacher, a simple but powerful technique was put
into operation.

One of the outcomes of the study was that the triangulation data convinced the teacher that in spite of his professed aspirations to implement enquiry/discovery methods his teaching was in fact formal/structured/directed and that behaviours like 'Do you all agree with that?' deliberately fostered his pupils' dependence on his authority position (10). As Walker explains, 'Having clarified and tested the theory implicit in his practice in this way he later dramatically switched to an unstructured/open-ended approach which he hoped would protect the self-directed learning of his pupils. His conscious switch to a new teaching approach reflected the development of a new theory, the applicability of which would require further self-monitoring.' Box 11.5 contains a short extract from a researcher's interview with pupils. For further extracts, we refer you to the reference cited.

It can be seen from this brief review that triangulation enables the teacher to make some assessment of his ability to self-monitor his teaching situation and was a significant way of constructing classroom realities.

Our second example is drawn from an ongoing research project into mixed ability teaching being conducted by a research team from the National Foundation of Educational Research.

It is the second phase of the project that is utilising the multimethod approach. Being a detailed study of some of the major issues in mixed ability teaching (12), it is concerned with: (1) organisation, preparation and in-service training for mixed ability teaching; (2) classroom methods and organisation; (3) the more able pupil — an examination of methods adopted to help him achieve in accordance with his capabilities; (4) the less able pupil — a study of strategies used to cater for his needs in a mixed ability class; (5) the implications of mixed ability teaching for methods of assessment; and (6) subject differences — the objectives and approaches employed by teachers in two subject areas (English and modern languages) where teachers' attitudes are known to differ, are being examined with a view to identifying factors associated with the ease or difficulty with which a subject can effectively be taught to mixed ability classes.

While a triangular approach is being used towards the project as a whole, units of investigation within the main project are also being subjected to a multimethod approach. For instance, one first-year class has been selected for detailed study in each school and three kinds of evidence are being sought: these arise from (1) the written material produced in class, (2) the observation of classes during group work, and (3) discussions with the teachers of the selected classes. For further details of this undertaking and of the instruments and schedules used, we refer you to the Foundation's report on the project.

References

1. Smith, H.W., *Strategies of Social Research: The Methodological Imagination* (Prentice Hall, London, 1975).
2. Lin, Nan, *Foundations of Social Research* (McGraw Hill, New York, 1976).
3. Boring, E.G., 'The role of theory in experimental psychology', *Amer. J. Psychol.*, 66 (1953) 169-84.
4. Denzin, N.K., *The Research Act in Sociology: A Theoretical Introduction to Sociological Method* (The Butterworth Group, London, 1970).
5. Levine, R.A., 'Towards a psychology of populations: the cross-cultural study of personality', *Human Development* 3 (1966) 30-46.
6. Campbell, D.T. and Fiske, D., 'Convergent and discriminant validation by the multi-trait multimethod matrix', *Psychol, Bull.*, 56 (1959) 81-105.
7. For example: Bennett, N., *Teaching Styles and Pupil Progress* (Open Books, London, 1975).
8. For example: Department of Education and Science, *Primary Education in England* (HMSO, London, 1978).
9. Isaac, S. and Michael, W.B., *Handbook in Research and Evaluation* (R.R. Knapp, California, 1971).
10. Walker, R. and MacDonald, B., *Curriculum Innovation at School Level*, (E 203. Units 27 and 28) (The Open University Press, Bletchley, 1976).
11. Adelman, C. and Walker, R., 'Developing pictures for other frames: action research and case study', in G. Chanan and S. Delamont (eds), *Frontiers of Classroom Research*, (NFER, 1975).
12. NFER, Research Project on Mixed Ability Teaching (ongoing project).

12 ROLE-PLAYING

Introduction

Much current discussion of role-playing occurs within the context of a protracted and continuing debate over the use of deception in experimental social psychology. Inevitably therefore, the following account of role-playing as a research tool involves some detailed comment on the 'deception' versus 'honesty' controversy. But role-playing has a much longer history of use in the social sciences than as a substitute for deceit. It has been employed for decades in assessing personality, in business training and in psychotherapy (1). In this latter connection, role-playing was introduced to the United States as a therapeutic procedure by Moreno in the 1930s. His group therapy sessions were called 'psychodrama', and in various forms they spread to the group dynamics movement which was developing in America in the 1950s. Current interest in encounter sessions and sensitivity training can be traced back to the impact of the originator of studies in role-taking and role-enactment, J.L. Moreno.

The focus of the present chapter is on the use of role-playing as a technique of educational research. Role-playing is defined as participation in simulated social situations that are intended to throw light upon the role/rule contexts governing 'real' life social episodes. The present discussion aims to extend some of the ideas set out in Chapter 10 which dealt with account gathering and analysis. We begin by itemising a number of role-playing methods that have been reported in the literature.

Various role-play methods have been identified by Hamilton (2) and differentiated in terms of a *passive-active* distinction. Thus, an individual may role play merely by reading a description of a social episode and filling in a questionnaire about it; on the other hand, a person may role play by being required to improvise a characterisation and perform it in front of an audience. This *passive-active* continuum, Hamilton notes, glosses over three important analytical distinctions.

First, the individual may be asked simply to imagine a situation or actually to perform it. Hamilton terms this an *imaginary-performed* situation. Second, in connection with performed role play, he distinguishes between structured and unstructured activities, the difference depending upon whether the individual is restricted by the experimenter to present forms or lines. This Hamilton calls a *scripted-improvised* distinction. And third, the participant's activities may be verbal responses, usually of the paper and pencil variety, or behavioural, involving something much more akin to acting. This distinction is termed *verbal-behavioural*. Turning next to the content of role play, Hamilton distinguishes between relatively involving or uninvolving contents, that is, where a subject is required to act or to imagine *himself* in a situation or, alternatively, to react as he believes *another* person would in those circumstances, the basic issue here being what *person* the subject is supposed to portray. Furthermore, in connection with the role in which the person is placed, Hamilton differentiates beween studies that assign the individual to the role of laboratory subject and those that place him in any other role. Finally, the content of the role play is seen to include the *context* of the acted or the imagined performance, that is, the elaborateness of the scenario, the involvement of other actors, and the presence or absence of an audience. The various dimensions of role-play methods identified by Hamilton are set out in Box 12.1. To illustrate the extremes of the range in the role-playing methods identified in Box 12.1 we have selected two studies, the first of which is *passive*, *imaginary* and *verbal*, typical of the way in which role-playing is often introduced to pupils; the second is *active*, *performed* and *behavioural*, involving an elaborate scenario and the participation of numerous other actors.

In a lesson designed to develop empathising skills (3), a number of magazine pictures were selected. The pictures included easily observed clues that served as the basis for inferring an emotion or a situation. Some pictures showed only the face of an individual, others depicted one or more persons in a particular social setting. The pictures exhibited a variety of emotions such as anger, fear, compassion, anxiety and joy. Pupils were asked to look carefully at a particular picture and then to respond to questions that included or were similar to those in Box 12.2.

The second example of a role-playing study is the well-known Stanford Prison experiment carried out by Zimbardo and his associates (4), a brief overview of which is given in Box 12.3.

Enthusiasts of role-playing as a research methodology cite experiments such as the Stanford Prison study to support their claim that where realism and spontaneity can be introduced into role play, then such experimental conditions do, in fact, simulate both symbolically and phenomenologically, the real-life analogues that they purport to

Box 12.1

Dimensions of role-play methods			
FORM		CONTENT	
Set: imaginary v.	performed	*Person:* self v. another	
Action:	scripted v. improvised	*Role:* subject role v. another role	
Dependent variables: verbal	verbal v. behavioural	*Context:*	scenario other actors audience

Source: Adapted from Hamilton (2)

Box 12.2.

Developing empathising skills

1. How do you think the individual (s) is (are) feeling?

2. Why do you think this is? (Encourage students to be specific about observations from which they infer emotions. Distinguish between observations and inferences.)

3. Might the person (s) be feeling a different emotion than the one you inferred? Give an example.

4. Have you ever felt this way? Why?

5. What do you think might happen next to this person?

6. If you inferred an unpleasant emotion, what possible action might the person (s) take in order to feel better?

Source Rogers and Atwood (3)

Box 12.3

The Stanford Prison experiment

The study was conducted in the summer of 1971 in a mock prison constructed in the basement of the psychology building at Stanford University. The subjects were selected from a pool of 75 respondents to a newspaper advertisement asking for paid volunteers to participate in a psychological study of prison life. On a random basis half of the subjects were assigned to the role of guard and half to the role of prisoner. Prior to the experiment subjects were asked to sign a form, agreeing to play either the prisoner or the guard role for a maximum of two weeks. Those assigned to the prisoner role should expect to be under surveillance, to be harassed, but not to be physically abused. In return, subjects would be adequately fed, clothed and housed and would receive 15 dollars per day for the duration of the experiment.

The outcome of the study was quite dramatic. In less than two days after the initiation of the experiment, violence and rebellion broke out. The prisoners ripped off their clothing and their identification numbers and barricaded themselves inside the cells while shouting and cursing at the guards. The guards, in turn, began to harass, humiliate and intimidate the prisoners. They used sophisticated psychological techniques to break the solidarity among the inmates and to create a sense of distrust among them. In less than 36 hours one of the prisoners showed severe symptoms of emotional disturbance, uncontrollable crying and screaming and was released. On the third day, a rumour developed about a mass escape plot. The guards increased their harassment, intimidation and brutality toward the prisoners. On the fourth day, two prisoners showed symptoms of severe emotional disturbance and were released. On the fifth day, the prisoners showed symptoms of individual and group disintegration. They had become mostly passive and docile, suffering from an acute loss of contact with reality. The guards on the other hand, had kept up their harassment, some behaving sadistically. Because of the unexpectedly intense reactions generated by the mock prison experience, the experimenters terminated the study at the end of the sixth day.

Source: Adapted from Banuazizi and Movahedi (5)

represent. Advocates of role play would concur with the conclusions of Zimbardo and his associates that the simulated prison developed into a psychologically compelling prison environment (4) and they, too, would infer that the dramatic differences in the behaviour of prisoners and guards arose out of their location in different positions within the institutional structure of the prison and the social psychological conditions that prevailed there rather than from personality differences between the two groups of subjects (5).

On the other hand, the passive, imaginary role play required of subjects taking part in the lesson cited in the first example has been the focus of much of the criticism levelled at role-playing as a research technique. Ginsburg (1) summarises the argument against role-playing as a device for generating scientific knowledge:

1. role-playing is unreal with respect to the variables under study in that the subject reports what he *would do**, and that is taken as though he did do it.
2. the behaviour displayed is not spontaneous even in the more active forms of role-playing.
3. the verbal reports in role-playing are very susceptible to artefactual influence such as social desirability.
4. role-playing procedures are not sensitive to complex interactions whereas deception designs are.

In general, Ginsburg (1) concludes, critics of role-playing view science as involving the discovery of natural truths and they contend that role-playing simply cannot substitute for deception — a sad but unavoidable state of affairs.

Role-playing Versus Deception: the Argument

As we shall shortly see, those who support role-playing as a legitimate scientific technique for systematic research into human social behaviour reject such criticisms by offering role-playing alternatives to deception studies of phenomena such as destructive obedience to authority and to conventional research in, for example, the area of attitude formation and change.

The objections to the current widespread use of deception in experimental research are articulated as follows:

1. Lying, cheating and deceiving contradict the norms that we typically try to apply in our everyday social interactions. The use of deception in the study of interpersonal relations is equally reprehensible. In a word, deception is unethical.
2. The use of deception is epistemologically unsound because it rests upon the acceptance of a less than adequate model of the subject *as a person*. Deception studies generally try to exclude the human capacities of the subject for choice and self-presentation. They tend therefore to focus upon 'incidental' social behaviour, that is,

---

* However, this is not what advocates of role play as an alternative to deception generally mean by role play. See Hamilton (2) and Forward, Canter and Kirsch (6) for a fuller discussion.

behaviours that are *outside* of the subject's field of choice, intention and self-presentation that typically constitute the main focus of social activity among human actors (6).

3. The use of deception is methodologically unsound. Deception research depends upon a continuing supply of subjects who are naive to the intentions of researchers. But word soon gets round and potential subjects come to expect that they will be deceived. It is a fair guess that most subjects are suspicious and distrustful of psychological research despite the best intentions of deception researchers.

Finally, advocates of role-playing methods deplore the common practice of comparing the outcomes of role-playing replications against the standard of their deception study equivalents as a means of evaluating the relative validity of the two methods. The results of role-playing and deception, it is argued (6), are not directly comparable since role-playing introduces a far wider range of human behaviour into experiments. If comparisons are to be made, then role-playing results should provide the yardstick against which deception study data are measured and not the other way round as is generally the case. We invite readers to follow this last piece of advice and to judge the well-known experiments of Milgram (7) on destructive obedience to authority against their role-playing replications by Mixon (8, 9).

Role-playing Versus Deception: the Evidence

Milgram's Obedience-to-authority Experiments

In a series of studies from 1963 to 1974, Milgram carried out numerous variations on a basic obedience experiment which involved individuals acting, one at a time, as 'teachers' of another subject (who was, in reality, a confederate of the experimenter). Teachers were required to administer electric shocks of increasing severity every time the learner failed to make a correct response to a verbal learning task. Over the years, Milgram involved over 1,000 subjects in the experiment — subjects, incidentally, who were drawn from all walks of life rather than from undergraduate psychology classes. Summarising his findings, Milgram (7) reported that typically some 67 per cent of his teachers delivered the maximum electric shock to the learner despite the fact that such a degree of severity was clearly labelled as highly dangerous to the physical well-being of the person on the receiving end.

Milgram's explanation of destructive obedience to authority is summarised in Box 12.4.

Box 12.4

Obedience to authority: an explanation

Milgram believes that an orientation to obedience to authority essentially
follows from the hierarchical organisation of all sorts of social systems.
Social hierarchy, he argues, is a form of organisation that has repeatedly
evolved in animal species because it promotes the survival of the species.
For human beings, too, various forms of social hierarchy have survival
value. When the individual operates in a hierarchy, he cedes control to
superior persons who co-ordinate the system. Since system coherence must
be the most important consideration in a hierarchy, the individual in the
hierarchy must be able to operate in what Milgram calls the *agentic mode*.
'The person entering into an authority system', Milgram explains, 'no
'no longer views himself as acting out of his own purposes but rather comes to
see himself as an agent for executing the wishes of another person.' Milgram's
experiments on obedience are said to reveal some of the factors that trigger the
agentic frame of mind.

Source: Adapted from Brown and Herrnstein (10)

Mixon's Role-playing Replications of the Milgram Experiment

Mixon's starting point was a disaffection for the deceit that played such
an important part in generating emotional stress in Milgram's subjects,
and a desire to explore alternative approaches to the study of destructive obedience to authority. Since Milgram's dependent variable was
a rule-governed action, Mixon (8) reasoned, the rule-governed behaviour
of Milgram's subjects could have been uniform or predictable. But it
was not. Why, then, did some of Milgram's subjects obey and some defy
the experimenter's instructions? The situation, Mixon notes, seemed
perfectly clear to most commentators; the command to administer an
electric shock appeared to be obviously immoral and all subjects *should*
therefore have disobeyed the experimenter. If defiance was so obviously
called for when looking at the experiment from the outside, why, asks
Mixon, was it not obvious to those taking part on the inside? Mixon
found a complete script of Milgram's experiment and proceeded to
transform it (8) into an active role-playing exercise.

One of the first things I did was to take the role of the naive subject
in order to look at the scene through his eyes. Later I took the roles
of both experimenter and victim and repeated the scene over and
over again using a different person each time in the role of naive
subject. The repetition allowed me to become thoroughly familiar
with each detail of the scene and by changing actors I was able to

question many people about what was going on.

Mixon's role-playing replication of the Milgram experiment involved an exploratory method that he calls the 'all-or-none' technique, an account of which is given in Box 12.5.

Box 12.5

Milgram's experiment: an alternative explanation

The 'all-or-none' method utilised continuous interaction and feedback from participants in the role-playing replication. Mixon succeeded in constructing several versions of the Milgram 'script' and produced the full range of possible obedience responses ranging from 0 per cent to 100 per cent. By exploring and specifying the particular meanings attributed to variations in the role/rule context of 'legitimate authority in experiments', and by being able to produce and observe the whole range of possible obedience responses, Mixon was better able to claim that he had an adequate conceptualisation and description of obedience in this particular social context.

Source: Adapted from Forward, Canter and Kirsch (6)

But let Mixon (8) speak for himself:

Previous interpretations [of the Milgram data] have rested on the assumption that obedient subjects helplessly performed an obviously immoral act. From the outside the situation seemed clear. It was otherwise to the actors. The actors in my role playing version could not understand why the experimenter behaved as if feedback from the 'victim' was unimportant. The feedback suggested that something serious had occurred, that something had gone badly wrong with the experiment. The experimenter behaved as if nothing serious had or could happen. The experimenter in effect contradicted the evidence that otherwise seemed so clearly to suggest that the 'victim' was in serious trouble . . . Using the 'all-or-none' method I found that when it became perfectly clear that the experimenter believed the 'victim' was being seriously harmed all actors indicated defiance to experimental commands. Briefly summarized, the 'all-or-none' analysis suggests that people will obey seemingly inhumane experimental commands so long as there is no good reason to think experimental safeguards have broken down; people will defy seemingly inhumane experimental commands when it becomes clear that safeguards have broken down — when consequences may indeed be what they appear to be. *When the experimental situation is confusing and mystifying as in Milgram's study, some people will obey and some will defy experimental commands* [our emphasis].

We leave readers to compare Mixon's explanations with Milgram's account set out in Box 12.4.

In summary, sophisticated role-playing methods such as those used by Mixon offer exciting possibilities to the educational researcher. They avoid the disadvantages of deception designs yet are able to incorporate many of the standard features of experiments such as constructing experimental conditions across factors of interest (in the Mixon studies for example, using scripts that vary the states of given role/rule contexts), randomly assigning actors to conditions as a way of randomising out individual differences, using repeated-measures designs, and standardising scripts and procedures to allow for replication of studies (6).

Despite what has just been said about the possibilities of incorporating experimental features into role-playing research, empirical studies have more commonly employed role-playing methodologies in exploratory rather than experimental settings, Harré and Secord (11) distinguish between *exploration* and *experiment* as follows.

Whereas the experiment is employed to test the authenticity of what is known, exploration serves quite a different purpose (11): 'In exploratory studies, a scientist has no very clear idea of what will happen, and aims to find out. He has a feeling for the direction in which to go . . . but no clear expectations of what to expect. He is not confirming or refuting hypotheses.' Increasingly, exploratory (as opposed to experimental) research into human social behaviour is turning to role-playing methodologies. The reason is plain enough. Where the primary objective of such research is the identification and elucidation of the role/rule frameworks governing social interaction, *informed* rather than *deceived* subjects are essential if the necessary data on how they genuinely think and feel are to be made available to the researcher. Contrast the position of the fully participating, informed subject in such research with that of the deceived subject under the more usual experimental conditions. Argyris's (12) experimenter speaks to his subject thus:

I want to design the environment in such a way that when you enter it, I will have done my best to have induced you to behave as I predicted you would. However, I must be certain that if you behaved in the way I predicted you would, it was because you wanted to, because it made sense to you to do so, because the choice was genuinely yours. In order to maximise this possibility, I must design the entire experiment rigorously and keep all of the key elements of the design secret from you until you have finished participating in it. Also I cannot permit or encourage you to learn (ahead of time or during the experiment) anything about the experiment. I cannot encourage you to confront it, or to alter it. The only learning that I permit is learning that remains within the purposes of the experiment.

It can be argued that many of the more pressing social problems that society faces today arise out of our current ignorance of the role/rule frameworks governing human interactions in diverse social settings. If this is the case, then role-playing techniques could offer the possibility of a greater insight into the natural episodes of human behaviour that they seek to elucidate than the burgeoning amount of experimental data already at hand. The danger may lie in too much being expected of role-playing as a key to such knowledge. Ginsburg (1) offers a timely warning. Role-playing, he urges, should be seen as a complement to conventional experiments, survey research and field observations. That is, it is an important addition to our investigative armamentarium, *not* a replacement.

Role-playing in Educational Settings

Role-playing, gaming and machine or computer simulation are three strands of development in simulation studies that have only recently found their way into British classrooms (13). Their discovery and introduction into primary and secondary schools in the late 1960s is somewhat surprising in view of the unqualified support that distinguished educational theorists from Plato onwards have accorded to the value of play and games in education (14).

The distinction between these three types of simulation — role-playing, games and machines/computers — is by no means clear-cut; for example, simulation games often contain role-playing activities and may be designed with computer back-up services to expedite their procedures (13).

In this section we focus particularly upon role-playing aspects of simulation, beginning with some brief observations on the purposes of role-playing in classroom settings and some practical suggestions directed towards the less experienced practitioners of role-playing methods.

The Uses of Role-playing

Van Ments (15) classifies the uses of role-playing as:

(1) *developing sensitivity and awareness*. The definitions of positions such as mother, teacher, policeman and priest, for example, explicitly or implicitly incorporate various role characteristics which often lead to the stereotyping of position occupants. Role-playing provides a means of exploring such stereotypes and developing a deeper understanding of the point of view and feelings of someone who finds himself in a particular role.

(2) *experiencing the pressures which create roles*. Role-playing provides study material for group members on the ways in which roles are created in, for example, a committee. It enables subjects to explore the interactions of formal structure and individual personalities in role taking.

(3) *testing out for oneself possible modes of behaviour*. In effect, this is *rehearsal*; trying out in one's mind in advance of some new situation that one has to face. Role-playing can be used for a wide variety of situations where the subject, for one reason or another, needs to learn to cope with the rituals and conventions of social intercourse and to practise them so that they can be repeated under stress.

(4) *simulating a situation for others (and possibly oneself) to learn from*. Here, the role-player provides materials for others to use and work upon. In the simplest situation, there is just one role-player acting out a specific role. In more complex situations such as the Stanford Prison study discussed in Box 12.3, role-playing is used to provide an environment structured on the interaction of numerous role incumbents.

Suggestions for Running Role-play Sessions

Van Ments offers the following practical suggestions in connection with three central aspects of role-playing methodology:

Preparation

From the outset, demystify the process of role-playing by pointing out that it is not really a new idea but is just an extension of the sort of things people do in everyday life. Avoid technical terminology and too much detail about the characters of personalities involved. Induct the group gently by introducing role-playing in stages. For example, divide the group into pairs or threes and allow all of them to role play the situation at the same time. Allocate key roles to the less shy or more experienced members.

Running the Simulation

Plan the timing of the simulation very carefully. Use suitable props and environments. Make sure that everyone is clear as to whether participants are 'in' or 'out' of role. Discourage people from getting more emotionally involved than they or the tutor wish by the judicious use of 'time out' periods.

Debriefing

The basic steps in debriefing any simulation involved (1) dealing with factual errors and tying up loose ends; (2) discussing what the participants thought happened; (3) discussing what the observers/tutors thought happened; (4) drawing out general conclusions about the session; and (5) deducing general lessons which can be extrapolated to the real world.

Strengths and Weaknesses of Role-playing and Other Simulation Exercises

Taylor and Walford (13) identify two prominent themes in their discussion of some of the possible advantages and disadvantages in the use of classroom simulation exercises. They are, first, the claimed enhancement of pupil motivation and second, the role of simulation in the provision of relevant learning materials. The motivational advantages of simulation are said to include (1) a heightened interest and excitement in learning; (2) a sustained level of freshness and novelty arising out of the dynamic nature of simulation tasks; (3) a transformation in the traditional pupil-teacher subordinate-superordinate relationship; and (4) the fact that simulation is a universal behavioural mode. As to the learning gains arising out of the use of simulation, the authors identify (1) the learning that is afforded at diverse levels (cognitive, social and emotional); (2) the decision-making experiences that participants acquire as well; (3) an increased role awareness; (4) the ability of simulation to provide a vehicle for free interdisciplinary communication; and (5) the success with which the concrete approach afforded by simulation exercises bridges the gap between 'schoolwork' and 'the real world'.

What reservations are there in connection with simulation exercises? Taylor and Walford identify the following: (1) simulations, however interesting and attractive, are time-demanding activities and ought therefore to justify fully the restricted timetabling allotted to competing educational approaches; (2) many simulation exercises are in the form of game kits and these can be quite expensive; and (3) simulation materials may pose problems of logistics, operation and general acceptance as legitimate educational techniques particularly by parent associations.

Our discussion of the strengths and weaknesses of role-playing has focused upon its application in pupil groups. To illustrate Taylor and Walford's point that simulation is a universal behavioural mode, the detailed example of a role-playing exercise that now follows is to do with adults in higher education.

Role-playing in an Educational Setting: an Example

Ferguson's (17) Toreside Comprehensive School is a simulation game for teachers in training that has been run successfully with PGCE students at Liverpool University School of Education. Its objectives are to encourage student teachers to think about the relationships between their subject disciplines in a social setting that is typical of many secondary school senior commonrooms. The simulation is structured on realism and conflict.

The game involves four distinct phases:

Phase 1: Volunteer subjects are assigned to subject departments in the imaginary Toreside Comprehensive School (hereinafter TCS). They are required to act out the roles of teachers in the actual subjects they themselves will eventually teach. They must devise and learn their own scripts. One person in each department is designated Head of Department.

Phase 2: TCS staff under the direction of the Headmaster (played by the University tutor) take part in a staffroom discussion the object of which is to reinforce their roles and establish their identities in the minds of other role-players.

Phase 3: The Headmaster injects a crisis in the staffroom discussion, forcing participants to justify their positions as subject specialists and to explore the overlap and interrelationships with other subjects. This is done within the atmosphere charged with those irrational elements that characterise the real situation.

Phase 4: The simulation game is terminated and participants are asked to discuss the exercise in which they have taken part.

Organising the Simulation Game

During the first briefing (Phase 1), Ferguson's instructions to his volunteers offer guidance by means of a role-proforma specifying personal and biographical details and requesting role-players to think out in advance of the actual game their role attitudes to potentially emotive issues such as corporal punishment, long hair, school uniforms and discipline in general. Each role-player also receives an information pack giving details of TCS — its pupil intake, system of organisation, timetabling, etc. At this first briefing, the purpose of the game is made clear to the participants but no mention is made of the crisis. The whole simulation exercise is to be recorded on TV and the reasons for this are explained.

At the second briefing (Phase 2), participants meet for the first time in the staffroom duly set out for the headmaster-led discussion. The locations of other rooms to be used during the simulation are identified and a detailed timetable of events for the rest of the simulation programme is handed out. The purpose of the third briefing (still Phase 2) is to reinforce the roles of participants. Each Head of Department is required to give a short resumé of his department to be followed by a short question period. This session gives participants opportunities to incorporate details from the role-proforma and information kit into their role portrayals.

Phase 3 constitutes the actual game in which the headmaster's policy announcement induces conflict into a situation in which some degree of tension may already be present following the role play in Phase 2. The conflict arises out of the headmaster's declared intention to introduce a scheme to break down subject boundaries in the first three years of the secondary school timetable. Staff are required to work out among themselves a basis for co-operation in implementing the head's wishes. Full details of his policy statement including financial implications for departments are provided in written form to all participants who then divide up, initially, into subject departments, to produce a departmental policy in relation to the crisis. At a second staff meeting, the headmaster asks for a progress report from each department and the negotiations and interdepartmental discussions become general knowledge. Later in the simulation game, at a final staff meeting, the difficulties and issues involved in integrating the school curriculum again became public knowledge and the arguments put forward bear a very close resemblance to what would probably be heard in a real school staffroom. The final staff meeting is the arena for negotiation and compromise among the role actors, including the headmaster.

The final session (Phase 4) is the debriefing period during which discussions of the exercise as a whole are held and participants are asked to complete a questionnaire about the simulation game and their reactions to it.

Ferguson reports on the comments of some of the student teachers with whom he has participated in the TCS simulation game. The great majority voted the experience as 'extremely interesting' on a Likert-type scale. The exercise was also found to be enjoyable by most of those taking part. Individual comments included the following:

It gave me a chance to meet and learn some of the problems of other departments.

It highlighted some interesting points in personal relationships.

It brought some aspects of the lectures [in the Certificate of Education course] into perspective.

It knitted a large part of our Education course together.

Evaluating Role-playing and Other Simulation Exercises

Because the use of simulation methods in classroom settings is growing, there is increasing need to evaluate claims concerning the advantages and effectiveness of these newer approaches against more traditional methods. Yet here lies a major problem. To date, as Megarry (14) observes, a high proportion of evaluation efforts has been directed towards the *comparative experiment* involving empirical comparisons between simulation-type exercises and more traditional teaching techniques in terms of specified learning pay-offs. One objection (14) to this approach to evaluation has been detailed earlier in the present chapter (p. 229) but is worth reiterating here:

the limitations [of the classical, experimental method] as applied to evaluating classroom simulation and games are obvious: not only are the inputs multiple, complex, and only partly known, but the outputs are disputed, difficult to isolate, detect or measure and the interaction among participants is considerable. Interaction forms, in some views, a major part of what simulation and gaming is about; it is *not* merely a source of 'noise' or experimental error.

What alternatives are there to the traditional type of evaluative effort? Megarry lists the following promising approaches to simulation evaluation: (1) using narrative reports; (2) using checklists gathered from students' recollections of outstanding positive and negative learning experiences; (3) encouraging players to relate ideas and concepts learned in games to other areas of their lives; and (4) using the instructional interview, a form of tutorial carried out earlier with an individual learner or a small group in which materials and methods are tested by an instructor who is versed not only in the use of the materials, but also in the ways in which pupils learn. (See also Percival's (16) discussion of observational and self-reporting techniques.)

Notice how each of the above evaluative techniques is primarily concerned with the *process* rather than the *product* of simulation.

By way of summary, simulation methods provide a means of alleviating a number of problems inherent in laboratory experiments. At the same time, they permit the retention of some of their virtues. Simulations, notes Palys (18), share with the laboratory experiment the characteristic that the experimenter has complete manipulative control over every aspect of the situation. At the same time, the subjects' humanity is left intact in that they are given a realistic situation in which to act in whatever way they think appropriate. The inclusion of the time dimension is another important contribution of the simulation, allowing as it does the subject to take an active role in interacting with the environment, and the experimenter the opportunity of observing a social system in action with its feedback loops, multi-directional causal connections and so forth. Finally, Palys observes, the high involvement normally associated with participation in simulations shows that the self-consciousness usually associated with the laboratory experiment is more easily dissipated.

References

1. Ginsburg, G.P., 'Role playing and role performance in social psychological research' in M. Brenner, P. Marsh and M. Brenner (eds), *The Social Context of Method* (Croom Helm, London, 1978).
2. Hamilton, V.L., 'Role play and deception: a re-examination of the controversy', *Journal for the Theory of Social Behaviour*, 6 (1976) 233-50.
3. Rogers, V.M. and Atwood, R.K., 'Can we put ourselves in their place', *Yearbook of the National Council for Social Studies*, 44 (1974) 80-111.
4. Haney, C., Banks, C. and Zimbardo, P., 'Interpersonal dynamics in a simulated prison', *International Journal of Criminology and Penology*, 1 (1973) 69-97.
5. Banuazizi, A. and Movahedi, A., 'Interpersonal dynamics in a simulated prison: a methodological analysis', *American Psychologist*, 30 (1975) 152-60.
6. Forward, J., Canter, R. and Kirsch, N., 'Role-enactment and deception methodologies', *American Psychologist*, 35 (1976) 595-604.
7. Milgram, S., *Obedience to Authority* (Harper and Row, New York, 1974).
8. Mixon, D., 'If you won't deceive, what can you do?' in N. Armistead (ed.), *Reconstructing Social Psychology* (Penguin Books, London, 1974).

9.   Mixon, D., 'Instead of deception', *Journal for the Theory of Social Behaviour*, 2 (1972) 146-77.
10. Brown, R. and Herrnstein, R.J., *Psychology* (Methuen, London, 1975).
11. Harré, R. and Secord, P.F., *The Explanation of Social Behaviour* (Basil Blackwell, Oxford, 1972).
12. Argyris, C., 'Dangers in applying results from experimental social psychology', *American Psychologist*, 30 (1975) 469-85.
13. Taylor, J.L. and Walford, R., *Simulation in the Classroom* (Penguin Books, London, 1972).
14. Megarry, J., 'Retrospect and prospect' in R. McAleese (ed.), *Perspectives on Academic Gaming and Simulation 3: Training and Professional Education* (Kogan Page, London, 1978).
15. van Ments, M., 'Role playing: playing a part or a mirror to meaning?' *Sagset Journal*, 8, 3 (1978) 83-92.
16. Percival, F., 'Evaluation procedures for simulating gaming exercises' in R. McAleese (ed.), *Perspectives on Academic Gaming and Simulation 3: Training and Professional Education* (Kogan Page, London, 1978).
17. Ferguson, S., 'Toreside Comprehensive School: a simulation game for teachers in training' in J. Megarry (ed.), *Aspects of Simulation and Gaming* (Kogan Page, London, 1977).
18. Palys, T.S., 'Simulation methods and social psychology', *Journal for the Theory of Social Behaviour*, 8 (1978) 341-68.

13 THE INTERVIEW

Introduction

Although the interview as a research technique is normally considered as one of a range of survey methods in social research, we treat it separately here chiefly to give us additional room to address ourselves more effectively to the details involved. The purposes of the interview in the wider context of life are many and varied. It may thus be used as a means of evaluating or assessing a person in some respect; for selecting or promoting an employee; for effecting therapeutic change, as in the psychiatric interview; for testing or developing hypotheses; for gathering data, as in surveys or experimental situations; or for sampling respondents' opinions, as in doorstep interviews. Although in each of these situations the respective roles of the interviewer and interviewee may vary and the motives for taking part may differ, a common denominator is the transaction that takes place between seeking information on the part of one and supplying information on the part of the other. As our interests lie primarily in reviewing research methods and techniques, we will subsequently limit ourselves to the use of the interview as a specific *research* tool. Interviews in this sense range from the *formal interview* in which set questions are asked and the answers recorded on a standardised schedule; through *less formal* interviews in which the interviewer is free to modify the sequence of questions, change the wording, explain them or add to them; to the *completely informal interview* where the interviewer may have a number of key issues which he raises in conversational style instead of having a set questionnaire. Beyond this point is located the *non-directive interview* in which the interviewer takes on a subordinate role.

The research interview has been defined (1) as 'a two-person conversation initiated by the interviewer for the specific purpose of obtaining research-relevant information, and focused by him on content specified by research objectives of systematic description, prediction, or explanation'. It is an unusual method in that it involves the gathering of data through direct verbal interaction between individuals. In this sense it differs from the *questionnaire* where the respondent is required to record in some way his responses to set questions. By way of interest, we illustrate the relative merits of the interview and the

241

questionnaire in Box 13.1. It has been pointed out (2) that the direct interaction of the interview is the source of both its advantages and disadvantages as a research technique. One advantage, for example, is that it allows for greater depth than is the case with other methods of data collection. A disadvantage, on the other hand, is that it is prone to subjectivity and bias on the part of the interviewer.

Box 13.1

Summary of relative merits of interviewing versus questionnaire		
Consideration	*Interview*	*Questionnaire*
1. Personal need to collect data	Requires interviewers	Requires a clerk
2. Major expense	Payment to interviewers	Postage and printing
3. Opportunities for response-keying (personalisation)	Extensive	Limited
4. Opportunities for asking	Extensive	Limited
5. Opportunities for probing	Possible	Difficult
6. Relative magnitude of data reduction	Great (because of coding)	Mainly limited to rostering
7. Typically, the number of respondents who can be reached	Limited	Extensive
8. Rate of return	Good	Poor
9. Sources of error	Interviewer, instrument, coding, sample	Limited to instrument and sample
10. Overall reliability	Quite limited	Fair
11. Emphasis on writing skill	Limited	Extensive

Source: Tuckman (3).

As a distinctive research technique, the interview may serve three purposes. First, it may be used as the principal means of gathering information having direct bearing on the research objectives. As Tuckman (3) describes it, 'By providing access to what is "inside a person's head", [it] makes it possible to measure what a person knows (knowledge or information), what a person likes or dislikes (values and preferences), and what a person thinks (attitudes and beliefs).' Second, it may be used to test hypotheses or to suggest new ones; or as an explanatory device to help identify variables and relationships. And third, the interview may be used in conjunction with other methods in a research undertaking. In this connection, Kerlinger (4) suggests that it might be used to follow up unexpected results, for example, or to validate other methods, or to go deeper into the motivations of respondents and their reasons for responding as they do.

There are four kinds of interview that may be used specifically as research tools: *the structured interview*; *the unstructured interview*; *the non-directive interview*; and *the focused interview*. The structured interview is one in which the content and procedures are organised in advance. This means that the sequence and wording of the questions are determined by means of a schedule and the interviewer is left little freedom to make modifications. Where some leeway is granted him, it too is specified in advance. It is therefore characterised by being a *closed* situation. In contrast to it in this respect, the unstructured interview is an *open* situation, having greater flexibility and freedom. As Kerlinger notes, although the research purposes govern the questions asked, their content, sequence and wording are entirely in the hands of the interviewer. This does not mean, however, that the unstructured interview is a more casual affair, for in its own way it also has to be carefully planned.

The non-directive interview as a research technique derives from the therapeutic or psychiatric interview. The principal features of it are the minimal direction or control exhibited by the interviewer and the freedom the respondent has to express his subjective feelings as fully and as spontaneously as he chooses or is able. As Moser and Kalton (5) put it,

> The informant is encouraged to talk about the subject under investigation (usually himself) and the course of the interview is mainly guided by him. There are no set questions, and usually no pre-determined framework for recorded answers. The interviewer confines himself to elucidating doubtful points, to rephrasing the

respondent's answers and to probing generally. It is an approach especially to be recommended when complex attitudes are involved and when one's knowledge of them is still in a vague and unstructured form.

The need to introduce rather more interviewer control into the non-directive situation led to the development of the focused interview. The distinctive feature of this type is that it focuses on a respondent's subjective responses to a known situation in which he has been involved and which has been analysed by the interviewer prior to the interview. He is thereby able to use the data from the interview to substantiate or reject previously formulated hypotheses. As Merton and Kendall (6) explain, 'In the usual depth interview, one can urge informants to reminisce on their experiences. In the focused interview, however, the interviewer can, when expedient, play a more active role: he can introduce more explicit verbal cues to the stimulus pattern or even *represent* it. In either case this usually activates a concrete report of responses by informants.'

We shall be examining both the non-directive interview and the focused interview in more detail later in the chapter.

Conceptions of the Interview

In his examination of views of the interview held by those who write theoretically about it and those who actually use it as a research tool, Kitwood (7) lucidly contrasts three conceptions of it. The first conception is that of a potential means of *pure information transfer*. He explains that

if the interviewer does his job well (establishes rapport, asks questions in an acceptable manner, etc.), and if the respondent is sincere and well-motivated, accurate data may be obtained. Of course all kinds of bias are liable to creep in, but with skill these can largely be eliminated. In its fullest expression, this view accords closely with that of the psychometricians, who apparently believe that there is a relatively permanent, consistent, 'core' to the personality, about which a person will give information under certain conditions. Such features as lying, or the tendency to give a socially desirable response, are to be eliminated where possible.

This conception of the interview appears to be widely held.

A second conception of the interview is that of *a transaction which inevitably has bias, which is to be recognised and controlled.* According to this viewpoint, Kitwood explains that 'each participant in an interview will define the situation in a particular way. This fact can be best handled by building controls into the research design, for example by having a range of interviewers with different biases.' The interview is best understood in terms of a theory of motivation which recognises a range of non-rational factors governing human behaviour, like emotions, unconscious needs and interpersonal influences. Kitwood points out that both these views of the interview regard the inherent features of interpersonal transactions as if they were 'potential obstacles to sound research, and therefore to be removed, controlled, or at least harnessed in some way'.

The third conception of the interview sees it as *an encounter necessarily sharing many of the features of everyday life.* Kitwood suggests that what is required, according to this view, is not a technique for dealing with bias, but a theory of everyday life that takes account of the relevant features of interviews. These may include role-playing, stereotyping, perception and understanding. One of the strongest advocates of this viewpoint is Cicourel (8) who lists five of the unavoidable features of the interview situation that would normally be regarded as problems. Briefly, these state that (7):

1. There are many factors which inevitably differ from one interview to another, such as mutual trust, social distance and the interviewer's control.
2. The respondent may well feel uneasy and adopt avoidance tactics if the questioning is too deep.
3. Both interviewer and respondent are bound to hold back part of what it is in their power to state.
4. Many of the meanings which are clear to one will be relatively opaque to the other, even when the intention is genuine communication.
5. It is impossible, just as in everyday life, to bring every aspect of the encounter within rational control.

The message that proponents of this view would express is that no matter how hard an interviewer may try to be systematic and objective, the constraints of everyday life will be a part of whatever interpersonal transactions he initiates. Kitwood concludes, 'The solution is to have as explicit a theory as possible to take the various factors into account. For those who hold this view, there are not good interviews and bad in the conventional sense. There are simply social encounters; goodness and badness are predicates applicable, rather, to the theories within which the phenomena are explained.'

Some Features of the Research Interview

We turn our attention now to the *structured interview* since this is one of the most frequently used methods of eliciting information in social and educational research. From here onwards, we shall comply with convention and refer to it as the *research interview*. After reviewing the types of schedule items used, we shall examine question format and the kinds of answers, or response modes, that may be elicited.

Three kinds of items are used in the construction of schedules used in research interviews (4): *fixed-alternative items*; *open-ended items*; and *scale items*.

The fixed-alternative items allow the respondent to choose from two or more alternatives. The most frequently used is the dichotomous item which offers two alternatives only: *yes-no* or *agree-disagree*, for instance. Sometimes a third alternative such as *undecided* or *don't know* is also offered.

Example:
Do you feel it is against the interests of a school
to have to make public its examination results?

Yes . . . .

No . . . .

Don't know . . . .

Kerlinger (4) has identified the chief advantages and disadvantages of fixed-alternative items. They have, for example, the advantage of achieving greater uniformity of measurement and therefore greater reliability; of making the respondents answer in a manner fitting the response category; and of being more easily coded. Disadvantages include their superficiality; the possibility of irritating respondents who find none of the alternatives suitable; and the possibility of forcing responses that are inappropriate, either because the alternative chosen conceals ignorance on the part of the respondent or because he may choose an alternative that does not accurately represent the true facts. These weaknesses can be overcome, however, if the items are written with care, mixed with open-ended ones, and used in conjunction with probes on the part of the interviewer.

Open-ended items have been succinctly defined by Kerlinger as 'those that supply a frame of reference for respondents' answers, but put a minimum of restraint on the answers and their expression'. Other than the subject of the question, which is determined by the nature of the problem under investigation, there are no other restrictions on either the content or the manner of the interviewee's reply.

Example:
What kind of television programmes do you most prefer to watch?

. . . .

. . . .

Open-ended questions have a number of advantages: they are flexible; they allow the interviewer to probe so that he may go into more depth if he chooses, or clear up any misunderstandings; they enable the interviewer to test the limits of a respondent's knowledge; they encourage co-operation and help establish rapport; and they allow the interviewer to make a truer assessment of what the respondent really believes. Open-ended situations can also result in unexpected or unanticipated answers which may suggest hitherto unthought-of relationships or hypotheses.

A particular kind of open-ended question is *the funnel*. This starts with a broad question or statement and then narrows down to more specific ones. Kerlinger quotes an example from the study by Sears, Maccoby and Levin (9):

All babies cry, of course. Some mothers feel that if you pick up a baby every time it cries, you will spoil it. Others think you should never let a baby cry for very long. How do you feel about this? What did you do about it? How about the middle of the night?

The *scale* is a set of verbal items to each of which the interviewee responds by indicating degrees of agreement or disagreement. The individual's response is thus located on a scale of fixed-alternatives. The use of this technique along with open-ended questions is a comparatively recent development and means that scale scores can be checked against data elicited by the open-ended questions.

Example:
Attendance at school after the age of 14 should be voluntary:

Strongly agree   Agree   Undecided   Disagree   Strongly disagree

It is possible to use one of a number of scales in this context: attitude scales, rank-order scales, rating scales, and so on. We touch upon this subject again subsequently.

We now look at the kinds of questions and modes of response associated with interviewing. First, the matter of question format: how is a question to be phrased or organised? One commentator (3) has listed four such formats that an interviewer may draw upon. Questions may, for example, take a *direct* or *indirect* form. Thus an interviewer could ask a teacher whether he likes teaching: this would be a direct question. Or else he could adopt an indirect approach by asking for the respondent's views on education in general and the ways schools function. From the answers proffered, the interviewer could make inferences about the teacher's opinions concerning his own job. Tuckman suggests that by making the purpose of questions less obvious, the indirect approach is more likely to produce frank and open responses.

There are also those kinds of questions which deal with either a *general* or *specific* issue. To ask a child what he thought of the teaching methods of the staff as a whole would be a *general* or *non-specific* question. To ask him what he thought of his teacher as a teacher would be a specific question. We have already made reference to that sequence of questions designated the funnel in which the movement is from the general and non-specific to the more specific. Tuckman comments, 'Specific questions, like direct ones, may cause a respondent to become cautious or guarded and give less-than-honest answers. Non-specific questions may lead circuitously to the desired information but with less alarm by the respondents.'

A further distinction is that between questions inviting *factual* answers and those inviting *opinions*. To ask a person what political party he supports would be a factual question. To ask him what he thinks of the current government's foreign policy would be an opinion question. Both fact and opinion questions can yield less than the truth, however: the former do not always produce factual answers; nor do the latter necessarily elicit honest opinions. In both instances, inaccuracy and bias may be minimised by careful structuring of the questions.

We may also note that an interviewee may be presented with either a *question* or a *statement*. In the case of the latter he will be asked for his response to it in one form or another. We illustrate the difference thus:

Do you think homework should be compulsory for all children

between 11 and 16? ....

And:

Homework should be compulsory for all children between 11 and 16.

Agree   Disagree   Don't know

If there are varied ways of *asking* questions, it follows there will be several ways in which they may be answered. It is to the different *response modes* that we now turn. In all, Tuckman lists seven such modes:

The first of these is the *unstructured response*. This allows the respondent to give his answer in whatever way he chooses. A *structured response*, by contrast, would limit him in some way. Thus:

Why did you not go to university?

And:

Can you give me two reasons for not going to university?

Although the interviewer has little control over the unstructured response, it does insure that the respondent has the freedom to give his own answer as fully as he chooses rather than being constrained in some way by the nature of the question. The chief disadvantage of the unstructured response concerns the matter of quantification. Data yielded in the unstructured response is more difficult to code and quantify than data in the structured response.

A *fill-in response* mode requires the respondent to supply rather than choose a response, though the response is often limited to a word or phrase. Consider the following examples:

What is your present occupation? ....

How long have you lived at your present address?   . . . .

The difference between the fill-in response and the unstructured response is one of degree.

A *tabular response* is similar to a fill-in response though more structured. It may demand words, figures or phrases. For example:

University	Subject	Degree	Dates	
			From	To

It is thus a convenient and short-hand way of recording complex information.

A *scaled response* is one structured by means of a series of gradations. The respondent is required to record his response to a given statement by selecting from a number of alternatives. Thus:

What are your chances of reaching a top managerial position within the next five years?

Excellent   Good   Fair   Poor   Very poor

Tuckman draws our attention to the fact that, unlike an unstructured response which has to be coded to be useful as data, a scaled response is collected in the form of usable and analysable data.

A *ranking response* is one in which a respondent is required to rank-order a series of words, phrases or statements according to a particular criterion. Here is an example:

Rank order the following persons in terms of their usefulness to you as sources of advice and guidance on problems you have encountered in the classroom. Use numbers 1 through 5 with 1 representing the person most useful: education tutor, subject tutor, class teacher, headteacher, other student.

Ranked data can be analysed by adding up the rank of each response across the respondents, thus resulting in an overall rank order of alternatives.

A *checklist response* requires that the respondent selects one of the alternatives presented to him. In that they do not represent points on a continuum, they are nominal categories. For example:

I get most satisfaction in college from:

> the social life
> studying on my own
> attending lectures
> college societies
> giving a paper at a seminar

This kind of response tends to yield less information than the other kinds considered.

Finally, the *categorical response* mode is similar to the checklist but simpler in that it offers respondents only two possibilities. For example:

Material progress results in greater
happiness for the people   True   False

Or:

In the event of another war, would you
be prepared to fight for your country?   Yes   No

Summing the numbers of respondents with the same responses yields a nominal measure.

Some Problems Surrounding the Use of the Interview in Research

A number of problems appear to attend the use of the interview as a research technique. One of these is that of invalidity, at least as far as the first two conceptions of the interview that we spoke of earlier are concerned. Studies reported by Cannell and Kahn (1), for instance, in which the interview was used seem to indicate that this was a persistent problem. In one such study (10), subjects interviewed on the existence and state of their bank accounts often presented a misleading picture: fewer accounts were reported than actually existed and the amounts declared frequently differed from bank records, often in the direction of understating assets. The reviewers suggest that inferences about validity are made too often on the basis of *face validity*, that is, whether the questions asked look as if they are measuring what they claim to measure. The cause of invalidity, they argue, is *bias*, which they define as 'a systematic or persistent tendency to make errors in the same direction, that is, to overstate or understate the "true value" of an attribute'. The problem, it seems, is not limited to a narrow range of data but is widespread. One way of validating interview measures is to compare the interview measure with another measure that has already been shown to be valid. This kind of comparison is known as *convergent validity*. If the two measures agree, it can be assumed that the validity of the interview is comparable with the proven validity of the other measure.

Perhaps the most practical way of achieving greater validity is to minimise the amount of bias as much as possible. The sources of bias are the characteristics of the interviewer, the characteristics of the respondent, and the substantive content of the questions. More particularly, these will include: the attitudes and opinions of the interviewer; a tendency for the interviewer to see the respondent in his own image; a tendency for the interviewer to seek answers that support his preconceived notions; misperceptions on the part of the interviewer of what the respondent is saying; and misunderstandings on the part of the respondent of what is being asked. Studies have also shown that colour, religion, social class and age can in certain contexts be potent sources of bias. Various writers have suggested the following as means of reducing bias: careful formulation of questions so that the meaning is crystal clear; thorough training procedures so that an interviewer is more aware of the possible problems; probability sampling of respondents; and sometimes by matching interviewer characteristics with those of the sample being interviewed.

In his critique of the interview as a research tool, Kitwood (7) draws attention to the conflict it generates between the traditional concepts of reliability and validity. Where increased reliability of the interview is brought about by greater control of its elements, this is achieved, he argues, at the cost of reduced validity. He explains,

In proportion to the extent to which 'reliability' is enhanced by rationalization, 'validity' would decrease. For the main purpose of using an interview in research is that it is believed that in an inter-personal encounter people are more likely to disclose aspects of themselves, their thoughts, their feelings and values, than they would in a less human situation. At least for some purposes, it is necessary to generate a kind of conversation in which the 'respondent' feels at ease. In other words, the distinctively human element in the interview is necessary to its 'validity'. The more the interviewer becomes rational, calculating, and detached, the less likely the interview is to be perceived as a friendly transaction, and the more calculated the response also is likely to be.

Where either of the first two conceptions of the interview outlined earlier is held, Kitwood suggests that a solution to the problem of reliability and validity might lie in the direction of a 'judicious compromise'; with the third conception, however, reliability and validity become 'redundant notions', for 'every interpersonal situation may be said to be valid, as such, whether or not it conforms to expectation, whether or not it involves a high degree of communication, and whether or not the participants emerge exhilarated or depressed'.

A cluster of problems surround the person being interviewed. Tuckman (3), for example, has observed that when formulating his questions an interviewer has to consider the extent to which a question might influence the respondent to show himself in a good light; or the extent to which a question might influence the respondent to be unduly helpful by attempting to anticipate what the interviewer wants to hear; or the extent to which a question might be asking for information about a respondent that he is not certain or likely to know himself. Further, interviewing procedures are based on the assumption that the person interviewed has insight into the cause of his behaviour. It has now come to be realised that insight of this kind is rarely achieved and that when it is, it is after long and difficult effort, usually in the context of repeated clinical interviews.

As the interview has some things in common with the self-administered questionnaire, it is frequently compared with it. Each has advantages over the other in certain respects. The advantages of the questionnaire, for instance, are: it tends to be more reliable; because it is anonymous, it encourages greater honesty; it is more economical than the interview in terms of time and money; and there is the possibility that it may be mailed. Its disadvantages, on the other hand, are: there is often too low a percentage of returns; the interviewer is able to answer questions concerning both the purpose of the interview and any misunderstandings experienced by the interviewee, for it sometimes happens in the case of the latter that the same questions have different meanings for different people; if only closed items are used, the questionnaire will be subject to the weaknesses already discussed; if only open items are used, respondents may be unwilling to write their answers for one reason or another; questionnaires present problems to people of limited literacy; and an interview can be conducted at an appropriate speed whereas questionnaires are often filled in hurriedly.

One of the problems that has to be considered when open-ended questions are used in the interview is that of developing a satisfactory method of recording replies. One way is to summarise responses in the course of the interview. This has the disadvantage of breaking the continuity of the interview and may result in bias because the interviewer may unconsciously emphasise responses that agree with his expectations and fail to note those that do not. It is sometimes possible to summarise an individual's responses at the end of the interview. Although this preserves the continuity of the interview, it is likely to induce greater bias because the delay may lead to the interviewer forgetting some of the details. It is these forgotten details that are most likely to be the ones that disagree with his own expectations.

Procedures

As a guide for those using the interview as a research technique perhaps for the first time, we outline a possible sequence of stages for such an undertaking.

The preliminary stage of an interview study will be the point where the purpose of the research is decided. It may begin by outlining the theoretical basis of the study, its broad aims, its practical value and the reasons why the interview approach was chosen. There may then follow the translation of the general goals of the research into more detailed and specific objectives. This is the most important step, for only careful formulation of objectives at this point will eventually produce the right kind of data necessary for satisfactory answers to the research problem.

This stage having been accomplished, there follows the preparation of the interview schedule itself. This involves translating the research objectives into the questions that will make up the main body of the schedule. This needs to be done in such a way that the questions adequately reflect what it is the researcher is trying to find out. It is quite usual to begin this task by writing down the variables to be dealt with in the study. As one commentator (3) says, 'The first step in constructing interview questions is to *specify your variables by name*. Your variables are what you are trying to measure. They tell you where to begin.'

Before the actual interview items are prepared, it is desirable to give some thought to the *question format* and the *response mode*. The choice of *question format*, for instance, depends on a consideration of one or more of the following factors: the objectives of the interview; the nature of the subject matter; whether the interviewer is dealing in facts, opinions or attitudes; whether specificity or depth is sought; the respondent's level of education; the kind of information he can be expected to have; whether or not his thought needs to be structured; some assessment of his motivational level; the extent of the interviewer's own insight into the respondent's situation; and the kind of relationship the interviewer can expect to develop with the respondent. Having given prior thought to these matters, the researcher is in a position to decide whether to use open and/or closed questions, direct and/or indirect questions, specific and/or non-specific questions, and so on.

As a general rule, the kind of information sought and the means of its acquisition will determine the choice of *response mode*. Data analysis, then, ought properly to be considered alongside the choice of response mode so that the interviewer can be confident that the data will serve his purposes and analysis of them can be duly prepared. Box 13.2 summarises the relationship between response mode and type of data.

Once the variables to be measured or studied have been identified, questions can be constructed so as to reflect them. If, for example, one of the variables was to be a new social education project that had recently been attempted with 15-year-olds in a comprehensive school, one obvious question would be: *How do you think the project has affected the pupils?* Or, less directly, *Do you think the children have been given too much or too little responsibility?* It is important to bear in mind that more than one question format and more than one response mode may be employed when building up a schedule. The final mixture will depend on the kinds of factors mentioned earlier — the objectives of the research, and so on.

Where an interview schedule is to be used as part of a field survey in which a number of trained interviewers are to be used, it will of course be necessary to include in it appropriate instructions for both interviewer and interviewees.

Setting up and conducting the interview will make up the next stage in the procedure. Where the interviewer is initiating the research himself, he will clearly select his own respondents; where he is engaged by another agent, then he will probably be given a list of people to contact.

Tuckman (3) has succintly reviewed the procedures to adopt at the interview itself. He writes,

Box 13.2

The selection of response mode			
Response mode	*Type of data*	*Chief advantages*	*Chief disadvantages*
Fill-in	Nominal	Less biasing; greater response flexibility	More difficult to score
Scaled	Interval	Easy to score	Time consuming; can be biasing
Ranking	Ordinal	Easy to score; forces discrimination	Difficult to complete
Checklist or categorical	Nominal (may be interval when totalled)	Easy to score; easy to respond	Provides less data and fewer options

Source: Tuckman (3).

At the meeting, the interviewer should brief the respondent as to the nature or purpose of the interview (being as candid as possible without biasing responses) and attempt to make the respondent feel at ease. He should explain the manner in which he will be recording responses, and if he plans to tape record, he should get the respondent's assent. At all times, an interviewer must remember that he is a data collection instrument and try not to let his own biases, opinions, or curiosity affect his behaviour. It is important that the interviewer should not deviate from his format and interview schedule although many schedules will permit some flexibility in choice of questions. The respondent should be kept from rambling away from the essence of a question, but not at the sacrifice of courtesy.

Once data from the interview have been collected, the next stage involves coding and scoring them. Coding has been defined by Kerlinger (4) as the translation of question responses and repondent information to specific categories for the purpose of analysis. As we have seen, many questions are precoded, that is, each response can be immediately and directly converted into a score in an objective way. Rating scales and checklists are examples of precoded questions.

Perhaps the biggest problem concerns the coding and scoring of open-ended questions. Two solutions are possible here. Even though a response is open-ended, the interviewer may precode his interview schedule so that while an interviewee is responding freely, the interviewer is assigning the content of his responses, or parts of it, to predetermined coding categories. Classifications of this kind may be developed during pilot studies. Here is an example:

Q. What is it that you like least about your job?
A. Mostly the way the place is run — and the long hours; and the prospects aren't too good.

Coding:	colleagues	. . . .
	organisation	. . . . .X. . . . .
	the work	. . . .
	conditions	. . . . .X. . . . .
	other	future prospects

Alternatively, data may be postcoded. Having recorded the interviewee's response, either by summarising it during or after the interview itself, or verbatim by tape recorder, the researcher may subject it to content analysis and submit it to one of the available scoring procedures — scaling, scoring, rank scoring, response counting, etc.

Finally, the data are analysed and interpreted in the light of the research objectives.

The Non-directive Interview and the Focused Interview

Originating from psychiatric and therapeutic fields with which it is most readily associated, the *non-directive interview* is characterised by a situation in which the respondent is responsible for initiating and directing the course of the encounter and for the attitudes he expresses in it (in contrast to the *structured* or *research interview* we have already considered, where the dominating role assumed by the interviewer results in, to use Kitwood's phrase, an asymmetry of commitment). It has been shown to be a particularly valuable technique because it gets at the deeper attitudes and perceptions of the person being interviewed in such a way as to leave them free from interviewer bias. We shall examine briefly the characteristics of the therapeutic interview and then consider its usefulness as a research tool in the social and educational sciences.

The non-directive interview as it is currently understood grew out of the pioneering work of Freud and subsequent modifications to his approach by later analysts. His basic discovery was that if one can arrange a special set of conditions and have his patient talk about his difficulties in a certain way, behaviour changes of many kinds can be accomplished (11). The technique developed was used to elicit highly personal data from patients in such a way as to increase their self-awareness and improve their skills in self-analysis. By these means they became better able to help themselves. As Madge (12) observes, it is these techniques which have greatly influenced contemporary interviewing techniques, especially those of a more penetrating and less quantitative kind.

The present-day therapeutic interview has its most persuasive advocate in Carl Rogers who has on different occasions testified to its efficacy. Basing his analysis on his own clinical studies, he has identified a sequence of characteristic stages in the therapeutic process, beginning with the client's decision to seek help (13). He is met by a counsellor who is friendly and receptive, but not didactic. The next stage is signalled when the client begins to give vent to hostile, critical and destructive feelings, which the counsellor accepts, recognises and clarifies. Subsequently, and *invariably*, these antagonistic impulses are used up and give way to the first expressions of positive feeling. The counsellor likewise accepts these until suddenly and spontaneously 'insight and self-understanding come bubbling through'. With insight comes the realisation of possible courses of action and also the power to make decisions. It is in translating these into practical terms that the client frees himself from dependence on the counsellor.

Rogers (14) subsequently identified a number of qualities in the interviewer which he deemed essential: that he bases his work on attitudes of acceptance and permissiveness; that he respects the client's responsibility for his own situation; that he permits the client to explain his problem in his own way; and that he does nothing that would in any way arouse the client's defences.

Such then are the principal characteristics of the non-directive interview technique in a therapeutic setting. But what of its usefulness as a purely *research* technique in societal and educational contexts? There are a number of features of the therapeutic interview which are peculiar to it and may well be inappropriate in other settings: for example, as we have seen, the interview is initiated by the respondent; his motivation is to obtain relief from a particular symptom; the interviewer is primarily a source of help, not a procurer of information; the actual interview is part of the therapeutic experience; the purpose of the interview is to change the behaviour and inner life of the person and its success is defined in these terms; and there is no restriction on the topics discussed.

A researcher has a different order of priorities, however, and what appear as advantages in a therapeutic context may be decided limitations when the technique is used for research purposes, even though he may be sympathetic to the spirit of the non-directive interview. As Madge explains, increasingly there are those 'who wish to retain the good qualities of the non-directive technique and at the same time are keen to evolve a method that is economical and precise enough to leave a residue of results rather than merely a posse of cured souls'.

One attempt to meet this need is to be found in a programme reported by Merton and Kendall (6) in which the *focused interview* was developed. While seeking to follow closely the principle of non-direction, the method did introduce rather more interviewer control in the kinds of questions used and sought also to limit the discussion to certain parts of the respondent's experience.

The focused interview differs from other types of research interview in certain respects. These have been identified by the authors as follows:

1. The persons interviewed are known to have been involved in a *particular situation*: they may, for example, have watched a TV programme; or seen a film; or read a book or article; or have been a participant in a social situation.
2. By means of the techniques of content analysis, elements in the situation which the researcher deems significant have previously been analysed by him. He has thus arrived at a set of hypotheses relating to the meaning and effects of the specified elements.
3. Using his analysis as a basis, the investigator constructs an *interview guide*. This identifies the major areas of enquiry and the hypotheses which determine the relevant data to be obtained in the interview.
4. The actual interview is focused on the *subjective experiences* of the persons who have been exposed to the situation. Their responses enable the researcher: (a) to test the validity of his hypotheses; and (b) to ascertain unanticipated responses to the situation, thus giving rise to further hypotheses.

From this it can be seen that the distinctive feature of the focused interview is *the prior analysis by the researcher of the situation in which subjects have been involved.*

The advantages of this procedure have been cogently explained by Merton and Kendall (6):

> Fore-knowledge of the situation obviously reduces the task confronting the investigator, since the interview need not be devoted to discovering the objective nature of the situation. Equipped in advance with a content analysis, the interviewer can readily distinguish the objective facts of the case from the subjective definitions of the situation. He thus becomes alert to the entire field of 'selective response'. When the interviewer, through his familiarity with the objective situation, is able to recognize symbolic or functional silences, 'distortions', avoidances, or blockings, he is the more prepared to explore their implications.

In the quest for what the authors term 'significant data', the interviewer must develop the ability to evaluate continuously the interview while it is in progress. To this end, they established a set of criteria by which productive and unproductive interview material can be distinguished. Briefly, these are: (1) *non-direction*: interviewer guidance should be minimal; (2) *specificity*: respondents' definitions of the situation should find full and specific expression; (3) *range*: the interview should maximise the range of evocative stimuli and responses reported by the subject; and (4) *depth and personal context*: the interview should bring out the affective and value-laden implications of the subjects' responses, to determine whether the experience had central or peripheral significance. It should elicit the relevant personal context, the idiosyncratic associations, beliefs and ideas.

Many instances of interview studies are to be found throughout the literature of social and educational research, the range varying from the comprehensiveness and sophistication of national polls at one extreme to small-scale investigations into educational issues at the other. We conclude this chapter with part of a transcript from the Newsons' longitudinal study of child-rearing practices (15). It illustrates the skills involved in focused interviewing; notice particularly the subtle ways in which the interviewer (I) is able to get beneath the rather conventional initial response of the mother (M) to Question 147.

Extract from a focused interview

Notes		Transcript
		147 Is there any special interest which you and Oliver share — something that the two of you follow together — would you say?
nothing yet	M	Mmmm . . . I don't *think* so.
		148 Is there anything which he and his Daddy are both specially interested in?
may be pause to think — but definite negative	M	(pause) . . . *No.*
		149 No special thing . . . would you say he's closer now to you or to his Daddy?
	M	He . . . is . . . closer . . .?
deliberately defuses by addition		149 Would you say Oliver is closer to you, or to his Daddy? . . . or is it about equal?
	M	About equal . . . might be a shade towards me.
		150 Does your husband like doing things with him?
ALERT quiet, but words quick and definite	M	(sigh) . . . Mmmm . . . not really — no.
WAIT — nothing comes — probe probe is a challenge, retreat expected	I	(pause) . . . How do you mean?
M retreats	M	Well — I suppose he *does* like doing things with him, but opportunity doesn't often present itself.
I accepts retreat	I	I see — yes . . . yes . . .
	M	He's . . . he's . . . well, he's home tonight, but some nights he's not home till 7 or 8, so he just sees them go to bed, really, and get up in the morning.
accepts, but probes from another angle, forcing issue	I	. . . yes, . . . and does he give Oliver a lot of attention when he *is* there — would you say, um, about average, or more or less than most fathers?
M enabled to advance again	M	Well, I sometimes think he could give *more* . . . um . . . he could perhaps take them *off* more — the boys — and *play* with them more;
voice rises		if the boys play games, they play games with *me!* (. . . yes . . .) — this is what I *find,* you know? (I see yes . . . yes . . .) 'Cause he's always . . . *out,* or *busy,* (. . . yes . . .) or doing something (. . . yes . . .)
semi-retreat		I suppose it's circumstances . . . not deliberate . . .
I accepts retreat	I	You're, sort of, more available . . .
M advances	M	Yes . . . yes. If we go to the cricket match — *he's playing* cricket — *I* play with the boys!

Notes		Transcript
unbiased re-statement (giving time)	I	(laughter in which M joins) . . . And the boys sort of *feel* really that you're more available — that, er, you're the person they play with, I suppose?
M advances, voice rising	M	Yes! Now Oliver asks *me* to take him swimming — he doesn't ask his Daddy!

(Interview continues, but this is now recognised as a sensitive area and may be
returned to if opportunity arises.)

Source: Adapted from Shipman (15).

References

1. Cannell, C.F. and Kahn, R.L., 'Interviewing' in G. Lindzey and E. Aronson
   (eds), *The Handbook of Social Psychology*, vol. 2, *Research Methods*
   (Addison Wesley, New York, 1968).
2. Borg, W.R., *Educational Research: An Introduction* (Longmans, London,
   1963).
3. Tuckman, B.W., *Conducting Educational Research* (Harcourt Brace
   Jovanovich, New York, 1972).
4. Kerlinger, F.N., *Foundations of Behavioural Research* (Holt, Rinehart and
   Winston, New York, 1970).
5. Moser, C.A. and Kalton, G., *Survey Methods in Social Investigation* (Heinemann Educational Books, London, 1977).
6. Merton, R.K. and Kendall, P.L., 'The focused interview', *Amer. J. Sociol.*,
   51 (1946) 541-57.
7. Kitwood, T.M., 'Values in adolescent life: towards a critical description',
   unpublished PhD dissertation, School of Research in Education (University
   of Bradford, 1977).
8. Cicourel, A.V., *Method and Measurement in Sociology* (The Free Press, New
   York, 1964).
9. Sears, R., Maccoby, E. and Levin, H., *Patterns of Child Rearing* (Harper and
   Row, New York, 1957).
10. Lansing, J.B., Ginsberg, G.P. and Braaten, K., *An Investigation of Response
    Error* (Bureau of Economic and Business Research, University of Illinois,
    1961). Reported in Cannell and Kahn (1).
11. Ford, D.H. and Urban, H.B., *Systems of Psychotherapy: a Comparative
    Study* (John Wiley and Sons, New York, 1963).
12. Madge, J., *The Tools of Social Science* (Longmans, London, 1965).
13. Rogers, C.R., *Counselling and Psychotherapy* (Houghton and Mifflin,
    Boston, 1942).
14. Rogers, C.R., 'The non-directive method as a technique for social research',
    Amer. J. Sociol., 50 (1945) 279-83.
15. Newson, J. and Newson, E., 'Parental roles and social contexts' in M.D.
    Shipman (ed.), *The Organization and Impact of Social Research* (Routledge
    and Kegan Paul, London, 1976) 22-48.

14 PERSONAL CONSTRUCTS

Introduction

One of the most interesting theories of personality to have emerged this century and one that has had an increasing impact on educational research is *personal construct theory*. Personal constructs are the basic units of analysis in a complete and formally stated theory of personality proposed by George Kelly in a book entitled *The Psychology of Personal Constructs* (1955). Because Kelly's own experiences were so intimately related to the development of his imaginative theory, we begin with some observations on Kelly, the man.

Kelly began his career as a school psychologist dealing with problem children referred to him by teachers. As his experiences widened, intead of merely corroborating a teacher's complaint about a pupil, Kelly tried to understand the complaint in the way the teacher construed it. This change of perspective constituted a significant reformulation of the problem. In practical terms, it resulted in an analysis of the teacher making the complaint as well as the problem pupil. By viewing the problem from a wider perspective Kelly was able to envisage a wider range of solutions.

The insights George Kelly gained from his clinical work led him to the view that there is no objective, absolute truth and that events are only meaningful in relation to the ways they are construed by the individual. Kelly's primary focus is upon the way an individual perceives his environment, the way he interprets what he perceives in terms of his existing mental structure, and the way in which, as a consequence, he behaves towards it. In *The Psychology of Personal Constructs*, Kelly proposes a view of man actively engaged in making sense of and extending his experience of the world. Personal constructs are the dimensions that man uses to conceptualise aspects of his day-to-day world. The constructs that man creates are used by him to forecast events and rehearse situations before their actual occurrence. Man, according to Kelly, takes on the role of scientist seeking to predict and control the course of events in which he is caught up. For Kelly (1), the ultimate explanation of human behaviour 'lies in scanning man's undertakings, the questions he asks, the lines of inquiry he initiates and the strategies he employs . . .' Kelly's ideas have a good deal in common with current educational thought and practice. Education, in Kelly's view, is necessarily experimental. Its ultimate goal is individual fulfilment and the maximising of individual potential. In emphasising the need of each individual to question and explore, construct theory implies a view of education that capitalises upon the child's natural motivation to engage in spontaneous learning activities. It follows that the teacher's task is to facilitate the child's ongoing exploration of the world rather than impose adult perspectives upon him. Kelly's ideas have much in common with those to be found in Rousseau's *Emile*.

The central tenets of Kelly's theory are set out in terms of a fundamental postulate and a number of corollaries. It is not proposed here to undertake a detailed discussion of Kelly's theoretical propositions. Good commentaries are available in Bannister (2) and Ryle (3). Instead, we look at the method suggested by Kelly of eliciting constructs and assessing the mathematical relationships between them, that is, repertory grid technique.

Characteristics of the Method

Kelly proposes that each person has access to a limited number of *constructs* by means of which he evaluates the phenomena that constitute his world. These phenomena — people, events, objects, ideas, institutions and so on — are known as *elements*. He further suggests that the constructs that each of us employ may be thought of as bipolar, that is, capable of being defined in terms of polar adjectives (good — bad) or polar phrases (makes me feel happy — makes me feel sad).

A number of different forms of repertory grid technique have been developed since Kelly's first formulation. All have the two essential characteristics in common that we have already identified, that is, *constructs* — the dimensions used by a person in conceptualising aspects of his world; and *elements* — the stimulus objects that the person evaluates in terms of the constructs he employs. In Box 14.1, we illustrate the empirical technique suggested by Kelly for eliciting constructs and identifying their relationship with elements in the form of a repertory grid.

Since Kelly's original account of what he called 'The Role Construct Repertory Grid Test', several variations of repertory grid have been developed and used in different areas of research. It is the flexibility and adaptability of repertory grid technique that has made it such an attractive tool to researchers in psychiatric, counselling, and more recently, educational settings. We now review a number of developments in the form and the use of the technique.

'Elicited' Versus 'Provided' Constructs

A central assumption of this 'standard' form of repertory grid is that it enables the researcher to elicit constructs that subjects customarily use in interpreting and predicting the behaviour of those people who are important in their lives. Kelly's method of eliciting personal constructs required the subject to complete a number of cards, 'each showing the name of a person in [his] life'. Similarly, in identifying elements, the subject was asked, 'Is there an important way in which two of [the elements] — any two — differ from the third?' This insistence upon

Box 14.1

Eliciting constructs and constructing a repertory grid

A person is asked to name a number of people who are significant to him. These might be, for example, mother, father, wife, friend, employer, priest. These constitute the *elements* in the repertory grid.

The subject is then asked to arrange the elements into groups of threes in such a manner that two are similar in some way but at the same time different from the third. The ways in which the elements may be alike or different are the *constructs*, generally expressed in bi-polar form (quiet — talkative; mean — generous; warm — cold). The way in which two of the elements are similar is called the *similarity pole* of the construct; and the way in which two of the elements are different from the third, the *contrast pole* of the construct.

A grid can now be constructed by asking the subject to place each element at either the *similarity* or the *contrast* pole of each construct. Let x = one pole of the construct, and blank = the other. The result can be set out as follows:

CONSTRUCTS	*ELEMENTS*					
	A	B	C	D	E	F
1. quiet — talkative	x	x	x			x
2. mean — generous	x			x	x	
3. warm — cold		x			x	

It is now possible to derive different kinds of information from the grid. By studying each *row*, for example, we can get some idea of how a person defines each construct in terms of significant people in his life. From each *column*, we have a personality profile of each of the significant people in terms of the constructs selected by the subjects. More sophisticated treatments of grid data are discussed in examples presented in the text.

Source: Adapted from Kelly (1)

important persons and important ways that they are alike or differ, where both constructs and elements are nominated by the subjects themselves, is central to Personal Construct Theory. Kelly gives it precise expression in his Individuality Corollary — 'Persons differ from each other in their construction of events.'

Several forms of repertory grid technique now in common use represent a significant departure from Kelly's individuality corollary in that they *provide* constructs to subjects rather than *elicit* constructs from them.

One justification for the use of provided constructs is implicit in Ryle's (3) commentary on the individuality corollary: 'Kelly paid rather little attention to developmental and social processes', Ryle observes, '. . . his own concern was with the personal and not the social.' Ryle believes that the individuality corollary would be strengthened by the additional statement that 'persons *resemble* each other in their construction of events'.

Can the practice of providing constructs to subjects be reconciled with the individuality corollary assumptions? A review (4) of a substantial body of research suggests a qualified 'yes' (but see Fransella and Bannister (8) on elicited versus supplied constructs as a 'grid-generated' problem).

> [While] it seems clear in the light of research that individuals prefer to use their own elicited constructs rather than provided dimensions to describe themselves and others . . . the results of several studies suggest that normal subjects, at least, exhibit approximately the same degree of differentiation in using carefully selected supplied lists of adjectives as when they employ their own elicited personal constructs.

Bannister and Mair (5) support the use of supplied constructs in experiments where hypotheses have been formulated and in those involving group comparisons. The use of elicited constructs alongside supplied ones can serve as a useful check on the meaningfulness of those that are provided, substantially lower intercorrelations between elicited and supplied constructs suggesting, perhaps, the lack of relevance of those provided by the researcher. The danger with supplied constructs, Bannister and Mair argue, is that the researcher may assume that the polar adjectives or phrases he provides are the verbal equivalents of the psychological dimensions in which he is interested.

Allotting Elements to Constructs

When a subject is allowed to classify as many or as few elements at the similarity or the contrast pole, the result is often a very lopsided construct with consequent dangers of distortion in the estimation of construct relationships. Bannister (5) suggests two methods for dealing with this problem which we illustrate in Box 14.2. The first, the *split-half form*, requires the subject to place half the elements at the similarity pole of each construct by instructing him to decide which element *most markedly* shows the characteristics specified by each of the constructs. Those elements that are left are allocated to the contrast pole. As Bannister observes, this technique may result in the discarding of constructs (for example, male – female) which cannot be summarily allocated. A second method, the *rank order form*, as its name suggests requires the subject to rank the elements from the one which most markedly exhibits the particular characteristic (shown by the similarity pole description) to the one which least exhibits it. As the second example in Box 14.2 shows, a rank order correlation coefficient can be used to estimate the extent to which there is similarity in the allotment of elements on any two constructs. Following Bannister, a construct *relationship* score can be calculated by squaring the correlation coefficient and multiplying by 100. (Because correlations are not linearly related they cannot be used as scores.) The construct relationship score gives an estimate of the percentage variance that the two constructs share in common in terms of the rankings on the two grids.

A third method of allotting elements is the *rating form*. Here, the subject is required to judge each element on a 7-point or a 5-point scale, for example, absolutely beautiful (7) to absolutely ugly (1). Commenting on the advantages of the rating form, Bannister (5) notes that it offers the subject greater latitude in distinguishing between elements than that provided for in the original form proposed by Kelly. At the same time the degree of differentiation asked of the subject may not be as great as that demanded in the ranking method. As with the rank order method, the rating form approach also allows the use of most correlation techniques. The rating form is the third example we illustrate in Box 14.2.

Laddering

The technique known as laddering arises out of Hinkle's (6) important revision of the theory of personal constructs and the method employed in his research. Hinkle's concern was for the location of any construct within an individual's construct system, arguing that a construct has

Box 14.2.

Allotting elements to constructs: three methods

Example 1: Split-half form

				Elements					
1	2	3	4	5	6	7	8	9	10
x		x	x		x		x		
	x	x		x		x			x
		x	x		x			x	x

Constructs

1. fast—slow
2. late—early
3. dangerous—safe

Since the subject is forced to allocate half of the elements to one pole, the chance expectancy of matchings occurring on 10 elements when two constructs are compared is 5. Deviation scores can be computed from chance level. Thus 5 matchings = 0; in constructs 1 and 2, matchings = −3; in constructs 1 and 3, matchings = +1; and in constructs 2 and 3, matchings = −1. The probability of particular matching scores being obtained can be had by reference to statistical tables.

Example 2: Rank-order form

				Elements					
1	2	3	4	5	6	7	8	9	10
10	1	2	5	8	7	3	4	9	6
9	4	10	1	6	8	5	2	3	7
7	9	5	6	10	2	1	4	8	3

Constructs

1. fast—slow
2. late—early
3. dangerous—safe

Spearman's rho (r_s)

Constructs 1 and 2 = .15
Constructs 1 and 3 = .24
Constructs 2 and 3 = −.16

Relationship scores

$(0.15)^2 \times 100 = +23$
$(0.24)^2 \times 100 = +58$
$(-0.16)^2 \times 100 = -26$

Example 3: Rating form

				Elements					
1	2	3	4	5	6	7	8	9	10
4	4	2	1	4	3	5	1	5	2
1	1	3	5	1	3	2	2	5	5
5	1	3	2	2	1	4	5	1	2

Constructs

1. fast
2. late
3. dangerous

A 5-point rating scale is shown in which, in this example, single poles of the constructs are rated as follows:

Not at all like		Average		Very much like
1	2	3	4	5

Bannister and Mair (5) suggest several methods for calculating relationships between constructs from the rating form (pp. 63-5). For a detailed discussion of measures of construct relationships, see Fransella and Bannister (8) (pp. 60-72).

Source: Adapted from Bannister and Mair (5)

differential *implications* within a given hierarchical context. He went on to develop an Implication Grid or Impgrid in which the subject is required to compare each of his constructs with every other to see which implies the other. The question *why?* is asked over and over again to identify the position of any construct in an individual's hierarchical construct system. In Box 14.3, we illustrate Hinkle's laddering technique with an example from educational research reported by Fransella (7).

Box 14.3

Laddering									
Constructs				Elements teachers					
		A	B	C	D	E	F	G	H
masculine		2	1	5	4	3	6	8	7
serious		6	2	1	3	8	4	5	7
good teacher									
authoritarian									
sexy									
old									
gets on with others									
lonely									
like me in character									
like I hope to become									

A matrix of rankings for a repertory grid with teachers as elements

You may decide to stop when you have elicited seven or eight constructs from the teacher elements. But you could go on to 'ladder' two or three of them. This process of laddering is in effect asking yourself (or someone else) to abstract from one conceptual level to another. You could ladder from *man—woman*, but it might be easier to start off with *serious—light-hearted*. Ask yourself which you would prefer to be — *serious or light-hearted*. You might reply *light-hearted*. Now pose the question 'why'. Why would you rather be a *light-hearted* person than a *serious* person? Perhaps the answer would be that *light-hearted* people *get on better with others* than do *serious* people. Ask yourself 'why' again. Why do you want to be the sort of person who gets on better with others? Perhaps it transpires that you think that people who do not get on well with others are *lonely*. In this way you elicit more constructs but ones that stand on the shoulders of those previously elicited. Whatever constructs you have obtained can be put into the grid.

Source: Adapted from Fransella (7)

Grid Administration and Analysis

The example of grid administration and analysis outlined below employs the split-half method of allocating elements to constructs and a form of *anchor analysis* devised by Bannister. We assume that 16 elements and 15 constructs have already been elicited by means of a technique such as the one illustrated in Box 14.1.

Procedures in Grid Administration

Draw up a grid measuring 16 (elements) by 15 (constructs) as in Figure 14.1 below, writing along the top the names of the elements, but first inserting the additional element, *self*. Alongside the rows write in the construct poles.

You now have a grid in which each intersection or cell is defined by a particular column (element) and a particular row (construct). The administration takes the form of allocating every element on every construct. If, for example, your first construct is 'kind—cruel', allocate each element in turn on that dimension, putting a cross in the appropriate box if you consider that person (element) kind, or leaving it blank if you consider that person cruel. Make sure that half of the elements are designated kind and half cruel.

Proceed in this way for each construct in turn, *always* placing a *cross* where the construct pole to the *left* of the grid applies, and leaving it blank if the construct pole to the *right* is applicable. Every element must be allocated in this way, and *half* of the elements must always be allocated to the left-hand pole.

Procedures in Grid Analysis

The grid may be regarded as a reflection of conceptual structure in which constructs are linked by virtue of their being applied to the same persons (elements). This linkage is measured by a process of matching construct rows.

To estimate the linkage between constructs 1 and 2 in Figure 14.1, for example, count the number of matches between corresponding boxes in each row. A match is counted where the same element has been designated with a cross (*or* a blank) on both constructs. So, for constructs 1 and 2 in Figure 14.1, we count 6 such matches. By chance we would expect 8 (out of 16) matches, and we may subtract this from the observed value to arrive at an estimate of such deviation from chance.

Figure 14.1 Elements

Construct	Self	1	2	3	4	5	6	7	8	9	10	11	12	13	14	15	Construct
KIND	x		x				x	x			x	x	x			x	CRUEL
CONFIDENT	x	x		x	x		x			x		x		x			UNSURE

Constructs	*Match*	*Difference score*
$1-2$	6	$6 - 8 = -2$

By matching construct 1 against all remaining constructs (3 . . . 15), we get a score for each comparison. Beginning then with construct 2, and comparing this with every other construct (3 . . . 15), and so on, every construct on the grid is matched with every other one and a difference score for each obtained. This is recorded in matrix form, with the reflected half of the table also filled in (see difference score for constructs $1 - 2$ in Figure 14.2). The *sign* of the difference score is retained. It indicates the direction of the linkage. A positive sign shows that the constructs are positively associated, a negative sign that they are negatively associated.

Figure 14.2

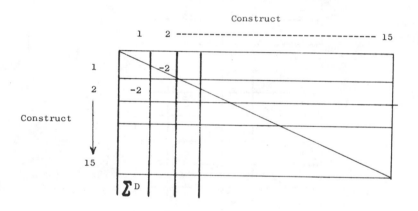

Now add up (without noting sign) the sum of the difference scores for each column (construct) in the matrix. The construct with the largest difference score is the one which, statistically, accounts for the greatest amount of variance in the grid. Note this down. Now look in the body of the matrix for that construct which has the largest non-significant association with the one which you have just noted (in the case of a 16-element grid as in Figure 14.1, this will be a difference score of ±3 or less). This second construct can be regarded as a dimension which is orthogonal to the first, and together they may form the axes for mapping the person's psychological space.

Figure 14.3

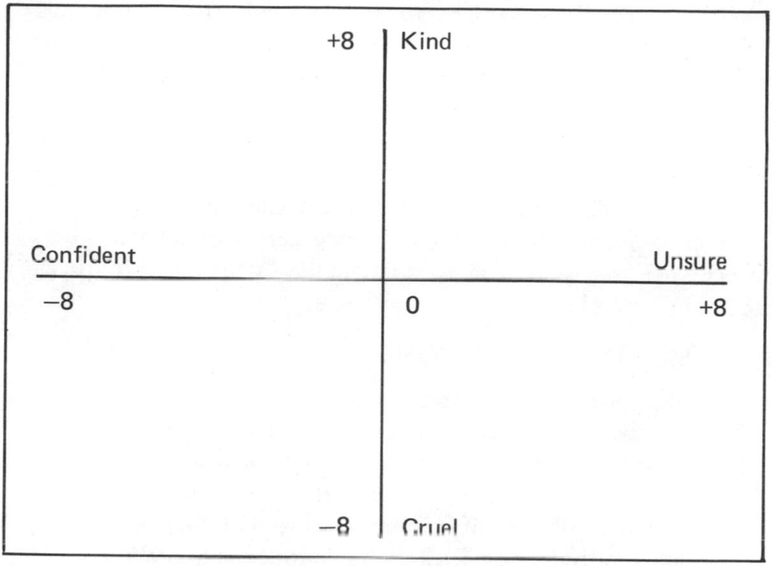

If we imagine the construct with the highest difference score to be 'kind–cruel' and the highest non-significant associated construct to be 'confident–unsure', then every other construct in the grid may be plotted with reference to these two axes. The co-ordinates for the map are provided by the difference scores relating to the matching of each construct with the two used to form the axes of the graph. In this way a pictorial representation of the individual's *personal construct space* can be obtained, and inferences made from the spatial relationships between plotted constructs.

By rotating the original grid 90° and carrying out the same matching procedure on the columns (figures), a similar map may be obtained for the people (figures) included in the grid.

Grid matrices can be subjected to analyses of varying degrees of complexity. We have illustrated one of the simplest ways of calculating relationships between constructs in Figure 14.2. For the statistically minded researcher, a variety of programs exist in GAP, the Grid Analysis Package developed by Slater and described by Chetwynd (9). GAP programs analyse the single grid, pairs of grids and grids in groups. Grids may be aligned either by construct, by element or both. A fuller discussion of metric factor analysis is given in Fransella and Bannister (8) (pp. 73-81).

Non-metric methods of grid analysis make no assumptions about the linearity of relationships between the variables and the factors. Moreover, where the researcher is primarily interested in the relationships between elements, multidimensional scaling may prove a more useful approach to the data than principal components analysis (see the educational example on p. 277).

The choice of one method rather than another must ultimately rest both upon what is statistically correct and what is psychologically desirable. The danger in the use of advanced computer programs, as Fransella and Bannister point out, is being caught up in the numbers game. Their plea is that grid users should have at least an intuitive grasp of the processes being so competently executed by their computers!

Strengths of Repertory Grid Technique

It is in the application of interpretive perspectives in classroom research, where the investigator seeks to understand the meaning of events to those participating, that repertory grid technique offers exciting possibilities. It is particularly able to provide the researcher with an abundance and a richness of interpretable material. Repertory grid technique is, of course, especially suitable for the exploration of relationships between an individual's personal constructs. It is equally adaptable to the problem of identifying changes in individuals that occur as a result of some educational experience as the studies of Ryle and Breen (10) and Lifshitz (11) show in the case of social work students undergoing professional training. In modified formats (the *dyad*, and the *double dyad*) repertory grid has employed *relationships between people* as elements rather than people themselves and demonstrated the increased sensitivity of this type of grid in identifying problems of adjustment between married partners (Ryle and Breen (12)) and the concerns of students attending psychiatric clinics (Ryle and Lunghi (13)). Finally, repertory grid technique can be employed in studying the changing nature of construing and the patterning of relationships between constructs in groups of children from relatively young ages as the work of Salmon (14) and Applebee (15) has shown.

Difficulties in the Use of Repertory Grid Technique

Fransella and Bannister (8) point to a number of difficulties in the development and use of grid technique, the most important of which is, perhaps, the widening gulf between technical advances in grid forms and analyses and the theoretical basis from which these are derived. There is, it seems, a rapidly expanding grid industry. Small wonder, then, as Fransella and Bannister wryly observe, that studies such as a one-off analysis of the attitudes of a group of people to asparagus, which bear little or no relation to personal construct theory, are on the increase.

A second difficulty relates to the question of bi-polarity in those forms of the grid in which customarily only one pole of the construct is used. Researchers may make unwarranted inferences about constructs' polar opposites. Yorke's illustration of the possibility of the researcher obtaining 'bent' constructs suggests the usefulness of the *opposite method* (Epting *et al.* (16)) in ensuring the bi-polarity of elicited constructs.

A third caution is urged with respect to the elicitation and laddering of constructs. Laddering, note Fransella and Bannister, is an art, not a science. Great care must be taken not to *impose* constructs. Above all, the researcher must learn to *listen* to his subject (s).

A number of practical problems commonly experienced in rating grids are identified by Yorke (17). These are:

1. Variable perception of elements of low personal relevance;
2. Varying the context in which the elements are perceived during the administration of the grid;
3. Halo effect intruding into the ratings where the subject sees the grid matrix building up;
4. Accidental reversal of the rating scale (mentally switching from 5 = high to 1 = high, perhaps because 'five points' and 'first' are both ways of describing high quality). This can happen both within and between constructs, and is particularly likely where a negative or implicity negative property is ascribed to the *pair* during triadic elicitation.
5. Failure to follow the rules of the rating procedure. For example, where the pair has had to be rated at the high end of a five-point scale triads have been found *in a single grid* rated as 5, 4, 4; 1, 1, 2; 1, 2, 4 which must call into question the constructs and their relationship with the elements.

Finally, growing sophistication in computer-based analyses of repertory grid forms leads inevitably to a growing language of concepts by which to describe the complexity of what can be found within matrices. It would be ironic, would it not, ask Fransella and Bannister, if repertory grid technique were to become absorbed into the traditions of psychological testing and employed in terms of the assumptions which underpin such testing. From measures to traits is but a short step, they warn.

Some Examples of the Use of Repertory Grid in Educational Research

What attributes of pupil achievement do teachers *actually* assess as opposed to those they are *supposed* to assess? This intriguing question formed the basis of a repertory grid study by Wood and Napthali (18). Twelve bi-polar constructs were elicited from each of 16 secondary school teachers in a London comprehensive school. The eight constructs which constituted the core of each teacher's judgemental repertoire were identified by requiring teachers to rank order their twelve constructs according to the criterion, 'If you were taking over a new class, which pieces of information about pupils contained in these constructs would you find the most useful?' Factor analysis of 23 correlation matrices showed that the highest correlations were between cognitive constructs. The thrust of Wood and Napthali's analysis was to discover whether some common framework existed that underpinned the construing of all 16 teachers with respect to pupil achievement. By further classifying the factors identified in the teachers' grids the researchers showed that on over 90 per cent of the occasions on which cognitive constructs were used to rate pupils a factor loading of $\geqslant 0.7$ was achieved. From the results of the study, it seems that teachers differentiated between pupils on the basis of all or some of the following derived constructs: (a) the overall ability of the pupil; (b) the ability of the pupil in the particular subject; (c) the involvement of the pupil in the learning situation; (d) the interest displayed by the pupil in the subject; (e) the quality and the tidiness of the work presented; and (f) the behaviour of the pupil.

The Wood and Napthali study was only concerned with teachers of mathematics and geography. It remains to be seen whether their results would hold across a wider range of subject specialisms. What other variables condition teachers' construing (do less experienced teachers use constructs such as *behaviour, discipline, quietness* more often than their experienced colleagues?) is yet to be systematically researched.

Another study of secondary school teachers used their construing of particular pupils as a means of understanding the differential treatment accorded to individual children by the teachers in the course of their day-to-day classroom work. Nash (19) used repertory grid to elicit a number of constructs commonly held by three secondary school teachers about a pupil called Alec. All agreed that Alec was *very bright, very lively, sociable* and *given to misbehave when bored*. Nash observed 36 lessons and made extensive field notes on the frequency and the quality of the interaction between Alec and his teachers. He was able to demonstrate a close association between the teachers' construing of Alec as a pupil, their behaviour towards him, and his behaviour towards them. Nash's summary is insightful:

> The point about Alec is that his sheer ability and obvious enthusiasm when his interest was sparked were sufficient to weight his teachers' perceptions heavily in his favour. They are not unaware of his tendency to disrupt things when he feels bored but there are signs that they don't blame him for it. My assessment of Alec's situation suggests that he knows that he is bright, knows that his teachers know he is bright. We can assume that his teachers have a parallel degree of knowledge and meta-knowledge. Alec's awareness of his teachers' knowledge and meta-knowledge enables him to negotiate successfully with them the behavioural concomitants of his identity as 'bright'. For example, when he asks his science teacher if he can write up the account of an experiment the class have just performed in his own words, rather than copy from the board, it is certain that he knows that the teacher will allow him to do this. And she does. But it is clear from her reply that she is making an exception for Alec. 'Most people', she says, 'had better stick pretty closely to what's on the board.' Alec is here transacting with the teacher an important aspect of his self-identity. The teacher implicitly recognizes his own evaluation of himself as 'bright'. In a similar way, Alec manages to transact with most of his teachers licence to pursue his own activities (often potentially disruptive) when he has finished his work.

A study by Ravenette (20) illustrates the ease with which techniques of linkage analysis (21) can be applied to grid data. Box 14.4 shows the constructs elicited from one pupil, the strength of the relationships between the constructs, and their groupings into two distinct clusters.

By contrast, Duckworth and Entwistle (22) developed a repertory grid to explore the attitudes of some 600 grammar school pupils towards their school subjects. Identifying appropriate constructs was ensured by preliminary interviews with pupils and by screening elicited constructs in a pilot grid with about 120 boys and girls. In the final

Box 14.4

Hierarchical linkage analysis applied to grid data

CORRELATION MATRIX TO SHOW CONSTRUCT RELATIONSHIPS

Constructs Most likely that/least likely that		1	2	3	4	5	6	7	8
1. You would be pleased with yourself	1.								
2. Teachers would think that you are different from other children in class	2.	0.95							
3. Other children would be pleased with you	3.	0.90	0.90						
4. Parents would think you are different from other children in the class	4.	0.60	0.64	0.55					
5. Parents would be pleased with you	5.	0.31	0.33	0.38	0.48				
6. Other children would think you were different from them	6.	0.60	0.57	0.62	0.93	0.62			
7. Teachers would be pleased with you	7.	0.90	0.88	0.93	0.64	0.64	0.74		
8. You would feel different from other children in the class	8.	0.31	0.26	0.31	0.79	0.76	0.90	0.55	

Pleased with self

Teachers see you as the same as other children

Other children pleased with you

Teachers pleased with you

Parents think you are the same as other children

Other children think you are the same as them

You would feel the same as other children

Parents would be pleased with you

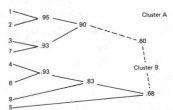

Hierarchical linkage analysis for constructs.

Source: Adapted from Ravenette (20)

form of the grid, the elements listed were school subjects. Analysis of
responses involved computing matching scores for elements on each
construct in the manner we have illustrated on p. 270. Each construct
was summed over the various elements to produce matrices of matching
scores for each pupil. Summary matrices were then constructed for
each subsample of pupils. From these summary matrices Kappa (K)
coefficients were calculated for the total sample. K is interpreted as
the proportion of agreement over and above that expected by chance
and is given by the formula:

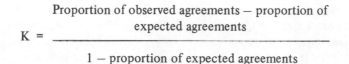

$$K = \frac{\text{Proportion of observed agreements} - \text{proportion of expected agreements}}{1 - \text{proportion of expected agreements}}$$

Duckworth and Entwistle went on to factor analyse their matrices of
K coefficients to identify the structuring of pupils' construing about
school subjects. Their report of the rank ordering of school subjects by
sex, interest, degree of difficulty and perceived freedom and social
benefit offers useful insights into the reasons behind subject choice in
the sixth form.

Recent Applications of Repertory Grid to Teaching and Learning

The 'Perception of Trouble in School' Technique

Harré and Rosser's (23) account of ethogenically-oriented research into
the rules governing disorderly behaviour among secondary school leavers
parallels both the spirit and the approach of an extension of repertory
grid described by Ravenette (24).

Ravenette's interest is in children's perception of troubles in school.
His approach is to offer the participant eight pictures of ordinary
situations in school that are purposely drawn with some ambiguity as
to detail but otherwise are straightforward. The individual is then
invited, by a series of questions, to isolate and describe the child who
might be troubled or upset. 'What do you think is happening?', he is
asked, and similarly, 'Who might be troubled and why?', 'How did this
come about?', etc.

Ravenette goes on to describe a method of 'shaking out' the personal
attributes' implications for the participant which shows how that
individual actually perceives various school situations, how he understands some of the interactions occurring there, how willingly he
identifies himself with these situations, and the extent of his grasp of

various ways of coping with them. Ravenette then uses an implications grid procedure to reduce to manageable proportions the wealth of ideas generated by the 'perception of troubles in school' technique.

'Impoverishing' Repertory Grid Data

In a study of student teachers' perceptions of the teaching practice situation, Osborne (25) employed 13 X 13 matrices to elicit elements (significant role incumbents) whose names remained secret from the researcher. Randomised triads were then identified and used to obtain constructs. Cluster analysis of the data provided a hierarchical picture of each student's grouping of constructs. Following a method devised by Smith and Leach (26), she then quantified the hierarchical structure by impoverishing each subject's construct system, all constructs inter-relating above the 0.05 level of significance being collapsed into one construct.

Osborne demonstrated the utility of her repertory grid data in illuminating case study reports of individual students compiled by teaching practice supervisors and headteachers over three teaching practice sessions.

Focused Grids, Non-verbal Grids, Exchange Grids and Sociogrids

A number of recent developments have been reported in the use of computer programs in repertory grid research (27). We briefly identify these as follows:

(a) Focusing a grid assists in the interpretion of raw grid data. Each element is compared with every other element and the ordering of elements in the grid is changed so that those most alike are clustered most closely together. A similar rearrangement is made in respect of each construct.

(b) Physical objects can be used as elements and grid elicitation is then carried out in non-verbal terms. Thomas claims that this approach enhances the exploration of sensory and perceptual experiences.

(c) Exchange grids are procedures developed to enhance the quality of conversational exchanges. Basically, one person's construing provides the format for an empty grid which is offered to another person for completion. The empty grid consists of the first person's verbal descriptions from which his ratings have been deleted. The second person is then invited to test his comprehending of the first person's point of view by filling in the grid as he believes the other has already completed it. Various computer programs (PAIRS, CORES and DIFFERENCE) are available to assist analysis of the processes of negotiation elicited in exchange grids.

(d) In the PAIRS analysis, all constructs in one grid are compared with all constructs in the other grid and a measure of commonality in construing is determined. PAIRS analysis leads on to SOCIOGRIDS in which the pattern of relationships between the grids of one group can be identified. In turn, SOCIOGRIDS can provide a mode grid for the whole group or a number of mode grids identifying cliques. Socionets which reveal the pattern of shared construing can also be derived.

With these brief examples, the reader will catch something of the flavour of what can be achieved using the various manifestations of repertory grid technique in the field of educational research.

References

1. Kelly, G.A., *Clinical Psychology and Personality: the Selected Papers of George Kelly*, edited by B.A. Maher (Wiley, New York, 1969).
2. Bannister, D. (ed.), *Perspectives in Personal Construct Theory* (Academic Press, London, 1970).
3. Ryle, A., *Frames and Cages: The Repertory Grid Approach to Human Understanding* (Sussex University Press, Brighton, 1975).
4. Adams-Webber, J.R., 'Elicited versus provided constructs in repertory grid technique: a review', *Brit. J. Med. Psychol.*, 43 (1970) 349-54.
5. Bannister, D. and Mair, J.M.M., *The Evaluation of Personal Constructs* (Academic Press, London, 1968).
6. Hinkle, D.N., 'The change of personal constructs from the viewpoint of a theory of implications', unpublished PhD thesis (Ohio State University, 1965).
7. Fransella, F., *Need to Change?* (Methuen, London, 1975).
8. Fransella, F. and Bannister, D., *A Manual for Repertory Grid Technique* (Academic Press, London, 1977).
9. Chetwynd, S.J., 'Outline of the analyses available with G.A.P., the Grid Analysis Package' (St George's Hospital, London, SW17, 1974).
10. Ryle, A. and Breen, D., 'Change in the course of social work training: a repertory grid study', *Brit. J. Med. Psychol.*, 47 (1974) 139-47.
11. Lifshitz, M., 'Quality professionals: does training make a difference? A personal construct theory study of the issue', *Brit. J. Soc. Clin. Psychol.*, 13 (1974) 183-9.
12. Ryle, A. and Breen, D., 'A comparison of adjusted and maladjusted couples using the double dyad grid', *Brit. J. Med. Psychol.*, 45 (1972) 375-82.
13. Ryle, A. and Lunghi, M., 'The dyad grid: a modification of repertory grid technique', *British Journal of Psychiatry*, 117 (1970) 323-7.
14. Salmon, P., 'Differential conforming of the developmental process', *Brit. J. Soc. Clin. Psychol.*, 8 (1969) 22-31.
15. Applebee, A.N., 'The development of children's responses to repertory grids', *Brit. J. Soc. Clin. Psychol.*, 15 (1976) 101-2.
16. Epting, F.R., Suchman, D.I. and Nickeson, K.J., 'An evaluation of elicitation procedures for personal constructs', *Brit. J. Psychol.*, 62 (1971) 513-17.
17. Yorke, D.M., 'Repertory grids in educational research: some methodological considerations', *Brit. Educ. Res. Journ.*, 4, 2 (1978) 63-74.

18. Wood, R. and Napthali, W.A., 'Assessment in the classroom: What do teachers look for?', *Educational Studies*, 1, 3 (1975) 151-61.
19. Nash, R., *Classrooms Observed* (Routledge and Kegan Paul, London, 1973).
20. Ravenette, A.T., 'Grid techniques for children', *Journal of Child Psychology and Psychiatry*, 16 (1975) 79-83.
21. McQuitty, L., 'Single and multiple hierarchical classification by reciprocal pairs and rank order types', *Educational and Psychological Measurement*, 26 (1966) 253-65.
22. Duckworth, D. and Entwistle, N.J., 'Attitudes to school subjects: a repertory grid technique', *Brit. J. Educ. Psychol.*, 44, 1 (1974) 76-83.
23. Harré, R. and Rosser, E., 'The rules of disorder', *The Times Educational Supplement*, 25 July 1975.
24. Ravenette, A.T., 'Psychological investigation of children and young people' in D. Bannister (ed.), *New Perspectives in Personal Construct Theory* (Academic Press, London, 1977).
25. Osborne, J.I., 'College of education students' perceptions of the teaching situation', unpublished MEd dissertation (University of Liverpool, 1977).
26. Smith, S. and Leach, C., 'A hierarchical measure of cognitive complexity', *Brit. J. Psychol.*, 63, 4 (1972) 561-8.
27. Thomas, L.K., 'A personal construct approach to learning in education, training and therapy', in F. Fransella (ed.), *Personal Construct Psychology* (Academic Press, London, 1978).

15 MULTIDIMENSIONAL MEASUREMENT

Introduction

However limited our knowledge of astronomy, most of us have learned to pick out certain clusterings of stars from the infinity of those that crowd the Northern skies and to name them as the familiar Plough, Orion, and the Great Bear. Few of us would identify constellations in the Southern Hemisphere that are instantly recognisable by our Australian friends. But we don't happen to live 'down under'.

Our predilection for reducing the complexity of elements that constitute our lives to a more simple order doesn't stop at star gazing. In numerous ways, each and every one of us attempts to discern patterns or shapes in seemingly unconnected events in order to better grasp their significance for us in the conduct of our daily lives. The educational researcher is no exception.

As research into a particular aspect of human activity progresses, the variables being explored frequently turn out to be more complex than was first realised. Investigation into the relationship between teaching styles and pupil achievement is a case in point. Global distinctions between behaviour identified as progressive or traditional, informal or formal, are vague and woolly and have led inevitably to research findings that are at worst inconsistent, at best, inconclusive. In reality, epithets such as informal or formal in the context of teaching and learning relate to *multidimensional concepts*, that is, concepts made up of a number of variables. *Multidimensional scaling*, on the other hand, is a way of analysing judgements of similarity between such variables in order that the dimensionality of those judgements can be assessed (1). As regards research into teaching styles and pupil achievement, it has been suggested that multidimensional typologies of teacher behaviour should be developed. Such typologies, it is believed, would enable the researcher to group together similarities in teachers' judgments about specific aspects of their classroom organisation and management, and their ways of motivating, assessing and instructing pupils.

Techniques for grouping such judgements are many and various. What they all have in common is that they are methods for 'determining the number and nature of the underlying variables among a large number of measures', a definition which Kerlinger (2) uses to describe

one of the best-known grouping techniques, *factor analysis*. We begin
the chapter by illustrating a number of methods of grouping or clustering variables ranging from *elementary linkage analysis* which can be
undertaken by hand, to *factor analysis* which is best left to the computer. We then outline two ways of analysing data cast into multidimensional tables.

Elementary Linkage Analysis: an Example

Seven constructs were elicited from an infant school teacher who was
invited to discuss the ways in which she saw the children in her class
(see Chapter 14, 'Personal constructs'). She identified favourable and
unfavourable constructs as follows: *intelligent* (+), *sociable* (+), *verbally-
good* (+), *well-behaved* (+), *aggressive* (−), *noisy* (−) and *clumsy* (−).

Four boys and six girls were then selected at random from the class
register and the teacher was asked to place each child in rank order
under each of the seven constructs, using rank position 1 to indicate
the child most like the particular construct, and rank position 10, the
child least like the particular construct. The teacher's rank ordering is
set out in Box 15.1. Notice that on three constructs, the rankings have
been reversed in order to maintain the consistency of favourable = 1,
unfavourable = 10.

Elementary linkage analysis (McQuitty (4)) is one way of exploring
the relationship between the teacher's personal constructs, that is, of
assessing the dimensionality of the judgements that she makes about
her pupils. It seeks to identify and define the clusterings of certain
variables within a set of variables. Like factor analysis which we shortly
illustrate, elementary linkage analysis searches for interrelated groups of
correlation coefficients. The objective of the search is to identify *types*.
By *type*, McQuitty refers to 'a category of people or other objects
(personal constructs in our example) such that the members are
internally self-contained in being like one another'. Box 15.2 sets out
the intercorrelations between the seven personal construct ratings
shown in Box 15.1 (Spearman's rho is the method of correlation used
in the present example).

Steps in Elementary Linkage Analysis

1. In Box 15.2, underline the strongest, that is the highest correlation
   coefficient in each *column* of the matrix. Ignore negative signs.
2. Identify the highest correlation coefficient in the *entire matrix*.
   The two variables having this correlation constitute the first two
   of Cluster 1.

Box 15.1

Rank ordering of ten children on seven constructs

		INTELLIGENT				SOCIABLE
(favourable)	1	Heather		(favourable)	1	Caroline
	2	Richard			2	Richard
	3	Caroline			3	Sharon
	4	Tim			4	Jane
	5	Patrick			5	Tim
	6	Sharon			6	Janice
	7	Janice			7	Heather
	8	Jane			8	Patrick
	9	Alex			9	Karen
(unfavourable)	10	Karen		(unfavourable)	10	Alex

		AGGRESSIVE				NOISY
(unfavourable)	10	Alex		(unfavourable)	10	Alex
	9	Patrick			9	Patrick
	8	Tim			8	Karen
	7	Karen			7	Tim
	6	Richard			6	Caroline
	5	Caroline			5	Richard
	4	Heather			4	Heather
	3	Jane			3	Janice
	2	Sharon			2	Sharon
(favourable)	1	Janice		(favourable)	1	Jane

		VERBALLY-GOOD				CLUMSY
(favourable)	1	Richard		(unfavourable)	10	Alex
	2	Caroline			9	Patrick
	3	Heather			8	Karen
	4	Janice			7	Tim
	5	Patrick			6	Richard
	6	Tim			5	Sharon
	7	Alex			4	Jane
	8	Sharon			3	Janice
	9	Jane			2	Caroline
(unfavourable)	10	Karen		(favourable)	1	Heather

		WELL BEHAVED
(favourable	1	Janice
	2	Jane
	3	Sharon
	4	Caroline
	5	Heather
	6	Richard
	7	Tim
	8	Karen
	9	Patrick
(unfavourable)	10	Alex

Source: Cohen (3).

Box 15.2

Intercorrelations between seven personal constructs

		(1)	(2)	(3)	(4)	(5)	(6)	(7)
Intelligent	(1)		53	−10	−16	<u>83</u>	−52	13
Sociable	(2)	53		−50	−59	44	−56	61
Aggressive	(3)	−10	−50		91	−07	79	<u>−96</u>
Noisy	(4)	−16	−59	91		−01	73	−93
Verbally-good	(5)	<u>83</u>	44	−07	−01		−43	12
Clumsy	(6)	−52	−56	79	73	−43		−81
Well-behaved	(7)	13	<u>61</u>	<u>−96</u>	<u>−93</u>	12	−81	

(decimal points omitted)

Source: Cohen (3).

Box 15.3

The structuring of relationships among the seven personal constructs

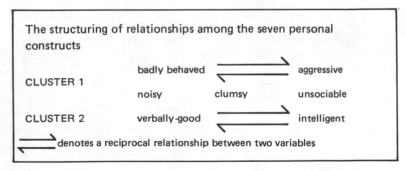

Source: Cohen (3)

3. Now identify all those variables which are most like the variables in Cluster 1. To do this, *read along the rows* of the variables which emerged in Step 2, selecting any of the coefficients which are underlined in the rows. In Box 15.3 we diagram the ways in which these new cluster members are related to the original pair which initially constituted Cluster 1.
4. Now identify any variables which are most like the variables elicited in Step 3. Repeat this procedure until no further variables are identified.
5. Excluding all those variables which belong within Cluster 1, repeat Steps 2 to 4 until all the variables have been accounted for.

Cluster Analysis*: an Example

Elementary linkage analysis is one method of grouping or clustering together correlation coefficients which show similarities among a set of variables. We now illustrate another method of clustering which was used by Bennett (5) in his study of teaching styles and pupil progress. His starting point was a disaffection for global descriptions such as progressive and traditional as applied to teaching styles in junior school classrooms. A more adequate theoretical and experimental conceptualisation of the elements constituting teaching styles was attempted through the construction of a questionnaire containing 28 statements illustrating six major areas of teacher classroom behaviour: (1) classroom management and control; (2) teacher control and sanctions; (3) curriculum content and planning; (4) instructional strategies; (5) motivational techniques; and (6) assessment procedures.

Bennett constructed a typology of teaching styles from the responses of 468 top junior school class teachers to the questionnaire. His cluster analysis of their responses involved calculating coefficients of similarity between subjects across all the variables that constituted the final version of the questionnaire. This technique involves specifying the number of clusters of subjects to which the researcher wishes the data to be reduced. Examination of the central profiles of all solutions from 22 to 3 clusters showed that at the 12-level cluster solutions, between-cluster differences were maximised in relation to within-cluster error (5). An essential prerequisite to the clustering technique employed in this study was the use of factor analysis (see p. 290) to ensure that the variables were relatively independent of one

---

* For a fuller discussion of clustering methods, see B. Everitt, *Cluster Analysis* (Heinemann Educational Books, London, 1974).

another and that groups of variables were not overweighted in the analysis. Principal components analysis followed by varimax rotation reduced the 28 variables in Bennett's original questionnaire to the 19 shown in Box 15.4. For purposes of exposition, Bennett ordered the types of teaching style shown in Box 15.4 from the most progressive cluster (type 1) to the most traditional cluster (type 12), noting, however, that whilst the extreme types could be described in these terms, the remaining types all contained elements of both progressive and traditional teaching styles. The figures in heavy typeface show percentage response levels that were considered significantly different from the total population distribution.

Bennett described the twelve types or teacher styles as follows.

Type 1: These teachers favour integration of subject matter, and, unlike most other groups, allow pupil choice of work, whether undertaken individually or in groups. Most allow pupils choice of seating. Less than half curb movement and talk. Assessment in all its forms, tests, grading and homework appears to be discouraged. Intrinsic motivation is favoured.

Type 2: These teachers also prefer integration of subject matter. Teacher control appears to be low, but offer less pupil choice of work. However, most allow pupils choice of seating, and only one-third curb movement and talk. Few test or grade work.

Type 3: The main teaching mode of this group is class teaching and group work. Integration of subject matter is preferred, associated with taking pupils out of school. They appear to be strict, most curbing movement and talk, and offenders are smacked. The amount of testing is average, but the amount of grading and homework is below average.

Type 4: These teachers prefer separate subject teaching but a high proportion allow pupil choice of work both in group and individual work. None seat their pupils by ability. They test and grade more than average.

Type 5: A mixture of separate subject and integrated subject teaching is characteristic of this group. The main teaching mode is pupils working in groups of their own choice on tasks set by the teacher. Teacher talk is lower than average. Control is high with regard to movement but not to talk. Most give tests every week and many give homework regularly. Stars are rarely used, and pupils are taken out of school regularly.

Type 6: These teachers prefer to teach subjects separately with emphasis on groups working on teacher-specified tasks. The amount of individual work is small. These teachers appear to be fairly low on

Box 15.4 Central profiles (percentage occurrence) at 12-cluster levels

Item						Type						
	1	2	3	4	5	6	7	8	9	10	11	12
1. Pupils have choice in where to sit	63	66	17	46	50	18	7	17	3	7	77	00
2. Pupils allocated to seating by ability	14	16	25	0	12	45	20	7	81	58	3	50
3. Pupils not allowed freedom of movement in the classroom	49	38	83	76	100	84	87	100	86	97	97	100
4. Teacher expects pupils to be quiet	31	34	92	61	23	55	56	90	81	74	90	100
5. Pupils taken out of school regularly as normal teaching activity	51	50	83	49	81	45	17	47	31	19	26	42
6. Pupils given homework regularly	9	22	8	27	65	3	13	43	36	29	21	56
7. *Teaching emphasis*												
(i) Above average teacher talks to whole class	29	16	79	58	30	74	83	73	33	94	85	70
8. (ii) Above average pupils working on groups on teacher tasks	46	13	83	12	77	92	3	3	22	68	10	8
9. (iii) Above average pupils working in groups of own choice	89	3	29	94	19	32	13	3	0	23	0	0
10. (iv) Above average pupils working individually on teacher tasks	9	97	0	3	42	0	73	83	100	0	72	92
11. (v) Above average pupils working individually on work of own choice	94	9	42	85	42	18	57	57	8	3	8	28
12. Pupils' work marked and graded	3	3	13	15	31	16	33	33	8	32	31	97
13. Stars given to pupils who produce best work	9	31	38	55	8	18	17	73	17	87	69	75
14. Arithmetic tests given at least once a week	9	9	71	88	100	8	10	70	50	94	56	81
15. Spelling tests given at least once a week	23	19	67	94	92	18	7	73	92	94	87	92
16. Teacher smacks for persistent disruptive behaviour	34	34	96	24	31	45	80	93	42	68	64	58
17. Teacher sends pupil out of room for persistent disruptive behaviour	11	25	13	6	8	3	7	10	25	0	33	11
18. Allocation of teaching time												
(i) Above average separate subject teaching	20	31	4	82	81	95	100	47	81	100	100	92
19. (ii) Above average integrated subject teaching	97	91	100	24	65	8	10	93	14	7	0	0
N in cluster	35	32	24	33	26	38	30	30	36	31	39	36

Source: Bennett (5).

control, and are below average on assessment and the use of extrinsic motivation.

Type 7: This group is separate subject oriented, with a high level of class teaching together with individual work. Teacher control appears to be tight, few allow movement or choice of seating, and offenders are smacked. Assessment, however, is low.

Type 8: This group of teachers has very similar characteristics to those in type 3, the difference being that these prefer to organise the work on an individual rather than group basis. Freedom of movement is restricted, and most expect pupils to be quiet.

Type 9: These teachers favour separate subject teaching, the predominant teaching mode being individuals working on tasks set by the teacher. Teacher control appears to be high; most curb movement and talk, and seat by ability. Pupil choice is minimal. Regular spelling tests are given, but few mark or grade work or use stars.

Type 10: All these teachers favour separate subject teaching. The teaching mode favoured is teacher talk to whole class, and pupils working in groups determined by the teacher, on tasks set by the teacher. Most curb movement and talk, and over two-thirds smack for disruptive behaviour. There is regular testing and most give stars for good work.

Type 11: All members of this group stress separate subject teaching by way of class teaching and individual work. Pupil choice of work is minimal, although most teachers allow choice of seating. Movement and talk are curbed, and offenders smacked.

Type 12: This is an extreme group in a number of respects. None favour an integrated approach. Subjects are taught separately by class teaching and individual work. None allow pupils' choice of seating, and every teacher curbs movement and talk. These teachers are above average on all assessment procedures, and extrinsic motivation predominates.

Bennett's typology of teacher styles and his analysis of pupil performance based on the typology has aroused considerable debate. Readers may care to follow up critical comments (6) on the cluster analysis procedures we have outlined here.

Factor Analysis: an Example

Factor analysis, we said earlier, is a way of determining the nature of underlying variables among a large number of measures. It is particularly appropriate in exploratory research where the investigator aims to impose an 'orderly simplification' (7) upon a number of interrelated measures. We illustrate the use of factor analysis in a study of the expectations of headteachers and their deputies for the role of the primary school deputy head. The exploratory nature of the enquiry is shown in the strategy adopted by Coulson, the researcher (8).

First, a search was undertaken to identify relevant issues from previous leadership studies. Once located, the issues provided the focus for interviews with headteachers, deputy heads, teachers and advisory staff. Second, arising out of the interviews, a tentative role definition instrument was constructed consisting of 114 statements describing a range of activities in the day-to-day work of a deputy head. Third, a small pilot sample of heads and deputy heads was given the task of winnowing out irrelevant items and rephrasing pertinent statements so that they were simple and unambiguous. The preliminary pilot work reduced the original group of statements to 40. These appeared to have some underlying structure, suggesting to Coulson six principal areas of concern for deputy heads which he identified as (a) interpersonal relations among teachers; (b) instrumental or task emphasis; (c) administrative control and procedural standardisation; (d) collegiality; (e) mediation and consultation; and (f) school leadership — subordination to the head. Later in the study, Coulson was able to check his *a priori* grouping of role statements against the structure which he derived by means of factor analysis. As Child (7) observes,

> In most instances, the factor analysis is preceded by a hunch as to the factors which might emerge. In fact, it would be difficult to conceive of a manageable analysis which started in an empty-headed fashion. In selecting test material in the first place it must have occurred to the experimenter that the tests have something in common or that some are markedly different. Even the 'let's see what happens' approach is pretty sure to have a hunch at the back of it somewhere. It is this testing and the generation of hypotheses which forms the principal concern of most factor analysts.

Finally, the 40-item role definition instrument (Box 15.5) was completed by 232 headteachers and 246 deputy heads using a five-point scale to indicate the direction and the intensity of their agreement/disagreement with the items contained therein.

The correlation matrix composed of the intercorrelations of the 40 role items was then factor analysed. The technical details of factor analysis are beyond the scope of this section. Briefly, however, the

Box 15.5

The deputy head role definition instrument

Item no.	Abbreviated form of item
1	Look out for personal welfare of individual teachers . . . . . .
2	Persuade teachers to try new methods . . . .
3	Put welfare of staff above that of individual teachers . . . . . .
4	Discourage 'outlandish' classroom methods . . . .
5	Help staff with personal teaching problems . . . .
6	Ensure recognition for jobs well done . . . .
7	Apply general school rules policy . . . .
8	Encourage equality between young and old teachers . . . . . .
9	Co-ordinate departments or year groups . . . .
10	Be friendly and accessible to all . . . .
11	Supervise and evaluate teachers' work . . . .
12	Secure teachers' approval on school matters . . . .
13	Allow individuality in teaching methods . . . .
14	Ask teachers to follow standard routines . . . .
15	Keep teachers informed about policy and changes . . . .
16	Inform teachers of expected standards . . . .
17	Put teachers' suggestions into operation . . . .
18	Keep informed of staff opinions on school issues . . . .
19	Reprimand teachers who don't conform to agreed procedures . . . .
20	Encourage teachers to work up to capacity . . . .
21	Be a good organiser of staff duties and schedules . . . .
22	Put over own ideas about teaching and organisation . . . .
23	Attend to welfare of children throughout school . . . .
24	Make own attitudes clear to staff . . . .
25	Emphasise the meeting of deadlines . . . .
26	Expect head to seek his agreement before proposing changes . . . .
27	Relay teachers' suggestion to the head . . . .
28	Have complete responsibility for some aspects of school life . . . .
29	Allow loyalty to head to precede loyalty to staff . . . .
30	Relay head's decisions and instructions to staff . . . .
31	Question head's decisions if these considered unwise . . . . . .
32	Have duties separate from those of the head . . . .
33	Expect head to make final decisions in all school matters . . . .
34	Have his own class . . . .
35	Act as a 'go-between' for head and teachers . . . .
36	Be a good classroom teacher . . . .
37	Have had varied teaching experience in other schools . . . . . .
38	Regard the post as a preparation for headship . . . .
39	Have his own room other than a classroom . . . .
40	Put head's point of view when staff are critical of policies . . . .

Source: Coulson (8).

Box 15.6

Deputy head role definition instrument loadings on ten promax factors											
Item no.	A priori group	Factors									
		I	II	III	IV	V	VI	VII	VIII	IX	X
1	A				−31			30			
2	B		55				32				
3	C	70									
4	B		65								
5	A			34							
6	D					31					
7	C	50						−35			
8	D						65				
9	D		45				39				
10	A			75							
11	B		73								
12	D						49				45
13	D		−48				36				
14	C	46									
15	A					34					
16	B		61								
17	D										64
18	A			55				32			
19	C		71								
20	B		39					43			
21	C			09							
22	B				36					−38	
23	F							75			
24	D							71			
25	C	43									
26	E										68
27	E					68					
28	F										
29	F	56								30	
30	E					65					
31	F								−61		
32	C	48									
33	F										68
34	F								−73		
35	E					80	−32				
36	B				60						
37	F				68						
38	F				61						
39	F								76		
40	E					44					
% variance accounted for		5.1	8.1	4.6	4.9	5.8	4.1	5.1	3.8	3.5	3.8

Decimal points omitted.   Loadings less than ± 0.3 omitted.

Source: Coulson (8).

procedures followed by Coulson involved a method called Principal Components by means of which ten factors or groupings were extracted. These were rotated to produce a more meaningful interpretation of the underlying structure than that provided by the Principal Components method. (Readable accounts of factor analysis may be found in Kerlinger (2) and Child (7).)

Box 15.6 shows the ten factors that were identified, together with what are called their *factor loadings*. These are like correlation coefficients, ranging from −1.00 to +1.00 and are interpreted similarly (2). This is to say, they indicate the correlations between the role items shown in Box 15.6 and the factors. Looking at Factor I, it can be seen that item 3 loads more highly than any of the other five items that go to make up the first factor. The footnote at the bottom of Box 15.6 to the effect that loadings less than ±0.3 are omitted refers to the criterion adopted when interpreting the significance of factor loadings. Because factor loadings are interpreted like correlation coefficients, Coulson would have been in order to have accepted loadings of about 0.12 as significant at p < 0.01 with a sample size of over 400. His adoption of ±0.3 was arbitrary though his decision shows commendable caution.

Having extracted factors, the researcher's next task was to interpret them and give them names. This part of the work can be relatively straightforward or extremely difficult. For example, the loadings on four of the six items (items 3, 7, 14 and 25) that constitute Factor 1 suggest a concern for the standardisation and routinisation of school procedures. The factor was appropriately named *Bureaucratic Organisation*. Notice how this interpretation squares with the hunch the researcher had about his data prior to factor analysis.

Factors VII and X, however, are obscure. Take Factor VII, for example. Start with the highest loading (item 23, loading 0.75) as the primary focus for its interpretation. The next highest loading (item 24, loading 0.71) is of no help in clarifying any underlying structure to the factor suggested by item 23. The addition of item 20 (loading 0.45) serves only to make the task of interpretation even more difficult. With the introduction of the negatively loaded item 7 (−0.35), confusion is total!

Because the ten factors extracted in the analysis shown in Box 15.7 (called the *first order* analysis) are correlated, the correlations between them can be treated as a correlation matrix and subjected to what is termed *second order* factor extraction. In effect, what this process does is to search for further underlying structures that may more parsimoniously describe the relationships between the factors identified in the first order analysis. Box 15.8 identifies four second order factors extracted by second order factor analysis.

By now the reader may well be asking where all this is leading to. Recall that the purpose of factor analysis and of other grouping or clustering techniques is to determine the 'nature and the number of the underlying variables among a large number of measures' (2). As a result of the factor analysis, Coulson was able to describe the nature of the deputy head's role with a greater degree of parsimony and refinement than in his initial Role Definition Instrument set out in Box 15.5. Moreover, the first order factor analysis brought out aspects of the deputy's role that the researcher's *a priori* classification failed to make explicit. Look at Factor IV in Box 15.6, for example. Its high loadings on items 36, 37 and 38, together with the negatively loaded item 1, suggest a *career orientation* factor — an important element in the deputy head's role not specified in the *a priori* classification. In reducing the data even further, the second order factor analysis illuminated the expressive leadership dimension of the deputy head's role with greater clarity.

Box 15.7

Matrix of correlations among ten first order factors									
	I	II	III	IV	V	VI	VII	VIII	IX	X
I	—									
II	−16	—								
III	09	−30	—							
IV	−22	14	03	—						
V	32	−17	21	−13	—					
VI	02	01	01	03	−13	—				
VII	30	−21	13	−14	34	−24	—			
VIII	02	05	−25	−07	−03	−09	18	—		
IX	−10	14	02	13	−15	01	−18	−17	—	
X	01	04	10	−01	−02	−02	16	13	02	—

Decimal points omitted.

Source: Coulson (8).

Box 15.8

Item loadings on second order factors

| Item | Factors | | | |
	I	II	III	IV
1		45		
2			31	
3				
4	32	33		
5		44	36	
6	30		44	
7	33			
8			46	
9			37	
10		33		
12			38	40
13			41	
14		45		−31
15			51	
16		44		
17				48
18		35	36	
19				
20		45		
21			55	
22	61			
23				
24	38		42	
25	52			
26				61
27			33	
28	55			
29	37			
30		30		
31	41			
36	30			
37	37			
38	39			
39	32			30
40	31			
% variance accounted for	16.6	15.6	13.7	11.4

Decimal points omitted   Loadings less than ±0.3 omitted

Source: Coulson (8).

Coulson interprets the second order factor loadings as follows:

Second Order Factor I: Quasi Headship

This associates a strong dimension of independent, 'head-like' career items ('Have own ideas which he should want to put over'; 'Regard post as preparation for headship') with alignment with and support of the head ('Loyalty to head to take precedence over loyalty to teachers'; 'Put head's point of view when teachers critical'). This appears to represent a joint leadership view of the deputy head partnership and is identified as *quasi headship*.

Second Order Factor II: Facilitation

This is loaded by items relating to administrative clarity and routine ('Be a good organiser and administrator'; 'Ask that teachers follow standard routines') and considerate interpersonal relations between the deputy and teachers ('Know staff well enough to help with personal problems': 'Encourage pleasant atmosphere'). Communication is predominantly downward and the factor seems to be concerned with the deputy head's part in keeping the school running smoothly and at the same time encouraging and helping the teachers to give of their best efforts (perhaps two sides of the same thing). The factor represents the deputy head as a considerate foreman and is tentatively identified as a *facilitation* dimension.

Second Order Factor III: Expressive Leadership

This gathers together the collegial items and the acts on behalf of teachers ('Keep teachers informed'; 'Encourage an equal voice to young and old'; 'Let teachers work in the way they think best') and is identified as *expressive leadership*.

Second Order Factor IV: Professionalism

Significant positive loadings on instrumental items in which the opinions of teachers or the deputy head are taken into account before changes are made ('Expect that head will seek agreement before proposing changes'; 'Put teachers' suggestions into operation'), and a significant negative loading on 'ask that teachers follow standard routines' suggest that this factor may have to do with professional *versus* bureaucratic forms of organisation. It is tentatively called *professionalism*.

Multidimensional Tables

Methods of analysing educational data cast into 2 X 2 contingency tables are well covered in most research methods texts. Increasingly, however, educational data are classified in multiple rather than two-dimensional formats. Everitt (9) has provided a useful exposition of methods for analysing multidimensional tables and has shown, incidentally, the erroneous conclusions that can result from the practice of analysing multidimensional data by summing over the variables to reduce them to two-dimensional formats. The example we use follows Everitt's treatment and discussion.

Multidimensional Educational Data: an Example

Box 15.9 shows data to do with the reading ability of a sample of seven year old Infant school girls. The three variables involved are:

1. an assessment of reading ability derived from a standardised reading test. Reading is classed as GOOD/POOR;
2. the method by which the children have been taught reading at school. PHONIC/LOOK AND SAY;
3. the degree to which teachers assess the additional reading support the children receive from home. This is classified as HIGH/MEDIUM/LOW.

Box 15.9

Reading ability in a sample of 7-year-olds girls

Method		High		Medium		Low		
		Phonic	Look and say	Phonic	Look and say	Phonic	Look and say	
R E A D I N G	GOOD	17	6	40	11	2	4	80
	POOR	1	2	2	4	3	8	20
		18	8	42	15	5	12	100

Unlike two-dimensional contingency tables involving a single hypothesis to do with the independence of the two variables, more than one hypothesis may be tested in a multidimensional table. For instance, the researcher may wish to test whether some variables are independent of others, or whether one particular variable is independent of the rest. Everitt suggests that the simplest hypothesis of interest for a multidimensional table is that of the *mutual independence of the variables.*

Testing the hypothesis of mutual independence of the variables involves calculating estimates of the expected frequencies in each of the cells of a multidimensional table. (Everitt (9) p. 6 ff. shows why these are *estimates of the expected frequencies* rather than *expected frequencies.* For convenience in presenting this section, we follow Everitt and use the term *expected values.*) Expected values are then compared with observed values by chi square, its significance being determined against the appropriate degrees of freedom. The method of calculating expected values is set out in Box 15.10.

By way of example, the expected value for the *good* reading, *phonic* method, *high* home support cell is given by:

$$\frac{H \times (A + C + E) \times (A + B)}{N^2} = \frac{80 \times (18 + 42 + 5) \times (18 + 8)}{100^2}$$

$$= 13.52$$

In Box 15.11, the full set of expected values is set out and the calculation of chi square completed. In our example, where we are testing the hypothesis of the mutual independence of the three variables, *degrees of freedom* (df) is given by:

$$df = rcl - r - c - l + 2$$

where r = rows, c = columns, and l = 'layer' categories; thus,

$$df = 3 \times 2 \times 2 - 3 - 2 - 2 + 2 = 7$$

The null hypothesis (H_0) with respect to the mutual independence of the variables is rejected. The researcher's task is now to identify which variables cause the null hypothesis to be rejected. As Everitt points out, however, because the test has given a significant result, we cannot assume that there are significant associations between all variables. For example, an association may exist between two of the variables whilst the third is completely independent. In this event,

Box 15.10

Calculating expected values for the data shown in Box 15.9

		Degree of home support					
		High		Medium		Low	
Method		Phonic	Look and say	Phonic	Look and say	Phonic	Look and say	
R E A D I N G	GOOD	$\dfrac{H\times(A+C+E)\times(A+B)}{N^2}$	$\dfrac{H\times(B+D+F)\times(A+B)}{N^2}$	$\dfrac{H\times(A+C+E)\times(C+D)}{N^2}$	$\dfrac{H\times(B+D+F)\times(C+D)}{N^2}$	$\dfrac{H\times(A+C+E)\times(E+F)}{N^2}$	$\dfrac{H\times(B+D+F)\times(E+F)}{N^2}$	H
	POOR	$\dfrac{G\times(A+C+E)\times(A+B)}{N^2}$	$\dfrac{G\times(B+D+F)\times(A+B)}{N^2}$	$\dfrac{G\times(A+C+E)\times(C+D)}{N^2}$	$\dfrac{G\times(B+D+F)\times(C+D)}{N^2}$	$\dfrac{G\times(A+C+E)\times(E+F)}{N^2}$	$\dfrac{G\times(B+D+F)\times(E+F)}{N^2}$	G
		A	B	C	D	E	F	N

Box 15.11

Calculation of chi square for data shown in Box 15.9

E

13.52	7.28	29.64	15.96	8.84	4.76
3.38	1.82	7.41	3.99	2.21	1.19

$(0 - E)^2 / E$

0.89	0.22	3.62	1.54	5.29	0.12
1.67	0.01	3.95	0.00	0.28	38.97

x^2 = 56.56 df 7 significant at $p < 0.001$

Box 15.12

Calculating expected values for hypothesis: reading ability is independent of scheme and home support

H × A	H × B	H × C	H × D	H × E	H × F
N	N	N	N	N	N
G × A	G × B	G × C	G × D	G × E	G × F
N	N	N	N	N	N

Everitt suggests that hypotheses of *partial independence* would be of interest. By way of example, let us hypothesise that reading ability is independent of the type of reading scheme employed in school and of the degree of support that the child receives from home. In testing this hypothesis, the method of calculating expected values is set out in Box 15.12. Degrees of freedom in this case are given by:

$$df = clr - cl - r + 1 = 5$$

Our obtained chi value in respect of the hypothesis that reading ability is independent of reading scheme and of degree of home support is *30.22*, df = 5, p < 0.001. We therefore reject the hypothesis and proceed to consider with which of the two variables is reading ability associated. We do this by collapsing our contingency table as shown in Box 15.13. Both *reading scheme* and *degree of home support*, it appears, are significantly associated with the children's reading ability. Everitt's discussion also deals with *conditional independence*, that is, the situation in which two of the variables are independent in each level of the third, but each are associated with this third variable. Everitt's outline, particularly Chapters 4 and 5, deserves close reading.

Multivariate Analysis of Ordinal Level Data

Spady (10) has outlined a convenient method of comparing the relative or partial effect of a given independent variable at the ordinal level of measurement upon a dependent variable which can be divided into ordered categories and expressed as a percentage. It does some of the same work as multiple regression analysis, suggests its author, but demands much less in the way of human and technical resources. Cohen (3) has shown how the method can be used in the analysis of educational data.

The Weighted Net Percentage Difference (WNPD): an Example

Suppose that in a study of a very large sample of secondary school pupils a researcher is trying to look at a variety of factors that he believes affect *staying on at school after 16 years of age*. Previous studies and some inspired guesses on his part suggest a number of causal (independent) variables that affect staying on at school (the dependent variable); for example, the type of school, the sex of the pupil, and the degree to which the pupil feels alienated from the school system.

Let us further suppose that the researcher now wishes to examine the *relative effect* of one particular causal factor upon the incidence of staying on, while holding constant or controlling for the effects of the other independent variables. How, for instance, is *alienation* related to *staying on after 16* (holding constant the effects of the *type* of school, the *sex* of the pupil, and *placement* in a high or low ability stream)? How does the strength of the proposed *alienation–staying on* relationship compare with, say, the strength of the relationship between high or low stream *placement* and staying on?

The hypothetical data are set out in Box 15.14. Each of the 16 cells by which the data are classified are identified by the cell numbers in

Box 15.13

Reading ability in a sample of 7-year-old girls (a) by reading scheme used in school and (b) degree of home support

(a) reading scheme used

		Phonic	Look and say
Reading ability	Good	59	21
	Poor	6	14

$\chi^2 = 11.60$ df 1 p < 0.001

(b) degree of home support

		Support		
		High	Medium	Low
Reading ability	Good	23	51	6
	Poor	3	6	11

$\chi^2 = 25.59$ df 2 p < 0.001

the small squares in the top left of each cell. The *unbracketed* number in each cell represents the *percentage* of the subjects whose *base N* is given in brackets below. Note that the variables in Box 15.14 have been arranged so as to follow as closely as possible a decreasing incidence of staying on at school after 16 as one moves down each column and across from left to right. Thus in Cell 1, 89 per cent of 27 grammar school boys in high ability streams who are low in their alienation from school intend to stay on. Compare this percentage with that shown in Cell 16. There, only 29 per cent of the 37 comprehensive school girls in low ability streams who are high in their alienation from school, intend to remain in school after 16.

Box 15.14

Intention of staying on at school after 16 years of age by alienation, ability stream placement, sex and type of school

Alienation	Ability Stream Placement	School			
		Grammar		Comprehensive	
		Boys	Girls	Boys	Girls
LOW	HIGH	1. 89 (27)	2. 83 (29)	3. 76 (42)	4. 71 (51)
	LOW	5. 73 (44)	6. 68 (48)	7. 52 (60)	8. 49 (49)
HIGH	HIGH	9. 81 (30)	10. 70 (33)	11. 57 (25)	12. 47 (37)
	LOW	13. 42 (19)	14. 33 (21)	15. 27 (43)	16. 29 (37)

Source: Cohen (3).

Box 15.15

Staying on at school and alienation (holding constant streaming, type of school and sex)

	(method)		(actual data)		
	rate differences	cell N's	rate differences	cell N's	sub-totals
	1–9 X	1 + 9 = .08	X	57	= 4.56
	2–10 X	2 + 10 = .13	X	62	= 8.06
	3–11 X	3 + 11 = .19	X	67	= 12.73
	4–12 X	4 + 12 = .24	X	88	= 21.12
cells					
	5–13 X	5 + 13 = .31	X	63	= 19.53
	6–14 X	6 + 14 = .35	X	69	= 24.15
	7–15 X	7 + 15 = .25	X	103	= 25.75
	8–16 X	8 + 16 = .20	X	86	= 17.20
				$\Sigma 595$	$\Sigma 133.10$

$$\text{WNPD} = \frac{\Sigma \text{ Subtotals}}{\Sigma \text{ Cell N's}} = \frac{133.1}{595} = 0.224 = 22.4\%$$

Source: Cohen (3).

Calculating the Weighted Net Percentage Difference

By way of illustrating the computation of the WNPD, Box 15.15 shows the relationship between *staying on at school* and *level of alienation*, when sex, type of school and high or low stream placement are controlled for.

The calculation of the WNPD involves a systematic comparison of matched pairs of cells. Thus we start with Cell 1 and match high ability grammar school boys who are *low* on alienation with high ability grammar school boys who are *high* on alienation, Cell 9. Next we match high ability grammar school girls who are *low* on alienation (Cell 2) with high ability grammar school girls who are *high* on alienation (Cell 10). We proceed to match all pairs of cells as shown in Box 15.15.

The comparison of each pair of matched cells allows us to calculate a *difference in percentage* of those staying on. This difference is then multiplied by the sum of the base Ns in the pair of matched cells to give the subtotal in the extreme right hand column in Box 15.15.

Example:
Cell 1 − Cell 9 = 89% − 81% = 8% or 0.08
0.08 multiplied by 57 (the sum of the Ns in Cells 1 and 9) = 4.56

Box 15.15 illustrates the full computation of the weighted net percentage difference in respect of *staying on at school after 16* and *level of alienation.*

Interpretation

Level of alienation explains 22.4 per cent of the variation in pupils' intentions to stay on after 16 years of age, when type of school, sex of pupil and placement in high or low ability stream have been held constant. In Box 15.16 we calculate the WNPD in respect of staying on at school and sex of pupil, holding constant the type of school, the placement in ability groups, and the degree of alienation. The computation in Box 15.16 usefully illustrates the case where the percentage

Box 15.16

Staying on at school and sex of pupil (holding constant streaming, type of school and level of alienation)

	(method)			(actual data)		
	rate differences	cell N's		rate differences	cell N's	sub-totals
	1–2	X	1 + 2 = .06	X	56	= 3.36
	3–4	X	3 + 4 = .05	X	93	= 4.65
	5–6	X	5 + 6 = .05	X	92	= 4.60
	7–8	X	7 + 8 = .03	X	109	= 3.27
cells						
	9–10	X	9 + 10 = .11	X	63	= 6.93
	11–12	X	11 + 12 = .10	X	62	= 6.20
	13–14	X	13 + 14 = .09	X	40	= 3.60
	15–16	X	15 + 16 = −.02	X	80	= −1.60
					$\Sigma 595$	$\Sigma 31.01$

$$\text{WNPD} = \frac{\Sigma \text{ Subtotals}}{\Sigma \text{ Cell N's}} = \frac{31.01}{595} = .052 = 5.2\%$$

Source: Cohen (3).

difference is *negative* (see Cells 15 and 16). In the case where a percentage difference is negative, the negative difference is treated algebraically in the summation of the subtotals in the extreme right-hand column in Box 15.16.

Sex of pupil explains only 5.2 per cent of the variation in pupils' intentions to stay on after 16 years of age, when type of school, placement in high or low ability group, and level of alienation have been held constant. Our final example poses the question, 'irrespective of level of alienation from school, what is the effect of high or low ability group placement on staying among girls in grammar schools as compared with girls in comprehensive schools?' The appropriate calculations of WNPD are set out in Box 15.17.

Placement in a high or a low ability grouping explains slightly more of the variation in girls' intentions to stay on after 16 in the grammar school than in the comprehensive, *level of alienation* having been held constant.

Box 15.17

Staying on at school among girls and placement in high or low ability groups (holding constant level of alienation)

(method)			(actual data)		
rate differences	cell N's		rate differences	cell N's	sub-totals
Grammar School Girls					
2 – 6 X	2 + 6	= .15 X		77	= 11.55
10 – 14 X	10 + 14	= .37 X		54	= 19.98
				Σ 131	Σ 31.53

$$\text{WNPD} = \frac{31.53}{131} = 24.07\%$$

Comprehensive School Girls					
4 – 8 X	4 + 8	= .22 X		100	= 22.00
12 – 16 X	12 + 16	= .18 X		74	= 13.32
				Σ 174	Σ 35.32

$$\text{WNPD} = \frac{35.32}{174} = 20.3\%$$

Source: Cohen (3).

Using the WNPD

In our example of factors affecting staying on at school after sixteen
we illustrated the computation of the WNPD by calculating (in Box
15.15) the effect of *level of alienation* upon the intention of remaining
at school after the statutory leaving age, holding constant the other
three variables thought to be associated with the phenomenon. Below,
we have calculated (from Box 15.14) the effects of each of the four
variables in turn, holding constant the remaining three and ranking the
obtained WNPDs according to their sizes.

	WNPD
Staying on and *placement in high ability group*	23.9%
Staying on and *level of alienation from school*	22.4%
Staying on and *type of school*	16.8%
Staying on and *sex of pupil*	5.2%
Total WNPD =	68.3%

We are able to conclude that the net simultaneous effects of each of
the four independent variables on the *intention to stay on at school*
show that the likelihood is strongest (in the following descending order)
among those in *high ability groups* who are *least alienated* from the
school system, who are in *grammar schools*, and who are *boys*. When
we summate the four WNPDs, we interpret the total WNPD of 68.3 per
cent as follows:

A male grammar school pupil in a *high ability group* and *low* in his
level of alienation is 68.3 per cent more likely to stay on at school after
16 than a female comprehensive school pupil in a *low ability group* and
high in her *level of alienation*.

If we examine the actual percentage difference between Cell 1 and
Cell 16, we see that our calculated total WNPD is a close approximation
to the actual percentage difference of 60 per cent. (Spady (10) points
out (footnote, p. 9) that these two percentages would be closer if there
were no reversals in the patterns in Box 15.14 and if the base Ns in
each cell were equivalent.)

Testing the Statistical Significance of the WNPD

It is possible to test the statistical significance of a WNPD although,
as Spady points out, with a large sample size, even the smallest
WNPD is likely to reach the 0.05 level of significance.

We illustrate the computation of the t test by reference to the data set out in the top section of Box 15.17 concerning the *staying on at school intentions* of two groups of grammar school girls, those placed in *high ability groups* and those placed in *low ability groups*.

$$t = \frac{WNPD}{[\bar{p}\,\bar{q}\,([n_1 + n_2]/[n_1 \times n_2])]}$$

where $\bar{p}$ is an estimate of the proportion of girls intending to stay on after 16. We obtain this by averaging out the percentages obtained from Cells 2, 6, 10 and 14 (i.e. 83% + 68% + 70% + 33% divided by 4).

$\bar{p} = 63\%$ or 0.63
$\bar{q} = 1 - p = 0.37$

$n_1 =$ the number of grammar school girls in *high ability groups* (i.e. 62)
$n_2 =$ the number of grammar school girls in *low ability groups* (i.e. 69)
$t = 24.07/[(0.63)(0.37)([62 + 69]/[62 \times 69])]$
$t = 286.55$ (p < 0.001)

References

1. Bennett, S. and Bowers, D., *An Introduction to Multivariate Techniques for Social and Behavioural Sciences* (Macmillan, London, 1977).
2. Kerlinger, F.N., *Foundations of Behavioural Research* (Holt, Rinehart and Winston, New York, 1970).
3. Cohen, L., *Educational Research in Classrooms and Schools: A Manual and Materials and Methods* (Harper and Row, London, 1977).
4. McQuitty, L.L., 'Elementary linkage analysis for isolating orthogonal and oblique types and typal relevancies', *Educational and Psychological Measurement*, 17 (1957) 207-29.
5. Bennett, N., *Teaching Styles and Pupil Progress* (Open Books, London, 1976); Bennett, N. and Jordan, J., 'A typology of teaching styles in primary schools', *Brit. J. Educ. Psychol.*, 45 (1975) 20-8.
6. Gray, J. and Satterly, D., 'A chapter of errors: teaching styles and pupil progress in retrospect', *Educational Research*, 19 (1976) 45-56.
7. Child, D., *The Essentials of Factor Analysis* (Holt, Rinehart and Winston, 1970).
8. Coulson, A.A., 'The attitudes of primary school heads and deputy heads to deputy headship', *Brit. J. Educ. Psychol.*, 46 (1976) 244-52.
9. Everitt, B.S., *The Analysis of Contingency Tables* (Chapman and Hall, London, 1977).
10. Spady, W.G., 'Simple techniques for multivariate analysis', *Interchange*, 1 (1970) 3-19.

BIBLIOGRAPHY

Adams, R.S. and Biddle, B.J., *Realities of Teaching* (Holt, Rinehart and Winston, New York, 1970)

Adams-Webber, J.R., 'Elicited versus provided constructs in repertory grid technique: a review', *Brit. J. Med. Psychol.*, 43 (1970) 349-54

Adelman, C. and Walker, R. 'Developing pictures for other frames: action research and case study' in G. Chanan and S. Delamont (eds), *Frontiers of Classroom Research* (NFER, 1975)

Applebee, A.N., 'The development of children's responses to repertory grids', *Brit. J. Soc. Clin. Psychol.*, 15 (1976) 101-2

Argyris, C., 'Dangers in applying results from experimental social psychology', *American Psychologist*, 30 (1975) 469-85

Armistead, N. (ed.), *Reconstructing Social Psychology* (Penguin Books, London, 1974)

Ary, D., Jacobs, L.C. and Razavieh, A., *Introduction to Research in Education* (Holt, Rinehart and Winston, New York, 1972)

Backstrom, C.H. and Hursh, G.D., *Survey Research* (Northwestern University Press, Evanston, 1963)

Bailey, K.D., *Methods of Social Research* (Collier-Macmillan, London, 1978)

Bannister, D. (ed.), *Perspectives in Personal Construct Theory* (Academic Press, London, 1970)

Bannister, D. (ed.), *New Perspectives in Personal Construct Theory* (Academic Press, London, 1977)

Bannister, D. and Mair, J.M.M., *The Evaluation of Personal Constructs* (Academic Press, London, 1968)

Banuazizi, A. and Movahedi, S., 'Interpersonal dynamics in a simulated prison: a methodological analysis', *American Psychologist*, 30 (1975) 152-60

Barratt, P.E.H., *Bases of Psychological Methods* (John Wiley and Sons, Australasia Pty Ltd, 1971)

Beard, R., Cohen, L. and Verma, G., *The Bradford Book Flood Experiment* (School of Research in Education, University of Bradford, 1978)

Bennett, N., *Teaching Styles and Pupil Progress* (Open Books, London, 1975)

Bennett, N. and Jordan, J., 'A typology of teaching styles in primary schools', *Brit. J. Educ. Psychol.*, 45 (1975) 20-8

Bennett, S. and Bowers, D., *An Introduction to Multivariate Techniques for Social and Behavioural Sciences* (Macmillan, London, 1977)

Berkowitz, L. (ed.), *Advances in Experimental Social Psychology*, vol. 10 (Academic Press, New York, 1977)

Bernstein, B., 'Sociology and the sociology of education: a brief acccount', in J. Rex (ed.), *Approaches to Sociology: an Introduction to Major Trends in British Sociology* (Routledge and Kegan Paul, London, 1974)

Best, J.W., *Research in Education* (Prentice Hall, Englewood Cliffs, New Jersey, 1970)

Borg, W.R., *Educational Research: An Introduction* (Longmans, London, 1963)

Boring, E.G., 'The role of theory in experimental psychology', *Amer. J. Psychol.*, 66 (1953) 169-84

Borkowsky, F.T., 'The relationship of work quality in undergraduate music curricula to effectiveness in instrumental music teaching in the public schools', *J. Exp. Educ.*, 39 (1970) 14-19

Bracht, G.H. and Glass, G.V., 'The external validity of experiments', *Amer. Educ. Res. Journ.*, 4, 5 (1968) 437-74

Brenner, M., Marsh, P. and Brenner, M., *The Social Context of Method* (Croom Helm, London, 1978)

Brown, J. and Sime, J.D., 'Accounts as a general methodology', Paper presented to the British Psychological Society Conference, Exeter University, 1977

Brown, R.K., 'Research and consultancy in industrial enterprises: a review of the contribution of the Tavistock Institute of Human Relations to the development of Industrial Sociology', *Sociology*, 1, 1 (1967) 33-60

Brown, R. and Herrnstein, R.J., *Psychology* (Methuen, London, 1975)

Butcher, H.J. and Pont, H.B. (eds), *Educational Research in Britain 3* (University of London Press, London, 1973)

Caldwell, O. and Coutis, S., *Then and Now in Education* (Harcourt, New York, 1925)

Campbell, D.T. and Fiske, D., 'Convergent and discriminant validation by the multi-trait multimethod matrix', *Psychol. Bull.*, 56 (1959) 81-105

Campbell, D.T. and Stanley, J.C., 'Experimental and quasi-experimental designs for research on teaching' in N.L. Gage (ed.), *Handbook of Research on Teaching* (Rand McNally, Chicago, 1963)

Cannell, C.F. and Kahn, R.L., 'Interviewing' in G. Lindzey and E. Aronson (eds), *The Handbook of Social Psychology*, vol. 2, Research

Methods (Addison Wesley, New York, 1968)

Cantor, L.M. and Matthews, G.F., *Loughborough: From College to University. A History of Higher Education at Loughborough 1909-1966*

Central Advisory Council for Education, *Children and their Primary Schools* (HMSO, London, 1967)

Chanan, G. and Delamont, S. (eds), *Frontiers of Classroom Research* (NFER, London, 1975)

Chapin, F.S., *Experimental Designs in Sociological Research* (Harper and Row, New York, 1947)

Chetwynd, S.J., 'Outline of the analyses available with G.A.P., the Grid Analysis Package' (St George's Hospital, London, SW17, 1974)

Child, D., *The Essentials of Factor Analysis* (Holt, Rinehart and Winston, London, 1970)

Christie, T. and Oliver, R.A.C., 'Academic performance at age 18+ as related to school organization', *Research in Education*, 2 (Nov 1969) 13-31

Cicourel, A.V., *Method and Measurement in Sociology* (The Free Press, New York, 1964)

Cohen, L., *Educational Research in Classrooms and Schools: a Manual of Materials and Methods* (Harper and Row, London, 1977)

Cohen, L. and Child, D., 'Some sociological and psychological factors in university failure', *Durham Research Review*, 22 (1969) 365-72

Cohen, L. and Manion, L. *Perspectives on Classrooms and Schools* (Holt-Saunders, Eastbourne, in preparation)

Cohen, L. and Manion, L. *Social Psychology for Teachers* (Holt-Saunders, Eastbourne, in preparation)

Corey, S.M., *Action Research to Improve School Practices* (Bureau of Publications, Teachers College, Columbia University, New York, 1953)

Coulson, A.A., 'The attitudes of primary school heads and deputy heads to deputy headship', *Brit. J. Educ. Psychol.*, 46 (1976) 244-52

Dahrendorf, R., *Class and Class Conflict in Industrial Society* (Routledge and Kegan Paul, London, 1959)

Davidson, J., *Outdoor Recreation Surveys: The Design and Use of Questionnaires for Site Surveys* (Countryside Commission, London, 1970)

Davie, R., 'The longitudinal approach', *Trends in Education*, 28 (1972) 8-13

Denscombe, M., 'The social organization of teaching: a study of teaching as a practical activity in two London comprehensive schools', unpublished PhD dissertation (University of Leicester, 1977)

Denzin, N.K., *The Research Act in Sociology: A Theoretical Introduction to Sociological Methods* (The Butterworth Group, London, 1970)

Department of Education and Science, *A Study of School Buildings* (HMSO, London, 1977)

Department of Education and Science, *Primary Education in England* (HMSO, London, 1978)

Dicsing, P., *Patterns of Discovery in the Social Sciences* (Aldine, Chicago, 1971)

Douglas, J.W.B., 'The use and abuse of national cohorts' in M.D. Shipman, *The Organization and Impact of Social Research* (Routledge and Kegan Paul, London, 1976)

Douglas, J.W.B. and Blomfield, J.M., *Maternity in Great Britain* (Oxford University Press, London, 1948)

Douglas, J.W.B., Ross, J.M. and Simpson, H.R., *All Our Future* (P. Davies, London, 1968)

Duck, S. (ed.), *Theory and Practice in Interpersonal Attraction* (Academic Press, London, 1977)

Duckworth, D. and Entwistle, N.J., 'Attitudes to school subjects: a repertory grid technique', *Brit. J. Educ. Psychol.*, 44, 1 (1974) 76-83

Ekehammar, B. and Magnusson, D., 'A method to study stressful situations', *Journal of Personality and Social Psychology*, 27, 2 (1973) 176-9

Epting, F.R., Suchman, D.I. and Nickeson, K.J., 'An evaluation of elicitation procedures for personal constructs', *Brit. J. Psychol.*, 62 (1971) 513-17

Eron, L.D., Huesman, L.R., Lefkowitz, M.M. and Walder, L.O., 'Does television violence cause aggression?', *Amer. Psychol.* (April 1972) 253-62

Evans, K.M., *Planning Small Scale Research* (NFER, Windsor, 1978)

Everitt, B.S., *Cluster Analysis* (Heinemann Educational Books, London, 1974)

Everitt, B.S., *The Analysis of Contingency Tables* (Chapman and Hall, London, 1977)

Ferguson, S., 'Toreside Comprehensive School: a simulation game for teachers in training' in J. Megarry (ed.), *Aspects of Simulation and Gaming* (Kogan Page, London, 1977)

Filstead, W.J. (ed.), *Qualitative Methodology: Firsthand Involvement with the Social World* (Markham Pub. Co., Chicago, 1970)

Ford, D.H. and Urban, H.B., *Systems of Psychotherapy: a Comparative Study* (John Wiley and Sons, New York, 1963)

Forgas, J.P., 'The perception of social episodes: categoric and dimensional representations in two different social milieu', *Journal of Personality and Social Psychology* 34, 2 (1976) 199-209

Forgas, J.P., 'Social episodes and social structure in an academic setting: the social environment of an intact group', *Journal of Experimental Social Psychology*, 14 (1978) 434-48

Forward, J., Canter, R. and Kirsch, N., 'Role-enactment and deception methodologies', *American Psychologist*, 35 (1976) 595-604

Fox, D.J., *The Research Process in Education* (Holt, Rinehart and Winston, New York, 1969)

Fransella, F., *Need to Change?* (Methuen, London, 1975)

Fransella, F. (ed.), *Personal Construct Psychology* (Academic Press, London, 1978)

Fransella, F. and Bannister, D., *A Manual for Repertory Grid Technique* (Academic Press, London, 1977)

Gage, N.L. (ed.), *Handbook of Research on Teaching* (Rand McNally, Chicago, 1963)

Gelwick, R., *The Way to Discovery: an Introduction to the Thought of Michael Polanyi* (Oxford University Press, New York, 1977)

Giddens, A., *New Rules of Sociological Method: a Positive Critique of Interpretative Sociologies* (Hutchinson, London, 1976)

Ginsburg, G.P., 'Role playing and role performance in social psychological research' in M. Brenner, P. Marsh and M. Brenner (eds), *The Social Context of Method* (Croom Helm, London, 1978)

Glaser, B.G. and Strauss, A.L., *The Discovery of Grounded Theory* (Aldine, Chicago, 1967)

Good, C.V., *Introduction to Educational Research* (Appleton Century Crofts, New York, 1963)

Gottschalk, L., *Understanding History* (Alfred A. Knopf, New York, 1951)

Gray, J. and Satterly, D., 'A chapter of errors: teaching styles and pupil progress in retrospect', *Educational Research*, 19 (1976) 45-56

Guilford, J.P. and Fruchter, B., *Fundamental Statistics in Psychology and Research* (McGraw Hill, New York, 1973)

Halsey, A.H. (ed.), *Educational Priority: Volume 1: E.P.A. Problems and Policies* (HMSO, London, 1972)

Hamilton, V.L., 'Role play and deception: a re-examination of the controversy', *Journal for the Theory of Social Behaviour*, 6 (1976)

233-50

Haney, C., Banks, C. and Zimbardo, P., 'Interpersonal dynamics in a simulated prison', *International Journal of Criminology and Penology*, 1 (1973) 69-97

Hargreaves, D.H., *Social Relations in a Secondary School* (Routledge and Kegan Paul, London, 1967)

Hargreaves, D.H., Hester, S.K. and Mellor, F.J., *Deviance in Classrooms* (Routledge and Kegan Paul, London, 1975)

Harré, R., 'Some remarks on "rule" as a scientific concept' in T. Mischel (ed.), *On Understanding Persons* (Basil Blackwell, Oxford, 1974)

Harré, R., 'The ethogenic approach: theory and practice' in L. Berkowitz (ed.), *Advances in Experimental Social Psychology*, vol. 10 (Academic Press, New York, 1977)

Harré, R., 'Friendship as an accomplishment' in S. Duck (ed.), *Theory and Practice in Interpersonal Attraction* (Academic Press, London, 1977)

Harré, R., 'Accounts, actions and meanings — the practice of participatory psychology' in M. Brenner, P. Marsh and M. Brenner (eds), *The Social Context of Method* (Croom Helm, London, 1978)

Harré, R. and Rosser, E., 'The rules of disorder', *The Times Educational Supplement*, 25 July 1975

Harré, R. and Secord, P.F., *The Explanation of Social Behaviour* (Basil Blackwell, Oxford, 1972)

Harvey, T.J. and Cooper, C.J., 'An investigation into some possible factors affecting children's understanding of the concept of an electric circuit in the age range 8-11 years old', *Educational Studies*, 4, 2 (1978) 149-55

Heather, N., *Radical Perspectives in Psychology* (Methuen, London, 1976)

Hill, J.E. and Kerber, A., *Models, Methods, and Analytical Procedures in Educational Research* (Wayne State University Press, Detroit, 1967)

Hinkle, D.N., 'The change of personal constructs from the viewpoint of a theory of implications', unpublished PhD thesis (Ohio State University, 1965)

Hockett, H.C., *The Critical Method in Historical Research* (Macmillan, London, 1955)

Hodgkinson, H.L., 'Action research — a critique', *J. Educ. Sociol.*, 31, 4 (1957) 137-53

Hoinville, G. and Jowell, R., *Survey Research Practice* (Heinemann

Educational Books, London, 1978)

Holsti, O.R., 'Content analysis' in G. Lindzey and E. Aronson, *The Handbook of Social Psychology*, vol. 2, Research Methods (Addison-Wesley, New York, 1968)

Isaac, S. and Michael, W.B., *Handbook in Research and Evaluation* (R.R. Knapp, California, 1971)

Jackson, B. and Marsden, D., *Education and the Working Class* (Routledge and Kegan Paul, London, 1962)

Jelinek, M.M., 'Multiracial education 3. Pupils' attitudes to the multiracial school', *Educational Research*, 19, 2 (1977) 129-41

Jelinek, M.M. and Brittan, E.M., 'Multiracial education 1. Inter-ethnic friendship patterns', *Educational Research*, 18, 1 (1975) 44-53

Kaplan, A., *The Conduct of Inquiry* (Intertext Books, Aylesbury, 1973)

Kelly, G.A., *Clinical Psychology and Personality: the Selected Papers of George Kelly*, edited by B.A. Maher (John Wiley and Sons, New York, 1969)

Kerlinger, F.N., *Foundations of Behavioural Research* (Holt, Rinehart and Winston, New York, 1970)

King, R., *All Things Bright and Beautiful?* (J. Wiley, Chichester, 1979)

Kitwood, T.M., 'Values in adolescent life: towards a critical description', unpublished PhD dissertation (School of Research in Education, University of Bradford, 1977)

Lacey, C., *Hightown Grammar* (Manchester University Press, Manchester, 1970)

Lambert, R., Bullock, R. and Millham, S., *The Chance of a Lifetime?* (Weidenfeld and Nicolson, London, 1975)

Lambert, R., Millham, S. and Bullock, R., *A Manual to the Sociology of the School* (Weidenfeld and Nicolson, London, 1970)

Lansing, J.B., Ginsberg, G.P. and Braaten, K., *An Investigation of Response Error* (Bureau of Economic and Business Research, University of Illinois, 1961)

Law, B., 'The role of the church school at Sowerby in local education', unpublished study submitted for the Certificate in Education (University of Leeds, 1978)

Levine, R.A., 'Towards a psychology of populations: the cross-cultural study of personality', *Human Development*, 3 (1966) 30-46

Lifshitz, M., 'Quality professionals: does training make a difference? A personal construct theory study of the issue', *Brit. J. Soc. Clin. Psychol.*, 13 (1974) 183-9

Lin, Nan, *Foundations of Social Research* (McGraw Hill, New York, 1976)

Lindzey, G. and Aronson, E., *The Handbook of Social Psychology*, vol. 2, Research Methods (Addison-Wesley, New York, 1968)

Lofland, J., *Analysing Social Settings* (Wadsworth Pub. Co., Belmont, Ca., 1971)

McAleese, R. (ed.), *Perspectives on Academic Gaming and Simulation 3: Training and Professional Education* (Kogan Page, London, 1978)

McAleese, R. and Hamilton, D., *Understanding Classroom Life* (NFER, Slough, 1978)

McQuitty, L.L., 'Elementary linkage analysis for isolating orthogonal and oblique types and typal relevancies', *Educational and Psychological Measurement*, 17 (1957) 207-9

McQuitty, L.L., 'Single and multiple hierarchical classification by reciprocal pairs and rank order types', *Educational and Psychological Measurement*, 26 (1966) 253-65

Madge, J., *The Tools of Social Science* (Longmans, London, 1965)

Magnusson, D., 'An analysis of situational dimensions', *Perceptual and Motor Skills*, 32 (1971) 851-67

Marris, P. and Rein, M., *Dilemmas of Social Reform: Poverty and Community Action in the United States* (Routledge and Kegan Paul, London, 1967)

Marsh, P., Rosser, E. and Harré, R., *The Rules of Disorder* (Routledge and Kegan Paul, London, 1978)

Megarry, J. (ed.), *Aspects of Simulation and Gaming* (Kogan Page, London, 1977)

Megarry, J., 'Retrospect and prospect' in R. McAleese (ed.), *Perspectives on Academic Gaming and Simulation 3: Training and Professional Education* (Kogan Page, London, 1978)

Menzel, H., 'Meaning – who needs it?' in M. Brenner, P. Marsh and M. Brenner (eds), *The Social Context of Method* (Croom Helm, London, 1978)

Merton, R.K. and Kendall, P.L., 'The focused interview', *Amer. J. Sociol.*, 51 (1946) 541-57

Milgram, S., *Obedience to Authority* (Harper and Row, New York, 1974)

Mischel, T. (ed.), *On Understanding Persons* (Basil Blackwell, Oxford, 1974)

Mixon, D., 'Instead of deception', *Journal for the Theory of Social Behaviour*, 2 (1972) 146-77

Mixon, D., 'If you won't deceive, what can you do?' in N. Armistead (ed.), *Reconstructing Social Psychology* (Penguin Books, London, 1974)

Moser, C.A. and Kalton, G., *Survey Methods in Social Investigation* (Heinemann Educational Books, London, 1977)

Mouly, G.J., *Educational Research: the Art and Science of Investigation* (Allyn and Bacon, Boston, 1978)

Nash, R., *Classrooms Observed* (Routledge and Kegan Paul, London, 1973)

National Educational Association of the United States, *Association for Supervision and Curriculum Development. Learning about Learning from Action Research* (Washington, DC, 1959)

NFER, Research Project on Mixed Ability Teaching (ongoing).

Newson, J. and Newson, E., *Infant Care in an Urban Community* (Allen and Unwin, London, 1968)

Newson, J. and Newson, E., *Four years old in an Urban Community* (Allen and Unwin, London, 1968)

Newson, J. and Newson, E., *Seven years old in an Urban Community* (Allen and Unwin, London, 1976)

Newson, J. and Newson, E., 'Parental roles and social contexts' in M.D. Shipman, *The Organization and Impact of Social Research* (Routledge and Kegan Paul, London, 1976)

Newson, J. and Newson, E., *Perspectives on School at seven years old* (Allen and Unwin, London, 1977)

Osborne, J.I., 'College of Education students' perceptions of the teaching situation', unpublished MEd dissertation (University of Liverpool, 1977)

Palmer, M., 'An experimental study of the use of archive materials in the secondary school history curriculum', unpublished PhD dissertation (University of Leicester, 1976)

Palys, T.S., 'Simulation methods and social psychology', *Journal for the Theory of Social Behaviour*, 8 (1978) 341-68

Parker, H.J., *View from the Boys* (David and Charles, Newton Abbott, 1974)

Parsons, T., *The Social System* (Free Press, New York, 1951)

Patrick, J., *A Glasgow Gang Observed* (Eyre Methuen, London, 1973)

Peevers, B.H. and Secord, P.F., 'Developmental changes in attribution of descriptive concepts to persons', *Journal of Personality and Social Psychology*, 27, 1 (1973) 120-8

Percival, F., 'Evaluation procedures for simulation gaming exercises' in R. McAleese (ed.), *Perspectives on Academic Gaming and Simulation 3: Training and Professional Education* (Kogan Page, London, 1978)

Pilliner, A., *Experiment in Educational Research* (E341. Block 5) (The Open University Press, Bletchley, 1973)

Ravenette, A.T., 'Grid techniques for children', *Journal of Child Psychology and Psychiatry*, 16 (1975) 79-83

Ravenette, A.T., 'Psychological investigation of children and young people' in D. Bannister (ed.), *New Perspectives in Personal Construct Theory* (Academic Press, London, 1977)

Rex, J. (ed.), *Approaches to Sociology: an Introduction to Major Trends in British Sociology* (Routledge and Kegan Paul, London, 1974)

Riley, M.W., *Sociological Research I: A Case Approach* (Harcourt, Brace and World, New York, 1963)

Rogers, C.R., *Counselling and Psychotherapy* (Houghton Mifflin, Boston, 1942)

Rogers, C.R., 'The non-directive method as a technique for social research', *Amer. J. Sociol.*, 50 (1945) 279-83

Rogers, V.M. and Atwood, R.K., 'Can we put ourselves in their place?', *Yearbook of the National Council for Social Studies*, 44 (1974) 80-111

Rutter, M., Maughan, B., Mortimore, P. and Ouston, J. *Fifteen Thousand Hours* (Open Books, London, 1979)

Ryle, A., *Frames and Cages: The Repertory Grid Approach to Human Understanding* (Sussex University Press, Brighton, 1975)

Ryle, A. and Breen, D., 'A comparison of adjusted and maladjusted couples using the double dyad grid', *Brit. J. Med. Psychol.*, 45 (1972) 375-82

Ryle, A. and Breen, D., 'Change in the course of social work training: a repertory grid study', *Brit. J. Med. Psychol.*, 47 (1974) 139-47

Ryle, A. and Lunghi, M., 'The dyad grid: a modification of repertory grid technique', *British Journal of Psychiatry* 117 (1970) 323-7

Salmon, P., 'Differential conforming of the developmental process', *Brit. J. Soc. Clin. Psychol.*, 8 (1969) 22-31

Sarnoff, I. *et al.*, 'A cross-cultural study of anxiety among American and English school children', *J. Educ. Psychol.*, 49 (1958) 129-36

Schutz, A., *Collected Papers* (Nijhoff, The Hague, 1962)

Sears, R., Maccoby, E. and Levin, H., *Patterns of Child Rearing* (Harper and Row, New York, 1957)

Secord, P.F. and Peevers, B.H., 'The development and attribution of person concepts' in T. Mischel (ed.), *On Understanding Persons* (Basil Blackwell, Oxford, 1974)

Selltiz, C., Wrightsman, L.S. and Cook, S.W., *Research Methods in Social Relations* (Holt, Rinehart and Winston, New York, 1976)

Sharp, R. and Green, A., *Education and Social Control* (Routledge and

Kegan Paul, London, 1975)

Shields, R.W., *A Cure of Delinquents* (Heinemann Educational Books, London, 1962)

Shipman, M.D., *The Limitations of Social Research* (Longmans, London, 1972)

Shipman, M.D., *Inside a Curriculum Project* (Methuen, London, 1974)

Shipman, M.D. (ed.), *The Organization and Impact of Social Research* (Routledge and Kegan Paul, London, 1976)

Smith, H.W., *Strategies of Social Research: The Methodological Imagination* (Prentice Hall, Lonodn, 1975)

Smith, S. and Leach, C., 'A hierarchical measure of cognitive complexity', *Brit. J. Psychol.*, 63, 4 (1972) 561-8

Social and Community Planning Research, *Questionnaire Design Manual No. 5* (London: 11 Duncan Terrace, N1 8BZ, 1972)

Social Science Research Council, *Research in Economic and Social History* (Heinemann, London, 1971)

Solomon, R.L., 'An extension of control group design', *Psychol. Bull.*, 46 (1949) 137-50

Spady, W.G., 'Simple techniques for multivariate analysis', *Interchange*, 1, 3 (1970) 3-19

Stenhouse, L., 'The humanities curriculum project' in H.J. Butcher and H.B. Pont (eds), *Educational Research in Britain 3* (University of London Press, London, 1973)

Sutherland, G., 'The study of the history of education', *History*, vol. LIV, no. 180 (Feb. 1969)

Taylor, J.L. and Walford, R., *Simulation in the Classroom* (Penguin Books, London, 1972)

Thomas, L.F., 'A personal construct approach to learning in education, training and therapy' in F. Fransella (ed.), *Personal Construct Psychology* (Academic Press, Lonodn, 1978)

Travers, R.M.W., *An Introduction to Educational Research* (Collier-Macmillan, London, 1969)

Tuckman, B.W., *Conducting Educational Research* (Harcourt Brace Jovanovich, New York, 1972)

van Ments, M., 'Role playing: playing a part or a mirror to meaning?', *Sagset Journal*, 8, 3 (1978) 83-92

Verma, G. and Bagley, C. (eds), *Race, Education and Equality* (Macmillan, London, 1979)

Walker, R. and MacDonald, B., *Curriculum Innovation at School Level* (E 203. Units 27 and 28) (The Open University Press, Bletchley, 1976)

Weber, M., *Essays in Sociology* (Routledge and Kegan Paul, London, 1948)

Weber, M., *The Theory of Social and Economic Organization* (Free Press, Glencoe, 1964)

Willis, P.E., *Learning to Labour* (Saxon House, London, 1977)

Wolcott, H.F., *The Man in the Principal's Office* (Holt, Rinehart and Winston, New York, 1973)

Wolcott, H.F., 'Criteria for an ethnographic approach to research in schools', *Human Organization*, 34, 2 (1973) 111-27

Wood, R. and Napthali, W.A., 'Assessment in the classroom: what do teachers look for?', *Educational Studies*, 1, 3 (1975) 151-61

Woods, P., *The Divided School* (Routledge and Kegan Paul, London, 1979)

Yorke, D.M., 'Repertory grids in educational research: some methodological considerations', *Brit. Educ. Res. Journ.*, 4, 2 (1978) 63-74

Young, J., *The Drugtakers* (Paladin, London, 1971)

INDEX